IMAGES
of America

BURLINGTON

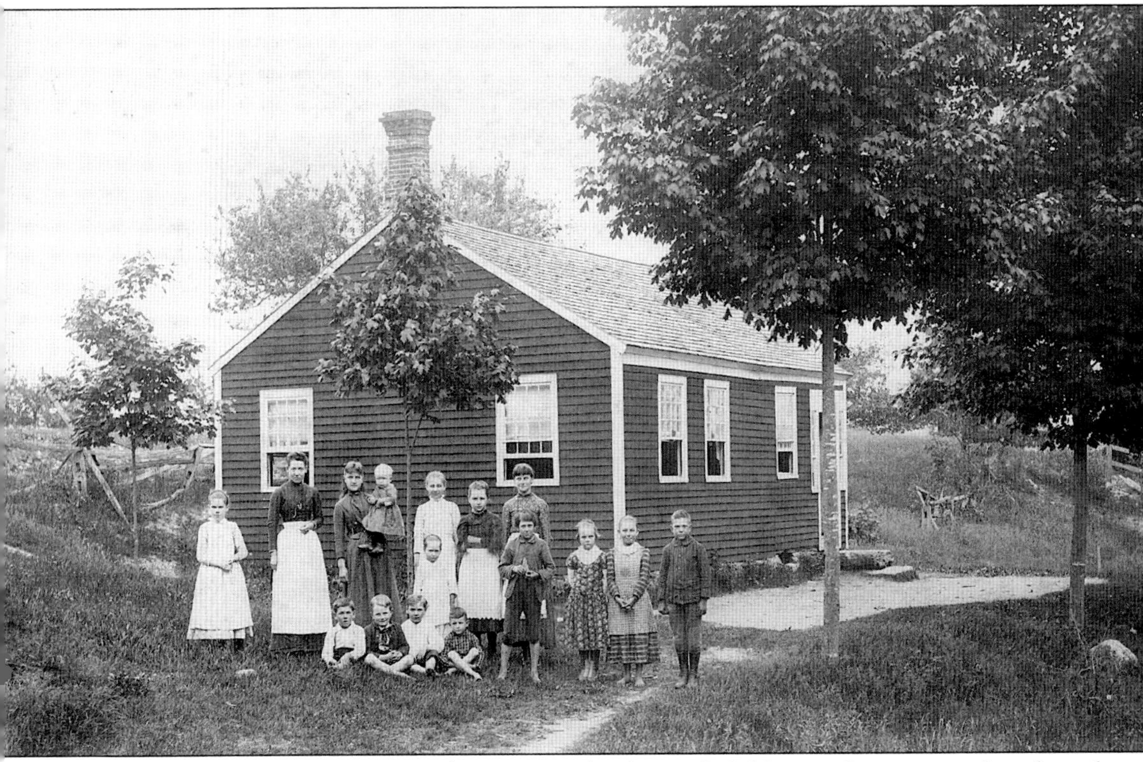

The Center School, 1890. The Center School served children within a one-mile radius of the center for over 100 years. Pictured outside the school in 1890 are, from left to right, the following: (front row, seated) Edwin Elton, Roy Turner, Orlando Gibbons, and Myron Butler; (middle row) Annie Nelson, Charles Nelson, Helen Beach, Mary Schwarzmann, and Roswell Elton; (back row) Edna Butler, teacher Lutie Bunnell Barnes, Maude Guilde holding Harry Elton, Susie Webster, Nellie Henry, and Grace Henry. (Lois Humphrey Collection, BPL.)

IMAGES
of America

BURLINGTON

Jean M. Martin

ARCADIA
PUBLISHING

ISBN 978-0-7385-0905-1

Published by Arcadia Publishing
Charleston, South Carolina

Printed in the United States of America

Library of Congress Catalog Card Number: 2001090301

For all general information contact Arcadia Publishing at:
Telephone 843-853-2070
Fax 843-853-0044
E-mail sales@arcadiapublishing.com
For customer service and orders:
Toll-Free 1-888-313-2665

Visit us on the Internet at www.arcadiapublishing.com

This book is dedicated to Gussie Poglitsch, who, when she heard of this project, was one of the first people to search for family photographs in her care. She encouraged her friends to do the same, and we are grateful. The Whigville area and the Grange have come to life through her efforts, since she has such a good memory for details. "I went to the attic for you," she said. She also shared with us her eighth-grade Citizenship Journal which is quoted a few times. Gussie, thank you so much! We hope Gussie and all other readers have many happy hours looking at everyone's pictures and reading about the town.

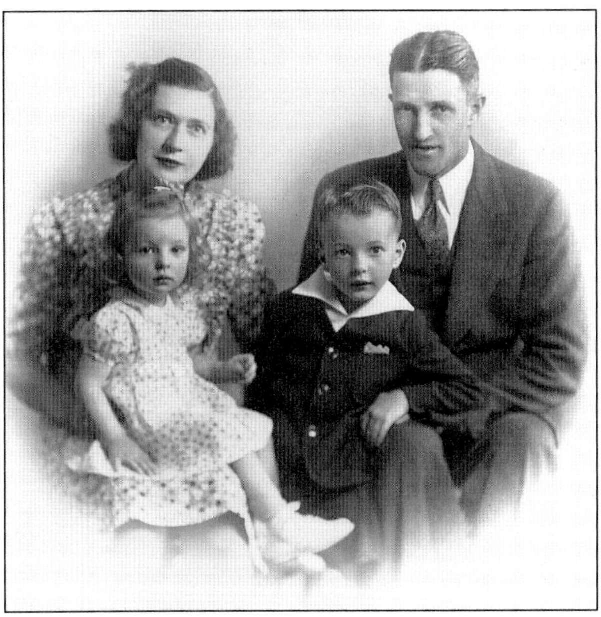

POGLITSCH FAMILY PORTRAIT. Rudy and Gussie Backes Poglitsch sat for this portrait in 1947 with their two children, Arlene and Rudy Jr. (ABP.)

Contents

ACKNOWLEDGMENTS

I wish to thank all of the lenders of the photographs in the book. The Burlington Public Library has a fine collection of books, photographs, manuscripts, letters, and newsletters in the Burlington Room. Many of the photographs and much of the information that accompanies them came from that room. On my visits there, I was made to feel like a part of the library family and a member of the community. I was warmly welcomed and well taken care of as I met with prospective lenders and listened to stories of Burlington's past. Thank you to all of the librarians, board members, and volunteers. Anne Walluk, Ann Mazeau, and Leonard Alderman were especially instrumental in encouraging me to compile this book and in supporting me at every opportunity. Leonard Alderman's materials in the library were helpful to me as I read the history and the stories he has compiled from thousands of sources. His *The Obituaries of Burlington People* has been my constant resource for birth dates and family genealogy. This and the volumes of *Burlington Articles of the Past* are his gift to current and future generations. Thank you Anne, Ann, and Leonard for all of your assistance. Wendy Cunningham, thank you for making Gussie aware of this project and then bringing to us her photographs and stories.

To my Farmington and Burlington friends who have fed and lodged me on several working trips for this book I am truly grateful. It was a special treat to spend the few extra moments with you. To my family in Virginia, especially my dear Charlie, thank you for your support and cheers at each successful trip. To our newest grandson, Miles Mandela Thompson, I say, "Welcome to the world, I hope you will come to enjoy history as much as your Nana does."

Thank you to everyone who brought in your cherished photographs so that they could be shared. Photographs from individuals and organizations are indicated throughout the book using the following abbreviations:

Clifford Alderman (CA.)
Lois and Leonard Alderman (LA.)
Richard Alderman (RA.)
Carol Mayer Bauer (CMB.)
Burlington Public Library (BPL.)
Mavis French Davis (MFD.)
Betty Hinman Douglas (BHD.)
Evelyn Ennis (EE.)
Lucretia Merriman Fortier (LMF.)
Walter and Mary Sakowski Krawiec (MSK.)
Emory G. Krish (EK.)
Margaret Lavoie (ML.)
Helen Hartigan Mullin (HHM.)
Augustina Backes Poglitsch (ABP.)
Harold W. Scheidel (HWS.)
Waldemar and Alice Brown Szczesniak (WABS.)
Virginia M. Vining (VMV.)
Russell and Dorothy Wollmann (RDW.)

INTRODUCTION

The year 2006 marks 200 years since the incorporation of Burlington. Originally part of Farmington, it became the northern part of the "West Woods District of Farmington," then New Cambridge, and finally Burlington in 1806. Farmington, in Hartford County, was settled in the 1720s and incorporated in 1745. In 1806, Burlington covered 30.6 square miles, which encompassed parts of five mountains. Its 20,160 acres of land included valleys filled with brooks, forests, rocks, fields, stone fences, and the Farmington River. The population in 1810 was 1,467 and the principal industry was agriculture. By 1990, the population was 7,026. This mountainous rocky land was settled for religious reasons. Seventh Day Baptists, Congregationalist, and Methodists built houses of worship here before the end of the 18th century. Among the early settlers were Jacob Bacon, Nathaniel Bunnell, Joseph Lankton, Enos Lewis, Abraham and Theodore Pettibone, John and Simeon Strong, Seth Wiard, Asa Yale, and their families. Most of the early settlers were farmers who had another trade, such as blacksmiths, millers, clock makers, tinsmiths, woodworkers, or ministers.

Isolated by its rocky steep terrain, this region to the west of Farmington was used as a route between Hartford and Litchfield. Little settlement occurred during the early 18th century. The few farms were scattered, and buildings were built at intersections. From 1740 to 1780, the population grew slowly. In 1760, the Burlington Congregational Church Board voted to erect five schools. Between 1770 and 1774, Gideon Beldon built his home at the center, which today houses the Farmington Savings Bank. By 1782, a gristmill was active in town, and two tavern licenses were recorded by 1790. The Hartford and Litchfield stage line went through in 1798, and there were several cider mills, five sawmills, tanneries, potash works, and distilleries. A large copper mine in Bristol was partially in Burlington.

Wood and water have been prime resources since Burlington began. The elevation of Burlington Center is near 800 feet and the highest point, at the top of Johnny Cake Mountain, is 1,150 feet above sea level. On the northern border, between Burlington and New Hartford, 676 acres between what was the Nepaug River and Phelps Brook make up the Nepaug Reservoir. The reservoir for New Britain is in Whigville, the southern section of town. The Connecticut state fish hatchery opened in 1922 on Beldon Road, now a short distance from the new post office and fire station on George Washington Turnpike.

Natural resources, especially the waterpower in the brooks and streams that turned the waterwheels of mills and distilleries, have provided a living for the inhabitants. Raceways and rock foundations testify to the early industries. The photographs in this book will share the essence of the past in this beautiful, wet, rocky, and natural place. Along with the residents and their household pets, the land is still home to foxes, wolves, squirrels, chipmunk, deer, skunks, and many lyrical birds. Lovely all year round, Burlington is breathtaking on a clear, sunny morning in winter following a snowfall, when ice coats each twig, rock, and tree and the brooks quietly tumble through the sparkling landscape. For many years, families have enjoyed excursions into the city of Hartford for outings and celebrations, and then have relished the opportunity to return to the quiet community life in the untamed and beautiful countryside.

The images of Burlington's past were fun to find and to learn about. The photographers captured the citizens in their everyday life, as well as the celebrations, the blizzard of 1888, and the flood of 1955. Several private and unpublished journals and old newspaper clippings supplied the information included in the captions. May all of you enjoy the selections chosen to tell Burlington's story.

—Jean M. Martin
Summer 2001

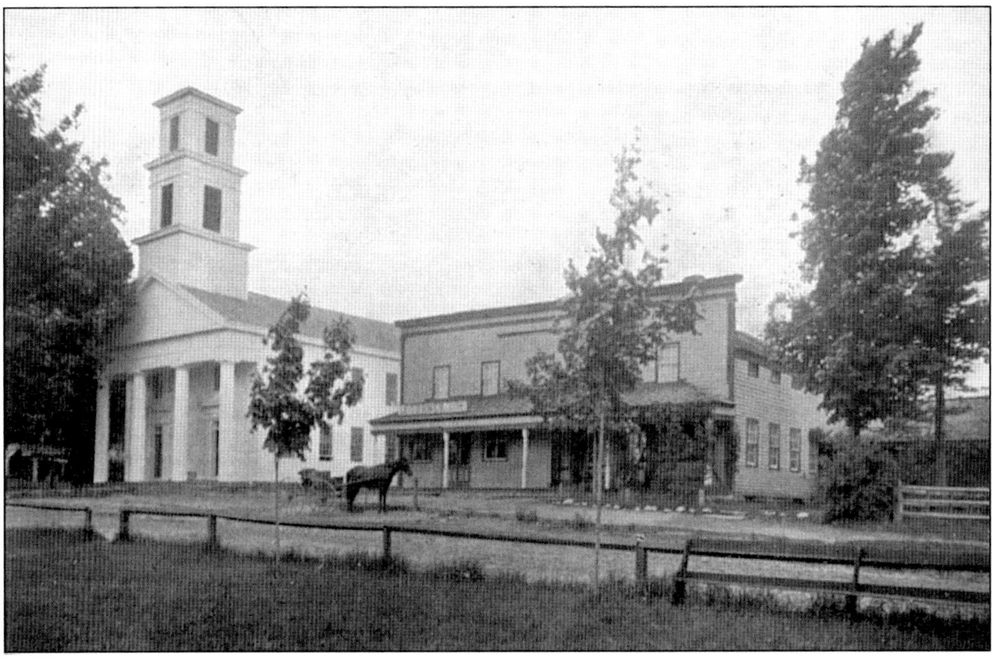

THE CHURCH, BURLINGTON, CONN. This postcard is No. 12 in a series of 15 that were printed for the centennial year of 1906. It shows the Congregational church and Turner's Store with a horse and carriage parked at the hitching post out front. The photographer was standing in the green looking northwest; on the right is a long bench. The storefront appears on the left side of the porch, nearest the church. On the right side was the house entrance with a fence and bushes to screen a family yard and garden. (BPL.)

One

Maple Shade and Watering Tubs

A small triangle of land at the center of town is called the Burlington Green. Over the years, it has changed shape and shrunk in size. By 1919, after the town had already celebrated its centennial, over 18 maple shade trees had been planted in and around the green; as Augustina "Gussie" Backes wrote that year in her Citizenship Journal, they were "about forty feet high and twenty-four inches in circumference. The branches are quite long near the ground but nearer the top they get shorter making very pretty shape trees. Which give excellent shade." In addition to the green, according to Gussie Backes, "The Town Property in Burlington are: Town hall, Public schools, Watering tubs, Highway, Bridges and School Books." The First Church of Christ stood facing the green then, as today. Burlington's first official church was the Seventh Day Baptist. In 1780, Rev. Jonathan Budick and Deacon Elisha Stillman led 19 families here from Westerly, Rhode Island. They set up their house of worship north of the present Burlington center. The Congregationalists, here from the beginning, did not officially record the society with its 26 members until 1783. Rev. John Miller of Torrington, then 22 years old, shepherded his flock until 1831. That first church, at the bottom of the slope east of the center, later gave its name to Meeting House Hill. It served Reverend Miller until 1808, when a larger one was built just to the northeast. For 28 years it remained there and then was taken down and rebuilt in its present location in the latest Greco-Roman style. The Methodists were meeting south of the village by 1814 and came into the center by 1835. One of their early pastors, Nathan Bangs, later became president of Wesleyan University. The Methodist church closed in 1892 and the building became town hall. Burlington Catholics worshiped at St. Patrick's Church in Collinsville until that church burned in 1925. Eleven years later, they dedicated a new church, built where the rectory had previously stood, just inside the Burlington boundary.

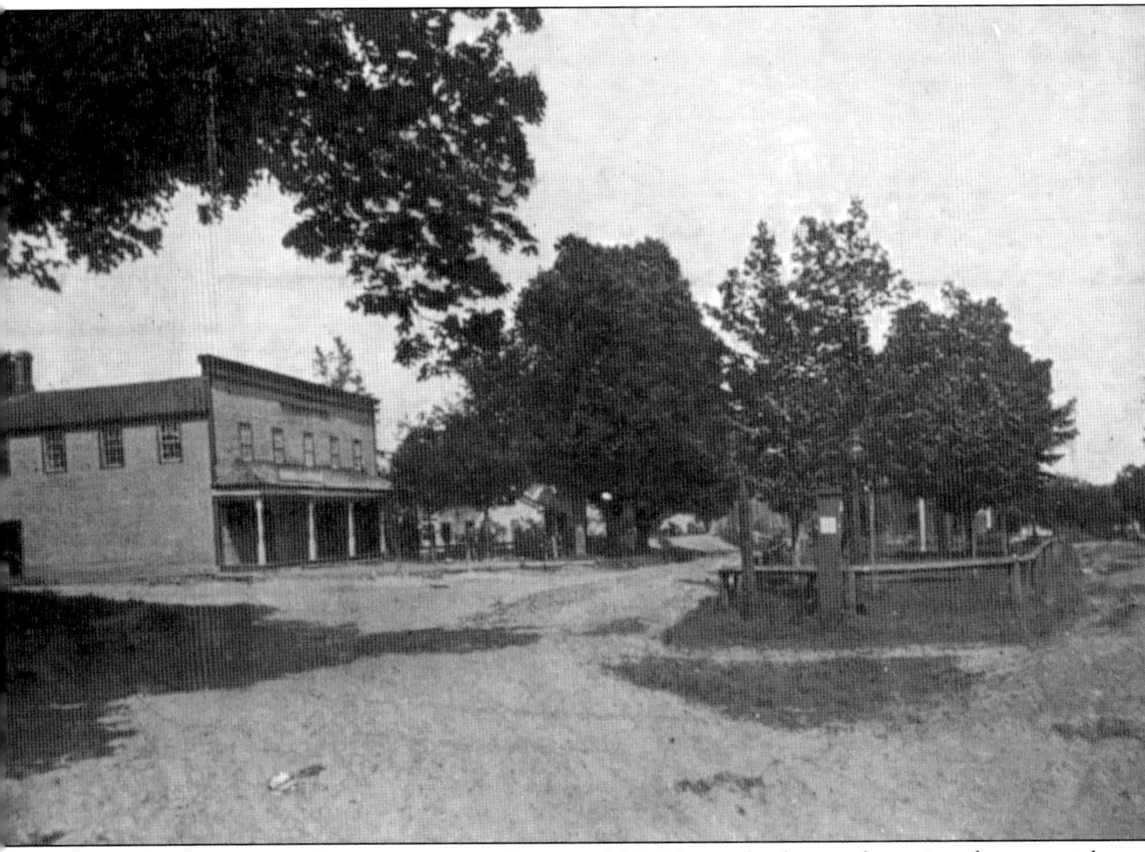

THE CENTER, THE GREEN, AND THE STORE, 1906. This is the first in the series of centennial postcards; it shows Turner's store on the left and the Burlington Green with a few shade trees. The unpaved roads look dry and dusty on this summer day. In the spring, they would have been wet and muddy for the stagecoach, horses, and pedestrians alike. The George Washington Turnpike is on the right, and just out of view is the tavern. (BPL.)

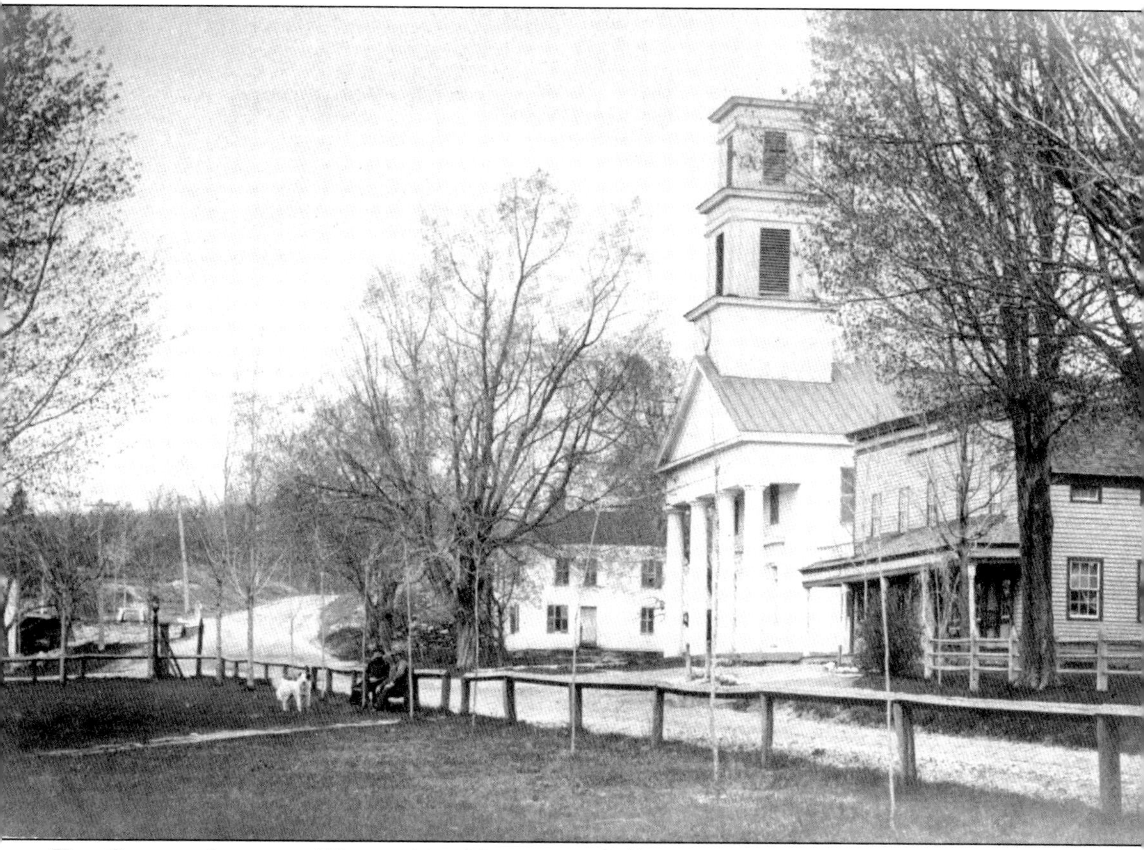

THE CENTER, LOOKING WEST, 1920. This postcard allows us to see farther along the road to Harwinton. One building beyond the tavern is on the left, and no other buildings appear as the road curves out of the center. The fence was built in 1889 by Linneus Turner to keep out large animals. At the same time, Turner planted the maple shade trees, which in this picture have not yet leafed out to provide their summer shade. The man and dog looking toward us are enjoying the fenced-in green space. (LA.)

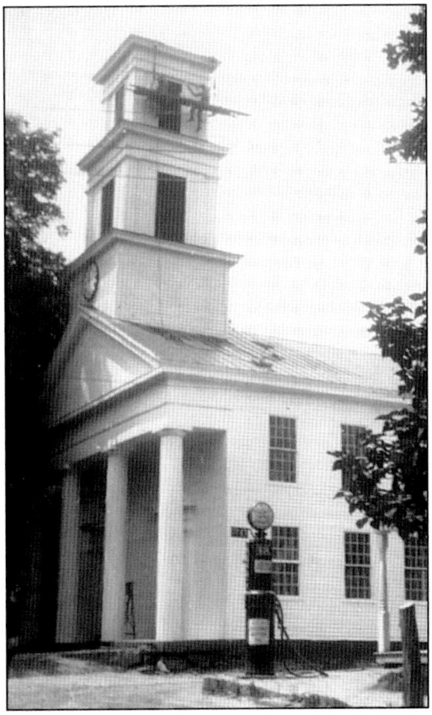

THE CHURCH STEEPLE BEING PAINTED, 1929. Arthur Ceder and his father, John Oscar "J.O." Ceder, are perched on scaffolding to paint the highest part of the wedding cake steeple. In 1906, the exterior received two coats of white paint and the blinds or shutters were painted green. The interior was decorated in sage green, blue green, and "fresco colors." The open Bible and the inscription in an arch over the pulpit were stenciled, and the seats were painted white enamel with mahogany trim. Renovations, intended to give a light, cheery aspect, were made thanks to the estate of W.F. Perkins. (LA.)

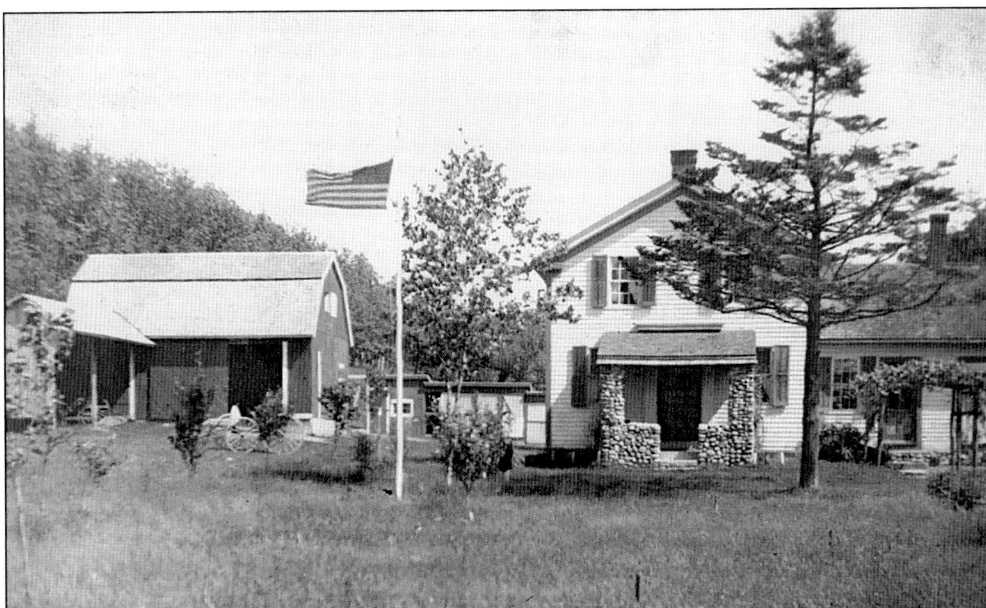

MABEL AND J.O. CEDER'S PLACE. Born in 1874, J.O. Ceder came to Burlington in 1912 from New York for his wife's health. He represented Burlington as a justice of the peace, as town treasurer, and in the state legislature. The Ceders' son Arthur had polio, but both the boy and his mother, Mabel Ceder, became "rugged" on the farm. Art and his brother Dave had the chores of filling the wood box and watering the animals. Before breakfast each boy made 6 trips to the 50-foot well, lowered buckets—one for each hand—and then ran with them to the barn, sheep pen, and chicken houses. The routine was repeated after school. (LA.)

A Church Wedding. On August 2, 1929, Reverend Thomas Campbell officiated at the wedding of Mildred Barnes and Howard Alderman. Jeanne Hinman, married here later, remembers: "There was a gray linoleum that seemed to be miserably cold looking and certainly most unattractive, but the red carpet did help." The organ and stenciling are still in place in 1929. (CA.)

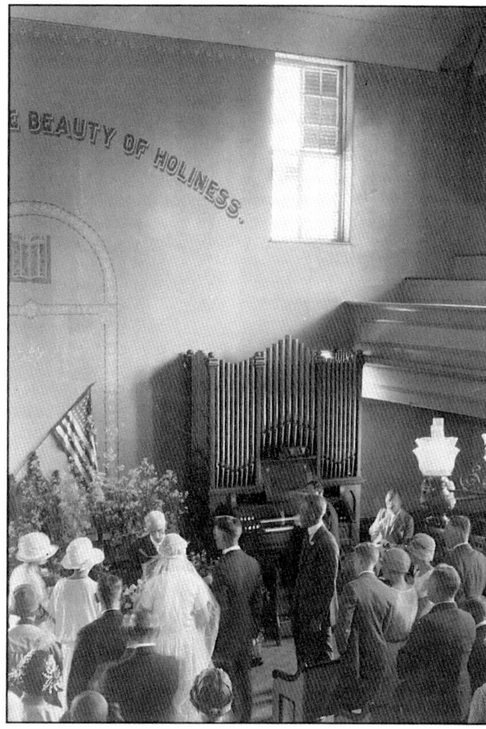

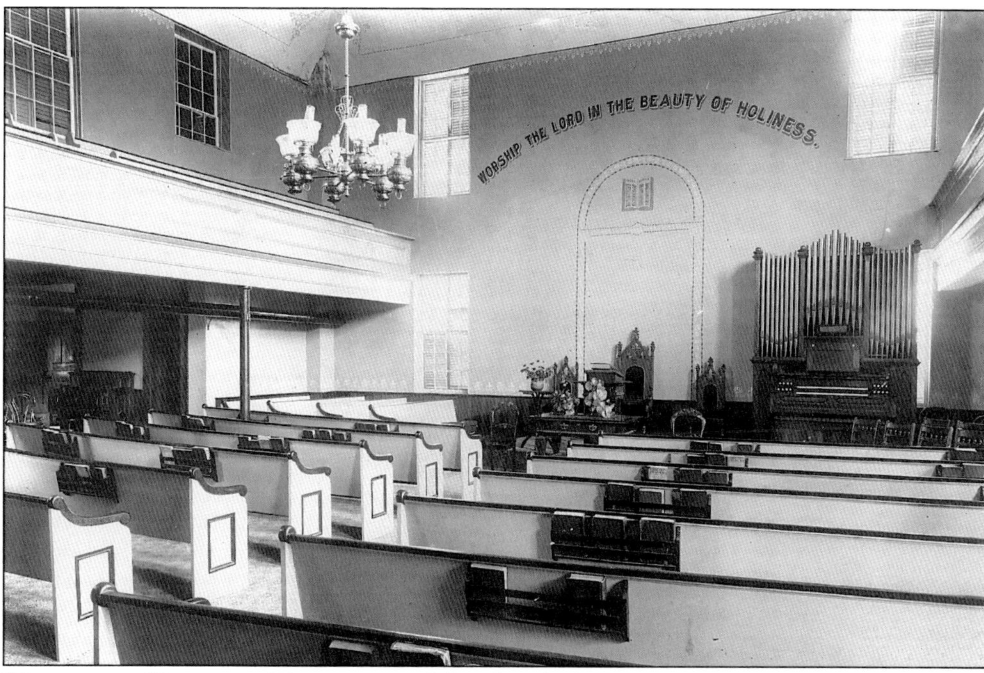

Worship in Holiness. This interior of the church shows the 1906 inscription and the new organ, which was purchased in 1912. The box pews have been removed, and the elevated pulpit has been replaced by this lower lectern with the table in front of it. Chairs for the minister, deacons, and choir show the hierarchy in seating. Jeanne Hinman recalls, "Before electricity there was a magnificent kerosene chandelier. No curtains on the windows." (CA.)

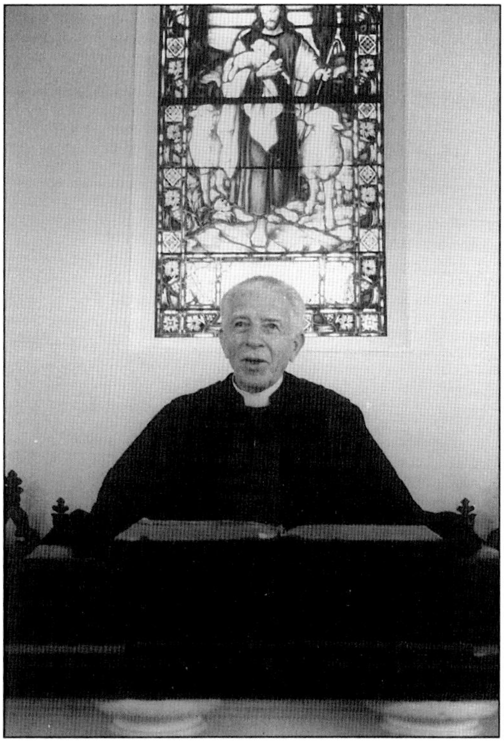

THE GOOD SHEPHERD. Rev. Dr. J. Good Brown preached his farewell sermon in 1976, after eight years of service in this church. He stands at the pulpit in front of the stained glass window that created such a controversy when it was installed. As a farewell gift, this beloved pastor compiled a history of the church and town called *The Burlington Pilgrims*. (CA.)

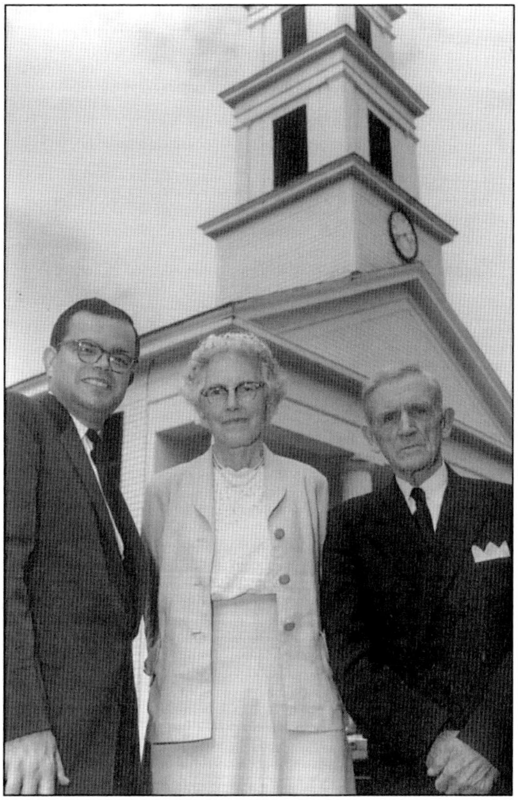

SESQUICENTENNIAL SPEAKERS. Rev. Nelson Cheney was the pastor who delivered the sesquicentennial sermon on June 16, 1956. Standing with him in front of the church are Laura R. Barnes, church historian, and Rev. Dr. Arza Keeler, son of a former pastor, John W. Keeler. A large parade with over 40 units in the line of march and a dance in the evening were part of Saturday's festivities. Sunday observances were held at the Burlington Congregational Church, and the festival culminated with a tea and anniversary cake reception in the church parlors. (CA.)

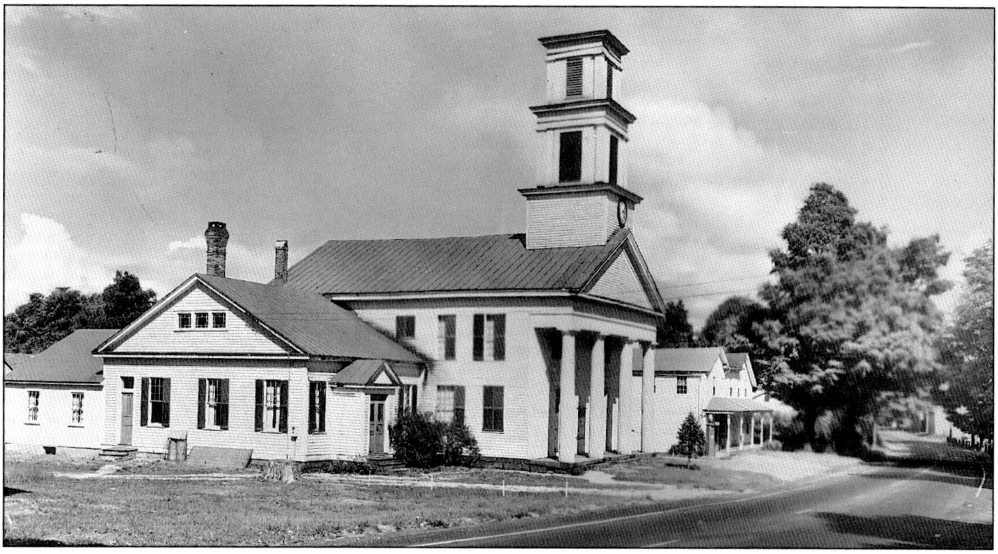

The Church Facing the Green, c.1950. This photograph shows the church over 100 years after it was moved to this location, where it has received an addition on the left. The new roofline for the store and a gas pump are visible; the hitching post is no longer needed and has been removed. Looking east, we see the paved, lined road as it goes toward the Farmington River, three miles down. We also see the large maple trees and the shade they provide for the green and the road. (LA.)

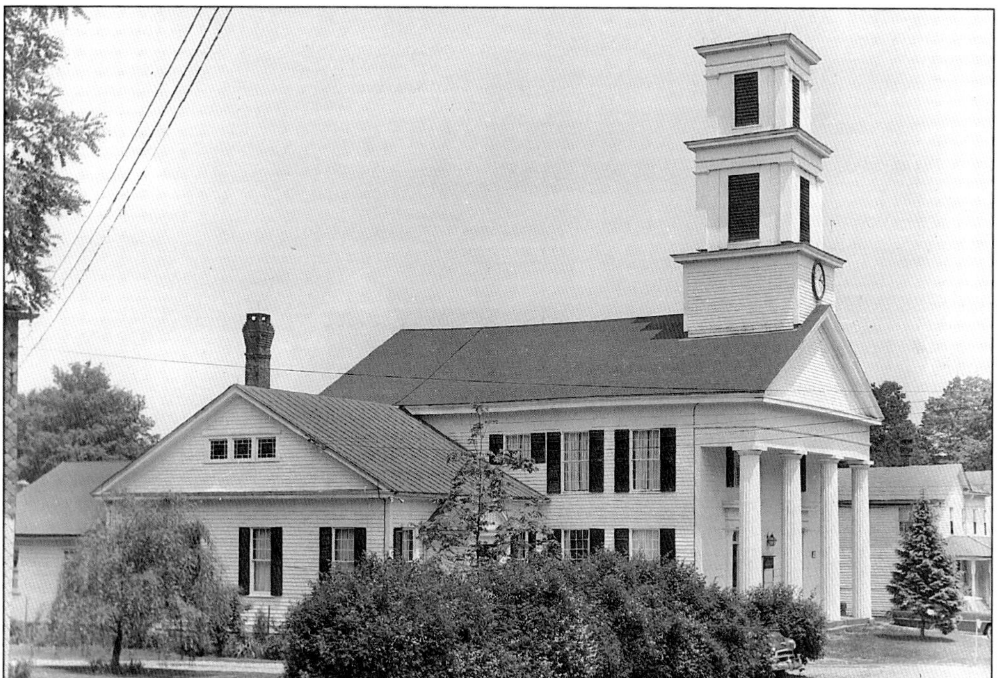

The Church Facing the Green. On June 16, 1956, the photographer captured the trees and shrubbery in full bloom outside the church parlors. Two vehicles face the Burlington Green on this bright sunny day. To the far left is the Sanford house, which is more clearly seen in the Flag Day photographs. (BPL.)

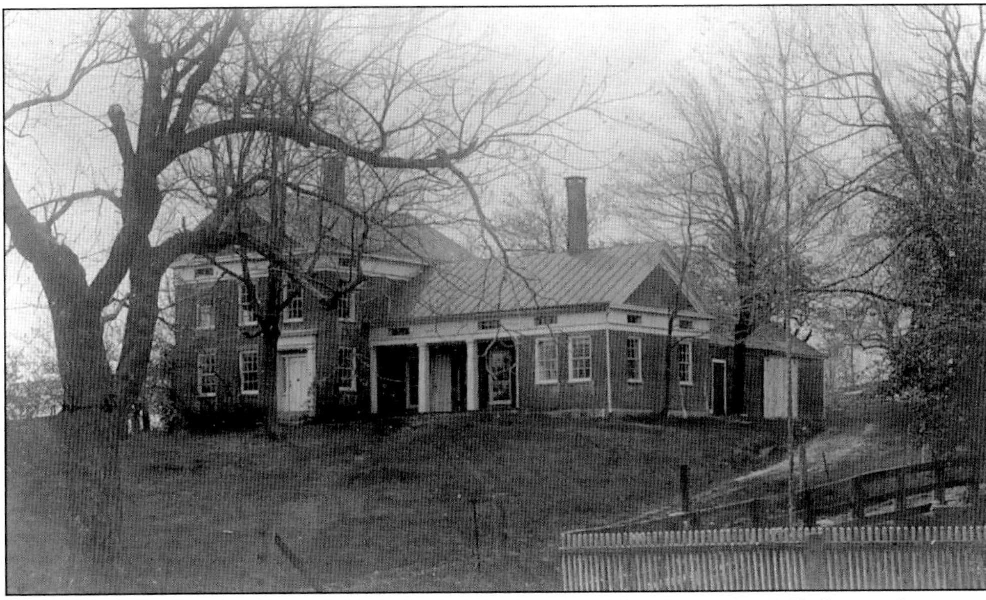

THE CONGREGATIONAL MANSE, C.1910. The brick mansion on the hill facing the green belonged to the church from 1849 until 1986. There is a steep driveway up to the back of the house and the barns. The fence on the right enclosed the yard of another early house, which is still there between the manse and the tavern. (LA.)

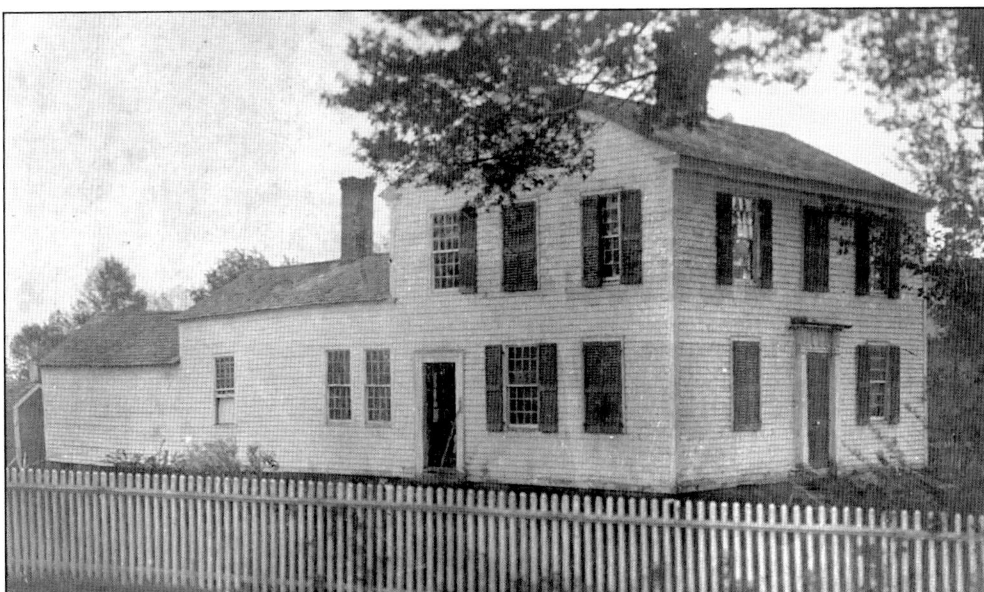

THE TURNER-LEWIS HOUSE. On the same side of the road as the church and a few doors to the east is this house, formerly owned by Linneus and Grace Turner. The Turners ran the general store on the Burlington Green for 43 years until 1924. The iron fence around the park was Grace Turner's idea, and she raised funds for the stone entrance to the cemetery. Robert and Marjorie Lewis were the last private owners; in the 1990s, the house was restored and became the Torrington Savings Bank. The Farmington Savings Bank has restored the house across the road. The Burlington Green is as lovely now as it was in the middle of the 19th century. (BPL.)

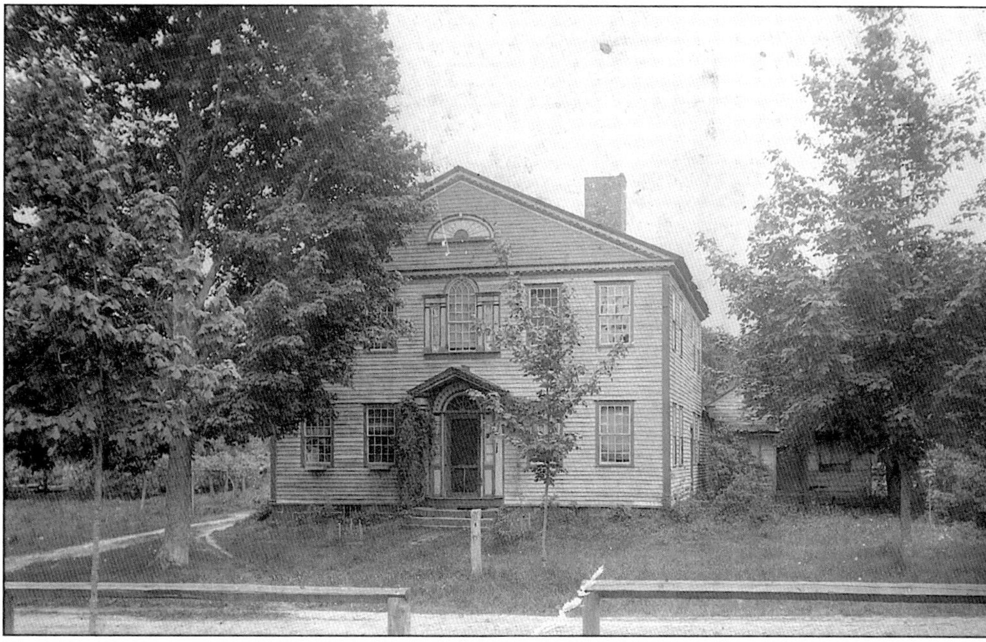

THE BROWN ELTON TAVERN IN SPRING AND SUMMER. These *c.* 1900 images show the beautiful classical architecture with a Palladian window above the front entry and a demilune window in the gable end. Twin chimneys balance the large roof, and a small canopy shelters the front entrance. Twelve-over-twelve windows allow plenty of light into all the rooms. The second-floor ballroom fills the front half of the house. A small building is on the northeast side, and a hitching post is out front. A grape arbor covered with vines stands on the other side of the driveway. Beyond the arbor are the privy and the barn. Stone walls and wooden fences abound on both sides of the tavern. Note the fence and shade trees on the green in the foreground of both views. Travelers on the Hartford & Litchfield Stage Line refreshed themselves at the tavern on the green while the stage driver changed horses. On the George Washington Turnpike, this tavern operated as an inn. The original photograph is owned by Shirley Johnson Tibbetts. (BPL.)

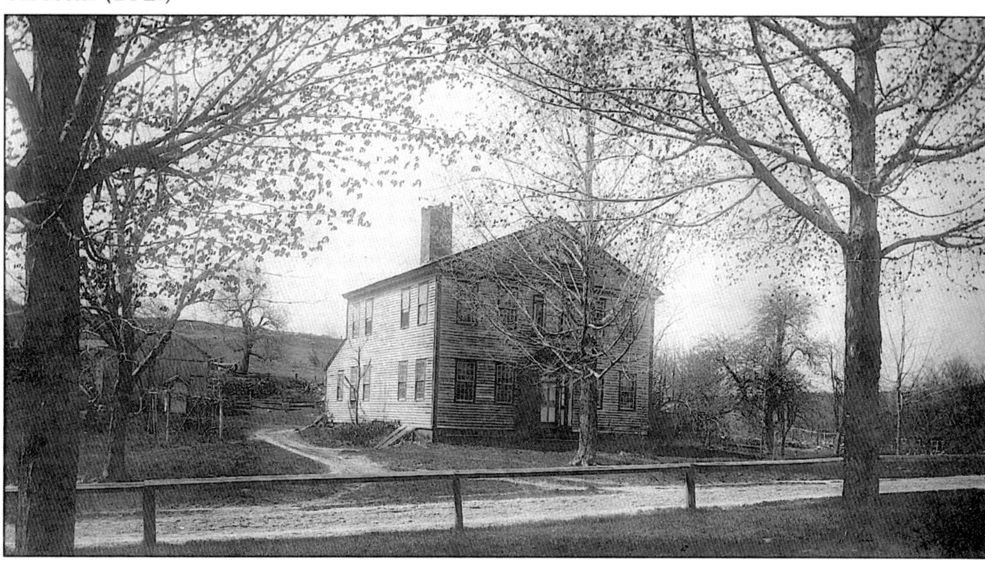

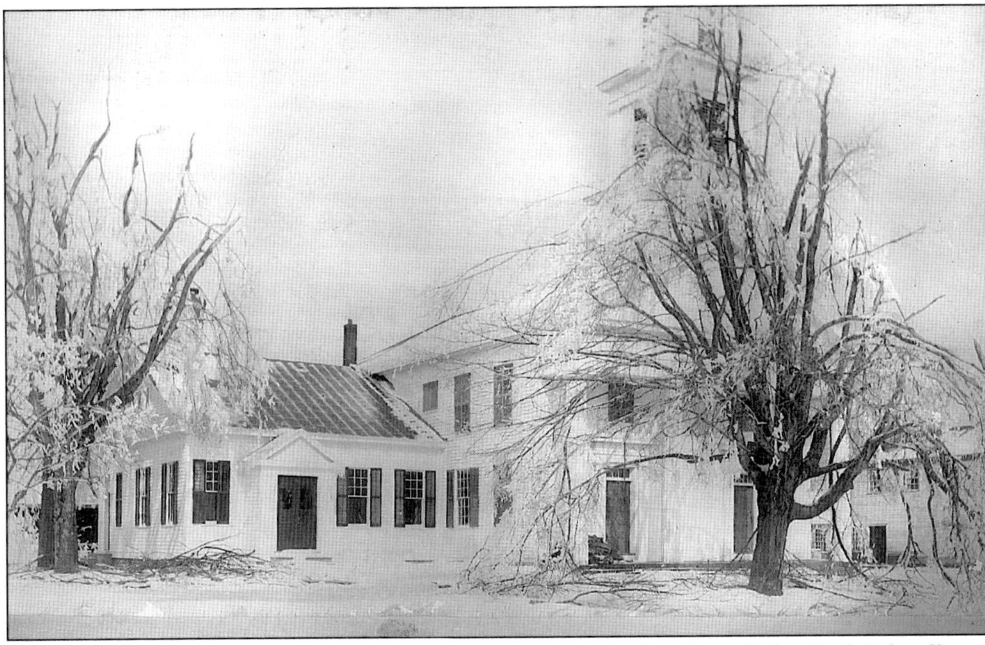

THE ICE STORM, FEBRUARY 1898. The Congregational church and the Red Schoolhouse on the green withstood the storm, but the trees were pruned mercilessly by the weight of the ice. (BPL.)

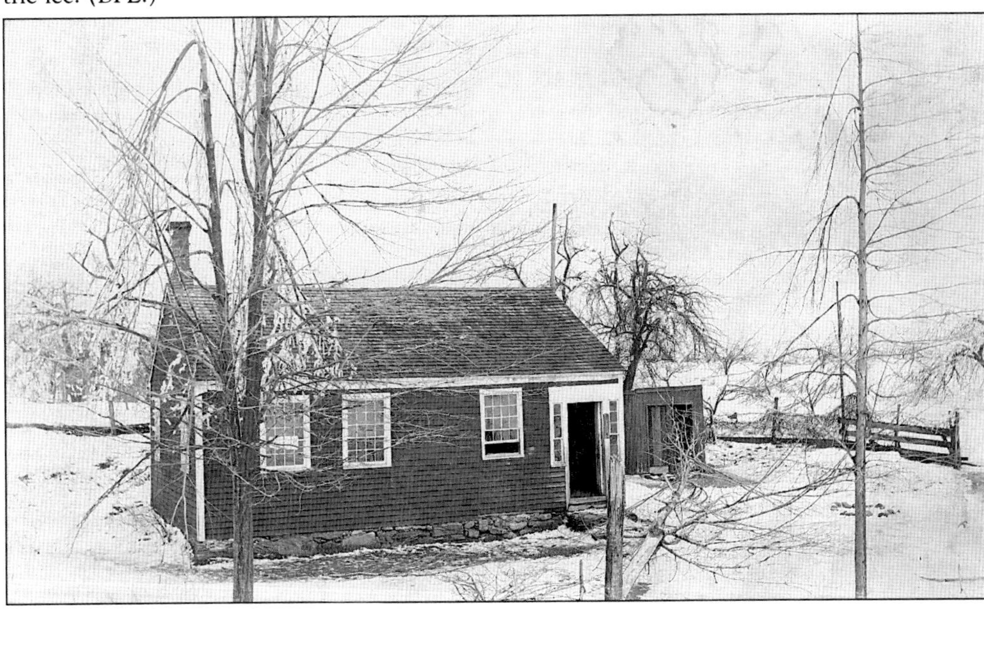

Two

Flagpoles and Patriots

The Burlington Green and the buildings around it are today referred to as the "Center." It is traditionally the place for celebrations and for honoring the people who have given their time, talents and, in many cases, their lives. Organized in 1823, the local militia practiced their maneuvers on the Burlington Green during Training Days, a community activity. Flag Day celebrations began in 1899, and now Tavern Day carries on the tradition. Photographers recorded large parades and celebrations in 1906 and 1956. Citizens of Burlington have served in all of the wars since the town's founding. There are 42 names on the American Revolutionary War Soldiers list for this area. Over 60 fought during the Civil War, and many of them were captured and imprisoned; 16 sons of Burlington did not return. World War I claimed 5 lives of the 43 men who served, and 125 men and women served in World War II. All of them are recognized in the traditional Memorial Day Parade and Remembrance Services. The photographs reflect the pride that the citizens of Burlington have had in their ancestors, schools, and heroes over the past two centuries.

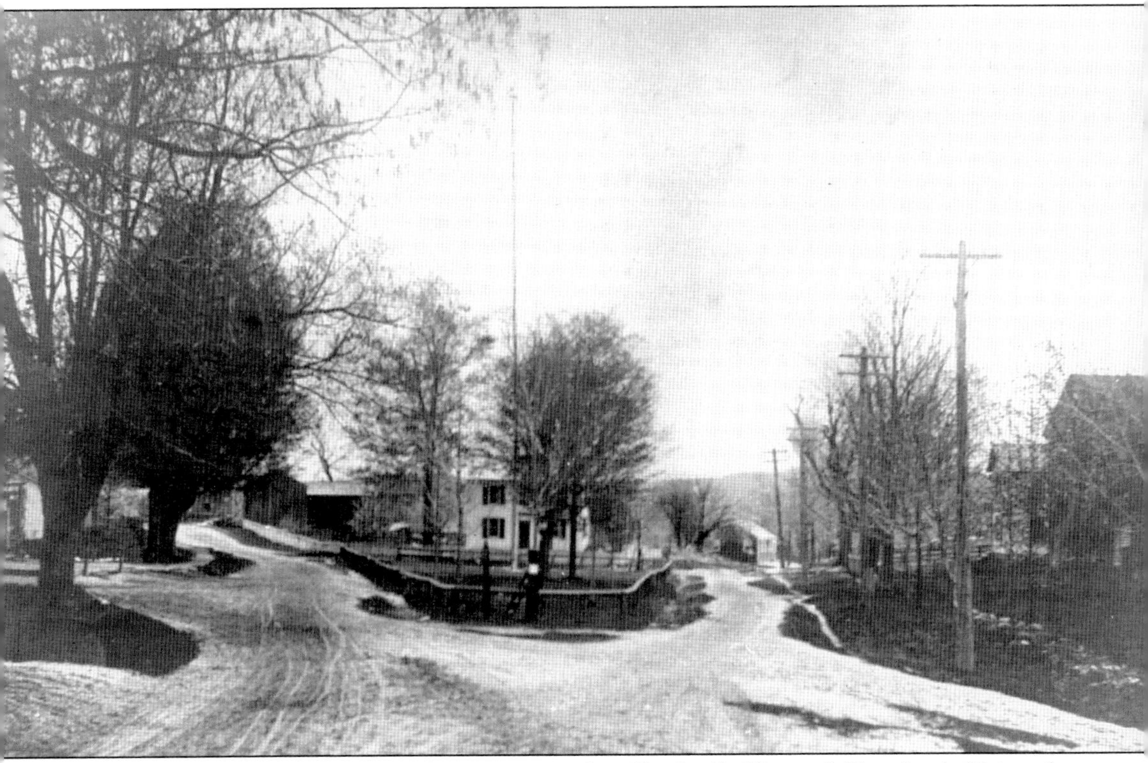

THE CENTER GREEN WITH A FLAGPOLE, 1920. Charles F. Olney of Cleveland, Ohio, whose wife, Abigail Bradley, was from Burlington, presented a large American flag to the Ladies Aid Association for Flag Day ceremonies. The pole, with the butt made of chestnut and the top of pine, was spliced together by Henry Winchester and was held by rings of steel made by Herman Wollman, the blacksmith. (LA.)

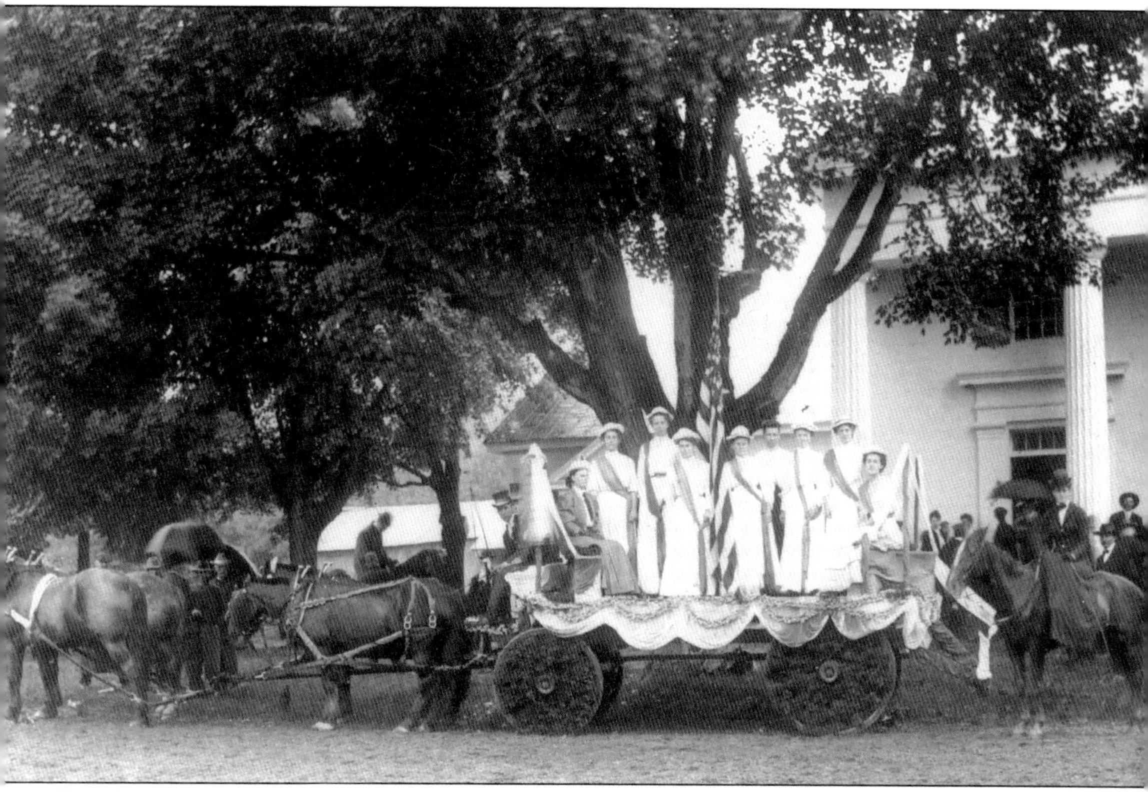

THE SUNSHINE SOCIETY, 1906. The active young women of the town who "never weary in well doing" had a float in the centennial parade. The sides and ends of the float were decorated with yellow-and-white draperies embellished with daisies. Seats on the float were arranged so the women, costumed in white dresses with yellow sashes, could face the sides. Wearing hats with yellow bands, they set the tone for the drivers, Louis Webster and Ernest Hinman, also in silk hats with yellow bands. Pulled by two teams of horses, the wheels of the wagon were camouflaged by pine branches. A large American flag floated from a central staff; along with a yellow-and-white banner, it brought sunshine to a rainy day. Those on the float are Sadie Scoville, Maida Green, Gertrude Wollmann, Edna Butler, Florence Smith, Sarah Jones, Addie Henry, Effie Dowd, and Julia and Elvira Webster. Clara Schwarzmann, Lila Turner, and Marshall D.E. Mills rode alongside on horses. (BPL.)

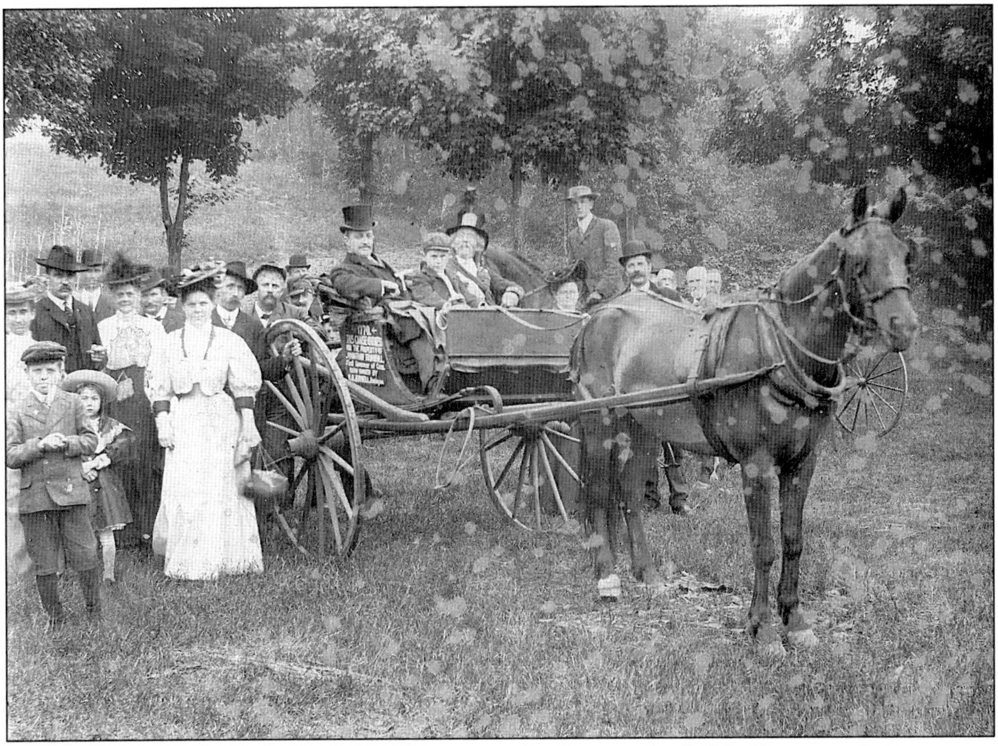

GOVERNOR ROBERTS IN GOVERNOR TRUMBULL'S CHAISE. In 1906, Governor Roberts gave an address at the centennial celebration. The governor is pictured with Warren Bunnell, his grandson, and a crowd of admiring townspeople. (BPL.)

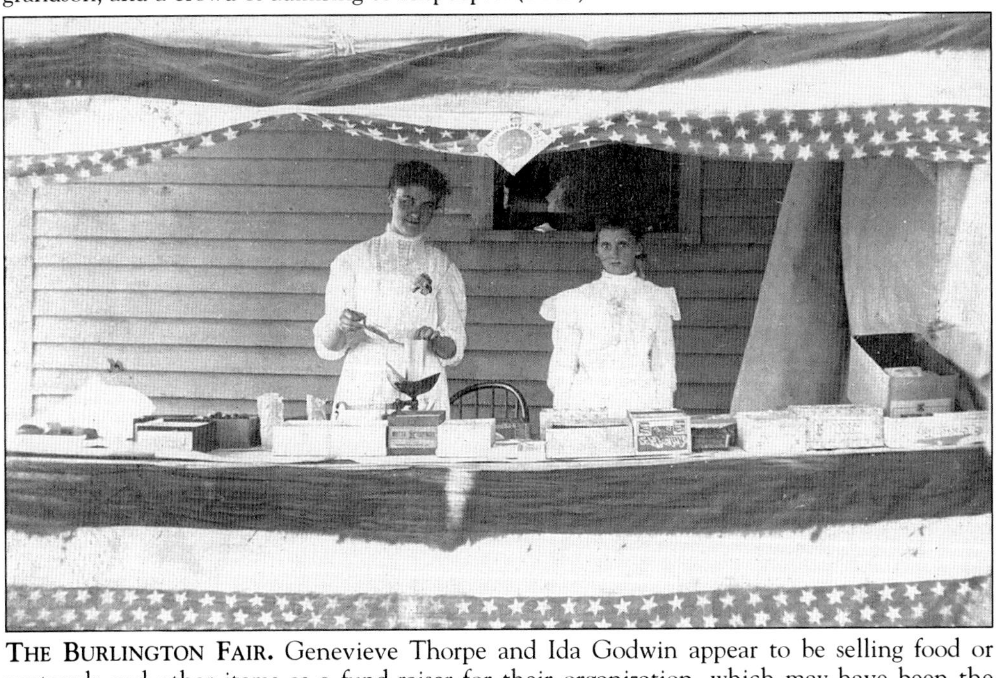

THE BURLINGTON FAIR. Genevieve Thorpe and Ida Godwin appear to be selling food or postcards and other items as a fund-raiser for their organization, which may have been the Sunshine Society. (CA.)

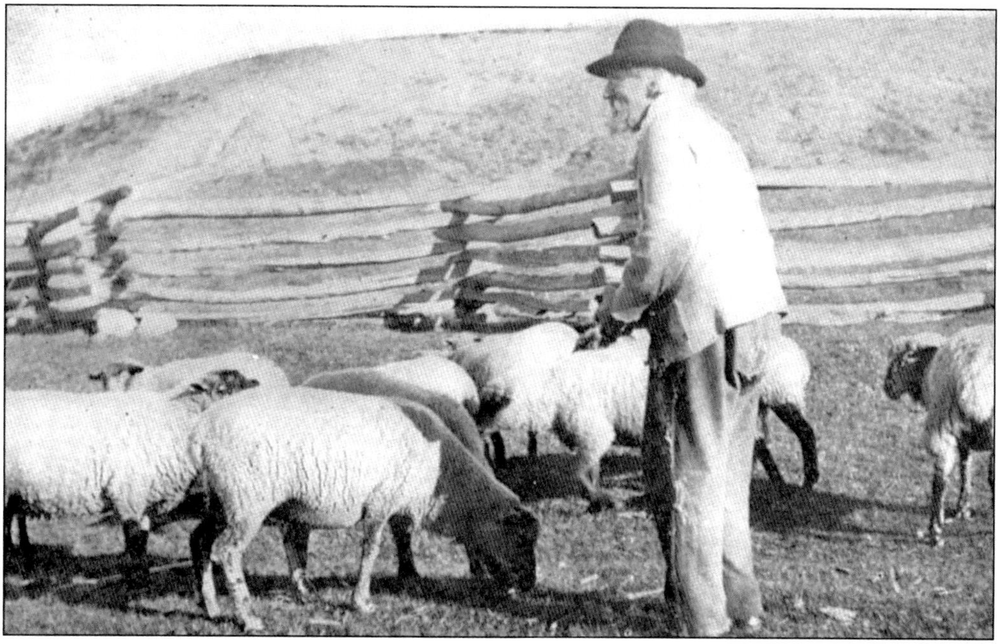

IN A BURLINGTON PASTURE. This 1906 postcard shows Warren Bunnell, age 86, and his sheep enclosed by a Virginia fence. Bunnell engineered the pole construction and installation of the 100-foot flagpole for Burlington Center. A successful farmer, the public-spirited Bunnell held many local offices, including town treasurer. (BPL.)

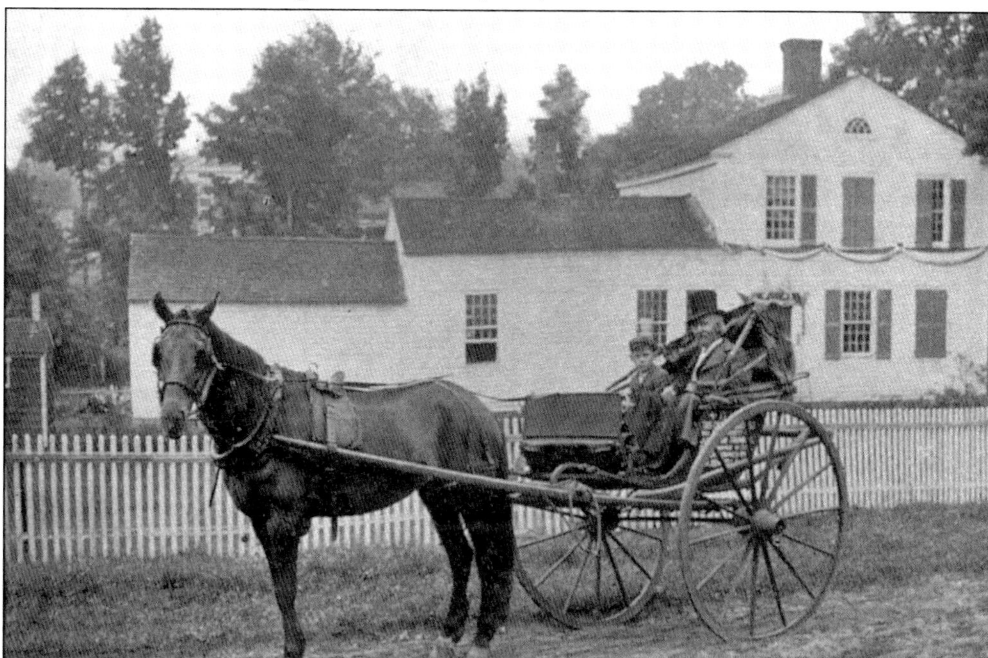

JONATHAN TRUMBULL'S CHAISE AND HARNESS. Warren Bunnell is in the carriage with his grandson in this postcard. They are in front of the mansion house built by Abraham Pettibone in the 1770s, (behind the flagpole in the Burlington Green photograph). Called the Barton House for its last owner, it is now the home of the Farmington Savings Bank. (LA.)

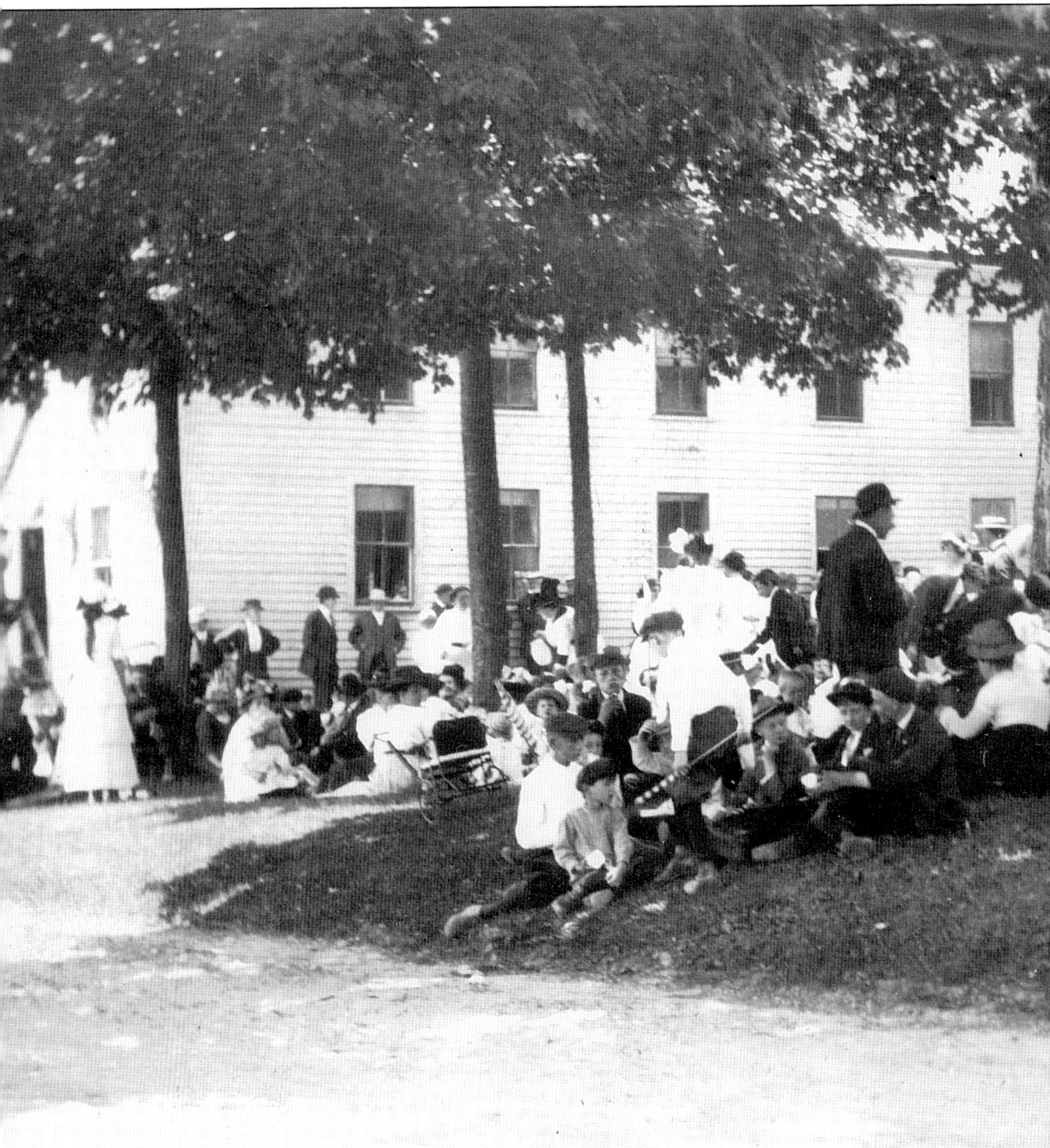

Flag Day. This Flag Day photograph is undated and unlabeled except for "Old Town Hall" and "Route 4, Drive to Cemetery." The building on the left was the town hall and the one

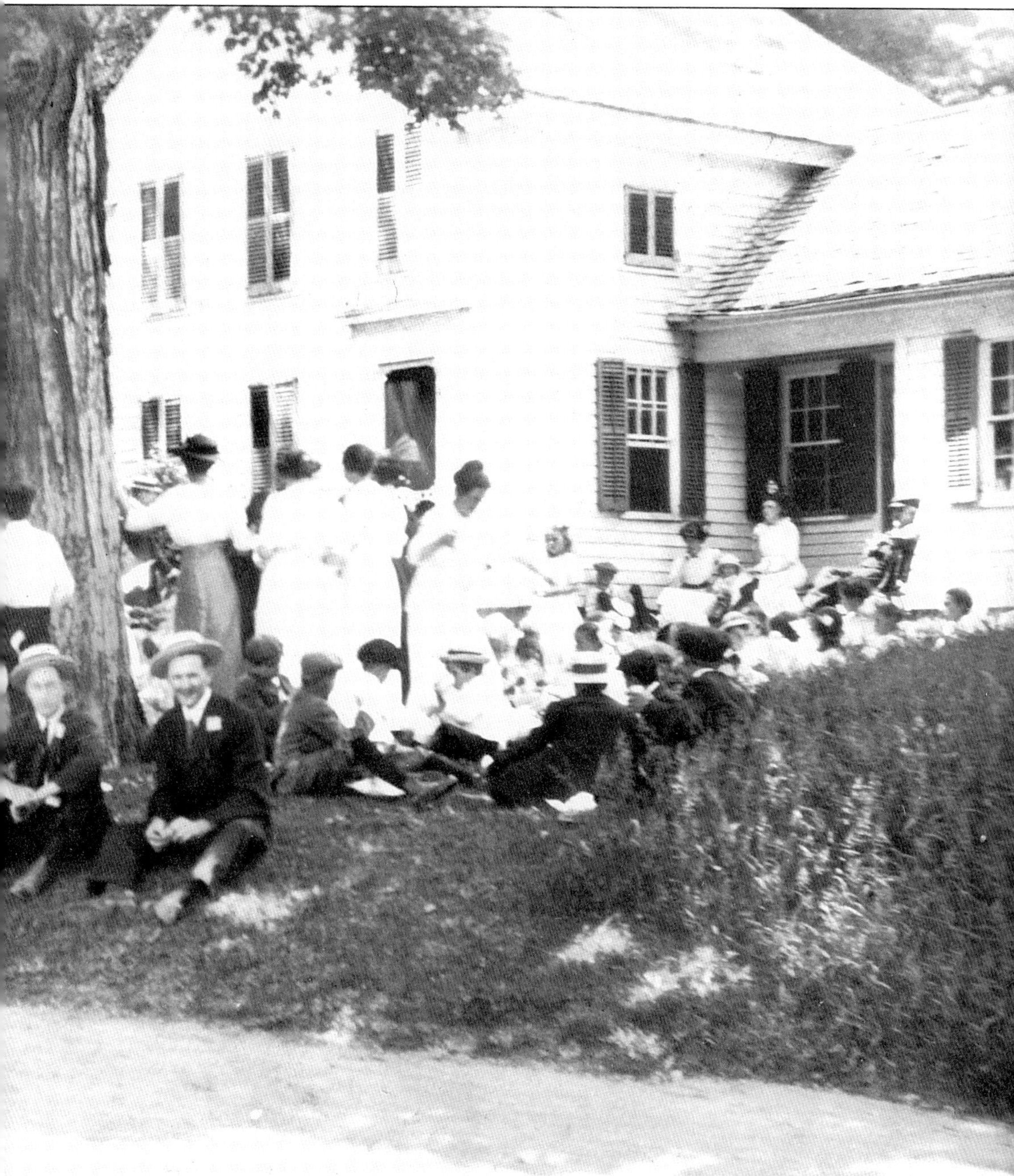

on the right served as the Methodist parsonage at one time. The entrance to the Burlington Center Cemetery is still in the same location, but the building on the left has changed. (LA.)

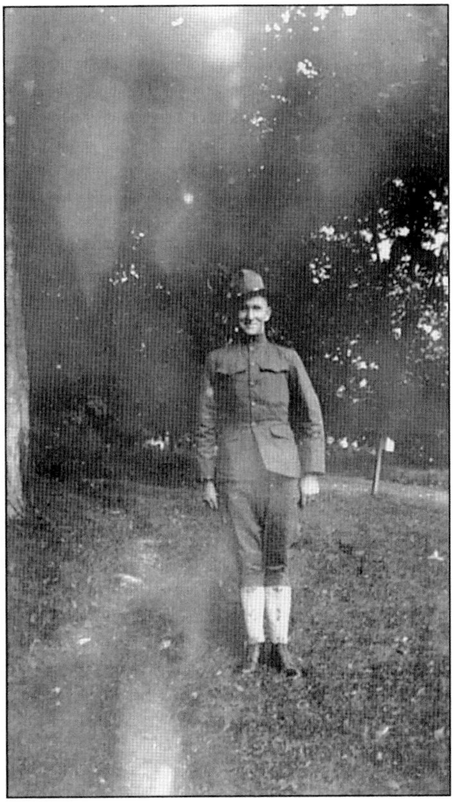

WILLARD RAYMOND REYNOLDS, WORLD WARS I AND II. Like many other Burlington men, Willard Raymond Reynolds saw service in more than one war. He was born in Harwinton in 1899, served in both World War I and World War II, and lived most of his life in the Harwinton-Burlington area. He died in 1969. (LA.)

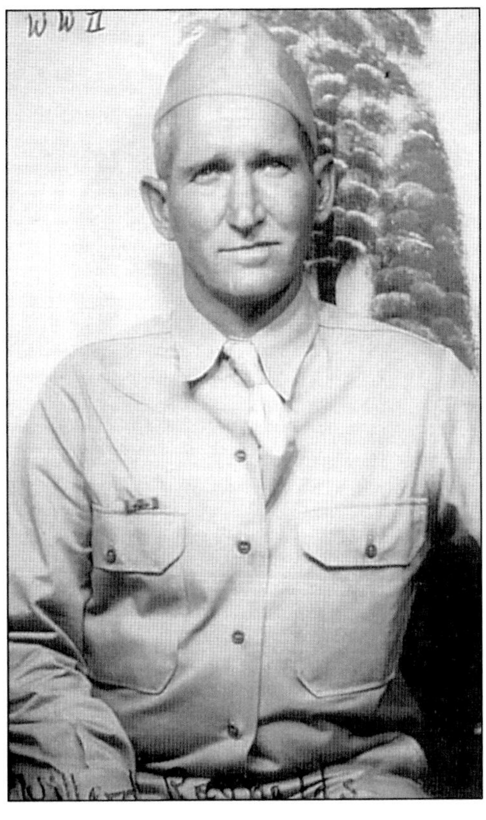

IN THE OLD CEMETERY. This postcard is No. 9 in the centennial series. The Katherine Gaylord Monument honors a brave wife and mother from the westward movement days of the United States. Her descendants and the Daughters of the American Revolution erected this stone to recognize her heroism at the 1778 Massacre of Wyoming, (a valley in the far western part of what was once Connecticut but now is Pennsylvania). (BPL.)

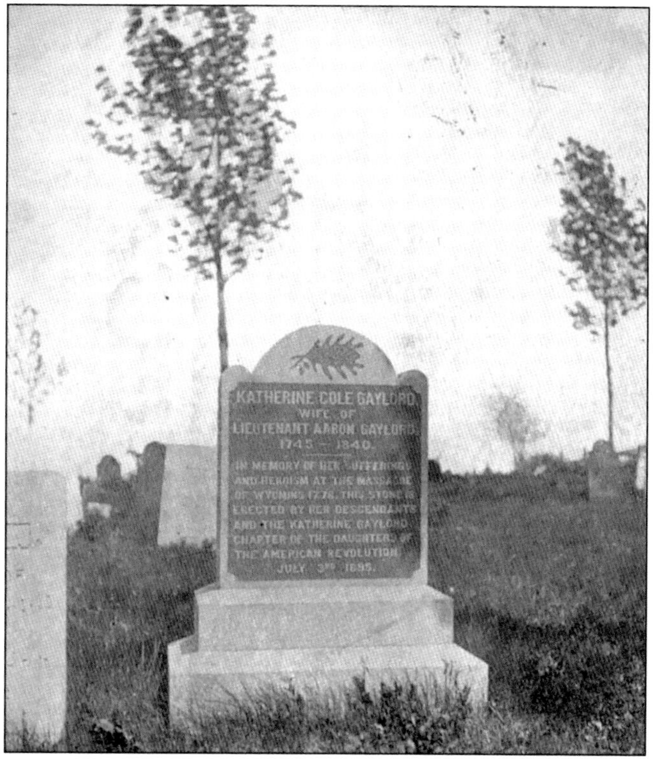

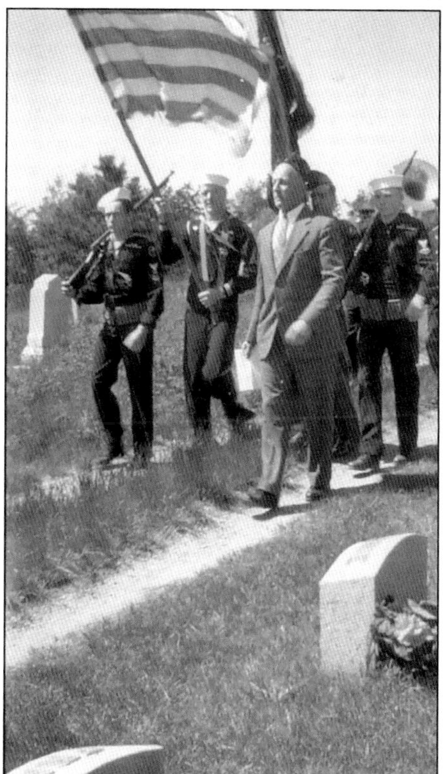

MEMORIAL DAY IN CENTER CEMETERY. Arthur Reeve Jr. (with the gun), Leonard Alderman (carrying the flag), David Twining, and John Daniels—all in navy uniform—accompany Arthur Reeve Sr. (see his wedding photograph on page 29) during a Memorial Day service. John Twining, David's father, was sexton of the church and of the cemetery for 20 years. (LA.)

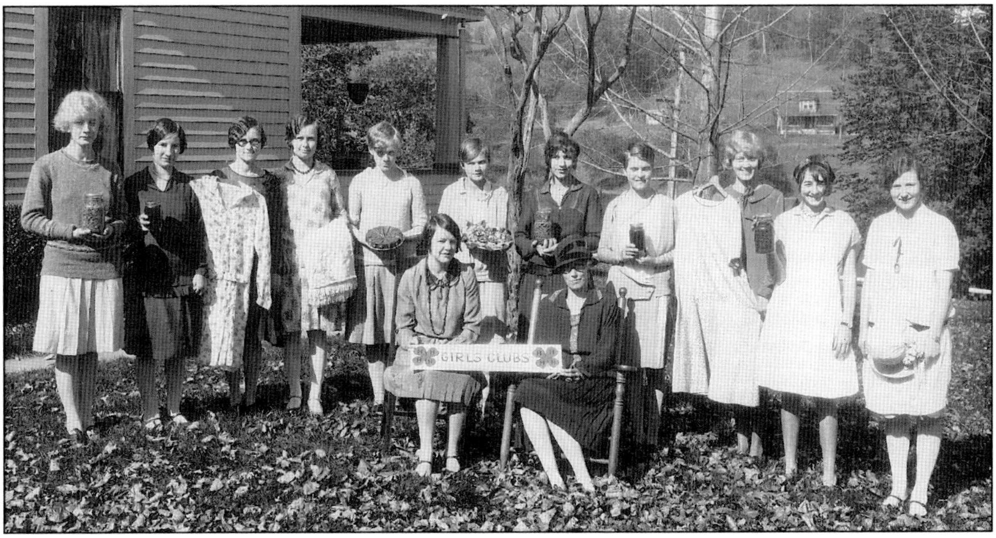

THE 4-H GIRLS CLUB, 1929. The Burlington Girls 4-H Club focused on sewing and cooking. This photograph was taken by Mildred Alderman outside Elliott Alderman's home, where Hazel, Doris, and Alice lived, on the west corner of Route 4 and Punch Brook Road. Each girl holds a project. Participating, from left to right, are the following: (front row) Elsie Tribou, head of 4-H in Connecticut, and Laura Barnes, 4-H leader; (back row) Doris Alderman, Marie Stieg, Nellie Szegda, Annie Szegda, Hazel Alderman, Gertrude Wuori, Loretta Scheidel, Mildred Winalski, Alice Alderman, Helen Hartigan, and Gertrude Warnecke. (HHM.)

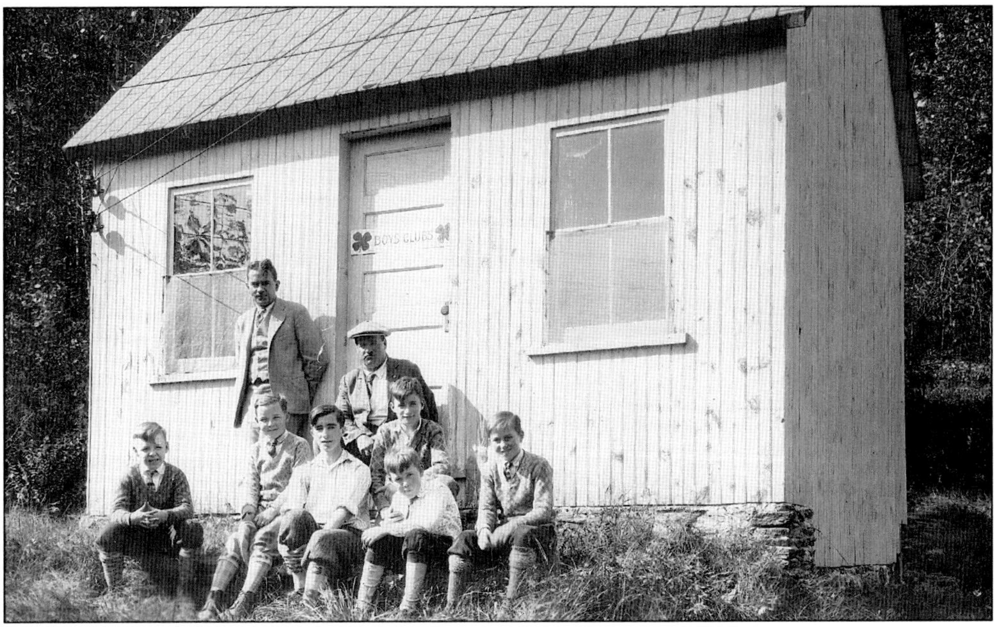

THE BOYS' 4-H POULTRY CLUB, 1929. The club meetinghouse stood beside Belden Road, about 150 yards northwest of the fish hatchery. It was later moved to a site near the hatchery. In this photograph taken by Mildred Alderman are, from left to right, the following: (front row) John and Howard Hinman, Michael Blanchard, Bernard Blanchard, and Chrysostom Blanchard; (back row) county 4-H agent Arthur Hale, club leader John "Jack" Larson, and Arthur Johnson. (BPL.)

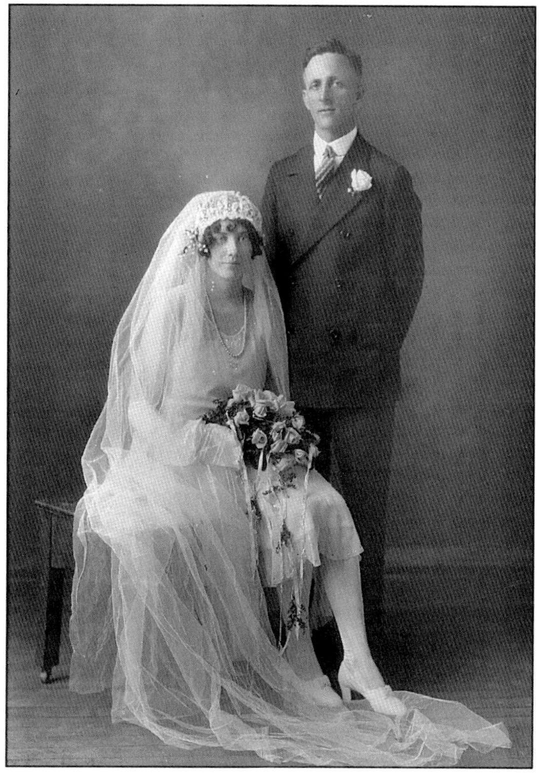

The Reeve Wedding. In 1925, Alice Watt and Arthur J. Reeve Sr. were married. Arthur Reeve was born in Burlington in 1895, was a veteran of World War I, and was town clerk of Burlington from 1935 to 1962. The couple had seven children. (ABP.)

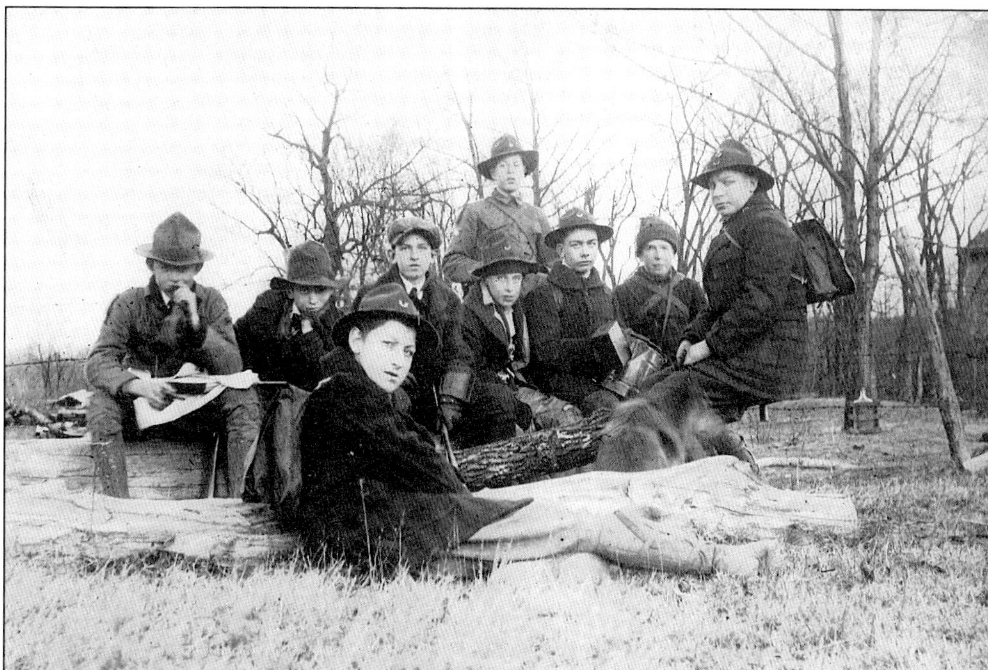

A Boy Scout Outing. In 1909, Carol Mayer Bauer's father's Boy Scout troop went into the woods off Ford Road near the Farmington River. Identified in the is Howard E. Mayer, far right. (CMB.)

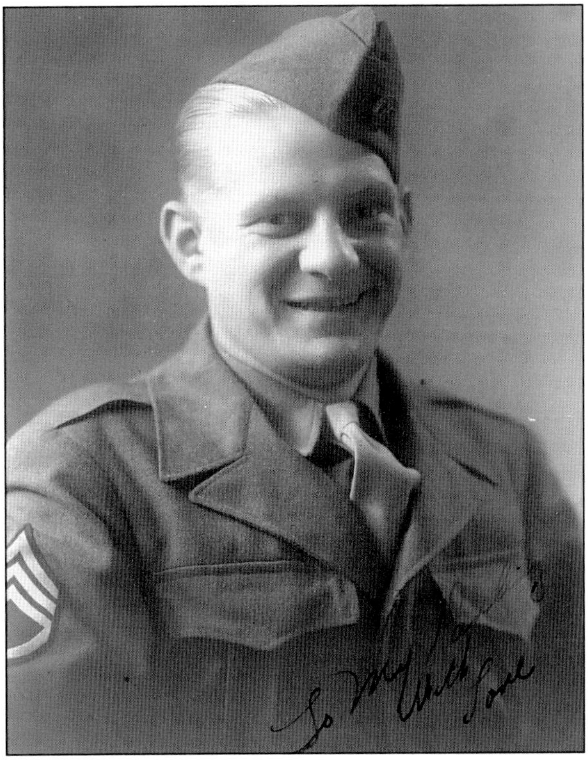

"To My Darling, with Love." In 1941, Anna Cswerko married Emory Krish and they sent frequent letters while he served in World War II. This pair of photographs was exchanged with XXX's and greetings on the back. After Krish returned, he and Anna, with their son Emory Jr., purchased five acres of land on Town Line Road and cleared it by hand. They built a small barn which they lived in while they made a foundation of local fieldstone and then built a Cape Cod–style house. (EK.)

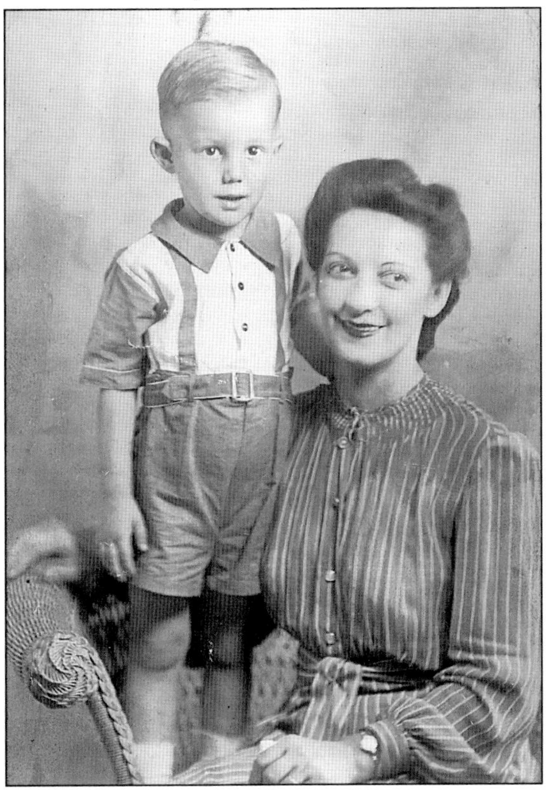

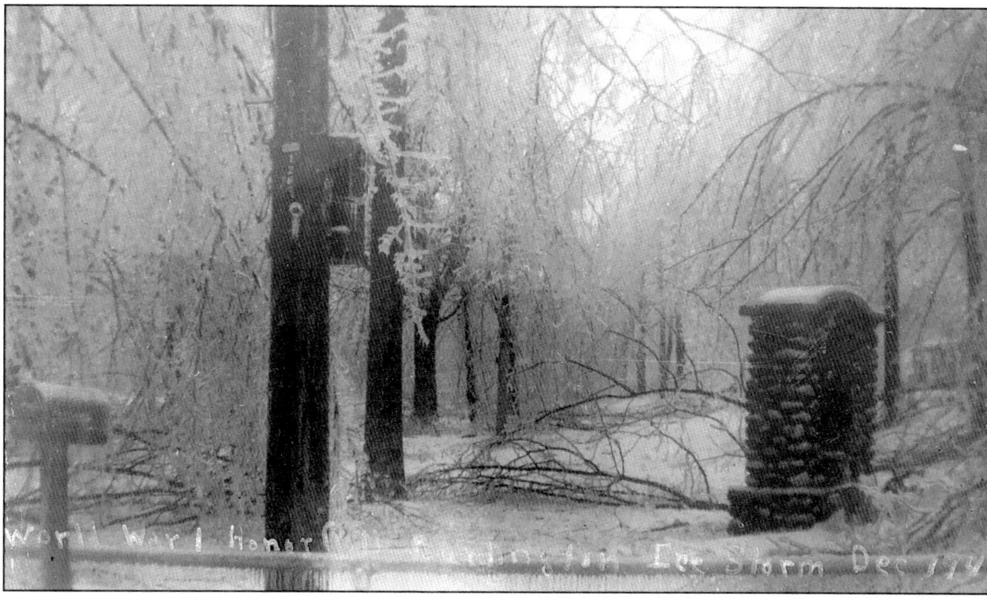

DECEMBER 11, 1942, POSTCARD OF WORLD WAR I HONOR ROLL MEMORIAL IN THE ICE STORM. On the back is written the date and "We took Leonard to New Haven in the A.M. to report to Newport, R.I. for Second World War." (LA.)

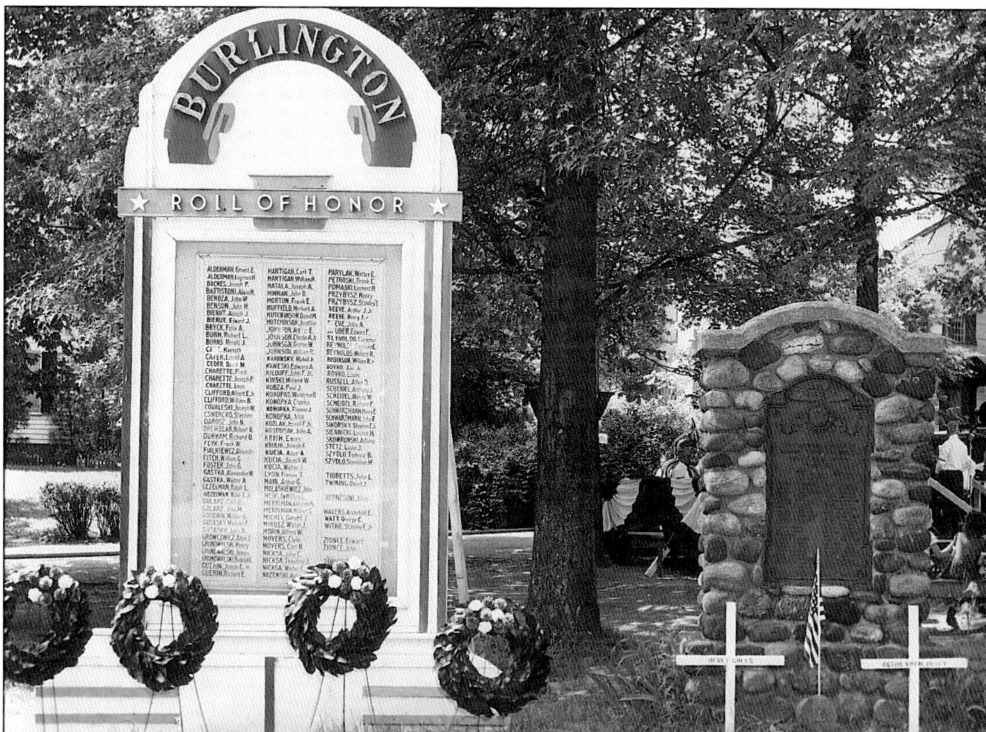

THE BURLINGTON ROLL OF HONOR, 1956. As part of the 1956 sesquicentennial celebration, the Roll of Honor and World War I Memorial are decorated with wreaths, flags, and crosses. This photograph was taken by E.L. Waldron. (BPL.)

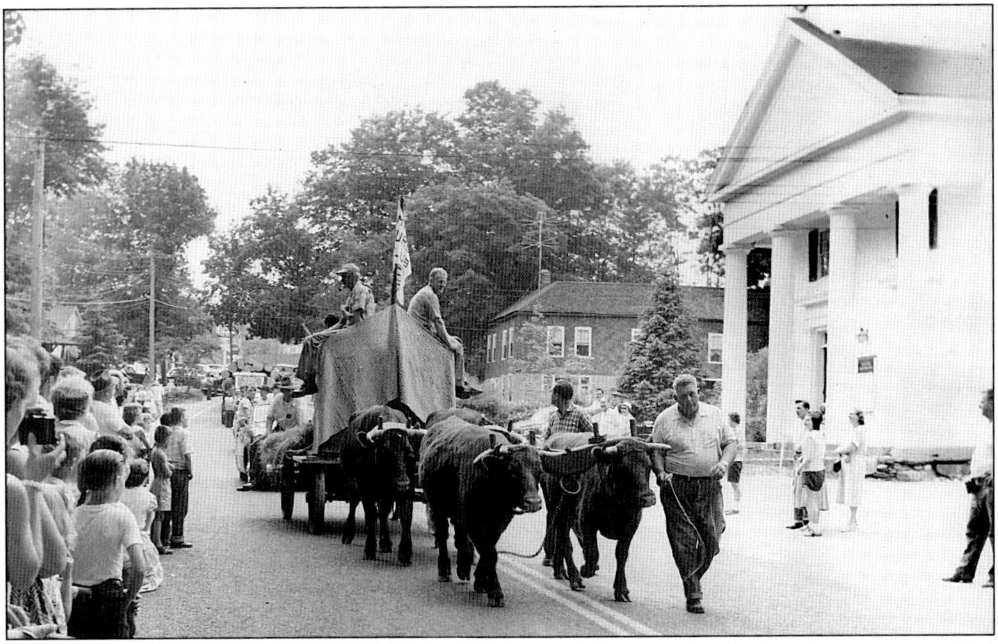

THE MEN'S CLUB CART AND OX TEAM. The entry following the donkey is a wagon pulled by two team of oxen with their handler Stoney. The men on this float enjoyed the crowds watching from the green. Antique cars made up the bulk of the next entries. E.L. Waldron took all of the 1956 parade photographs. (BPL.).

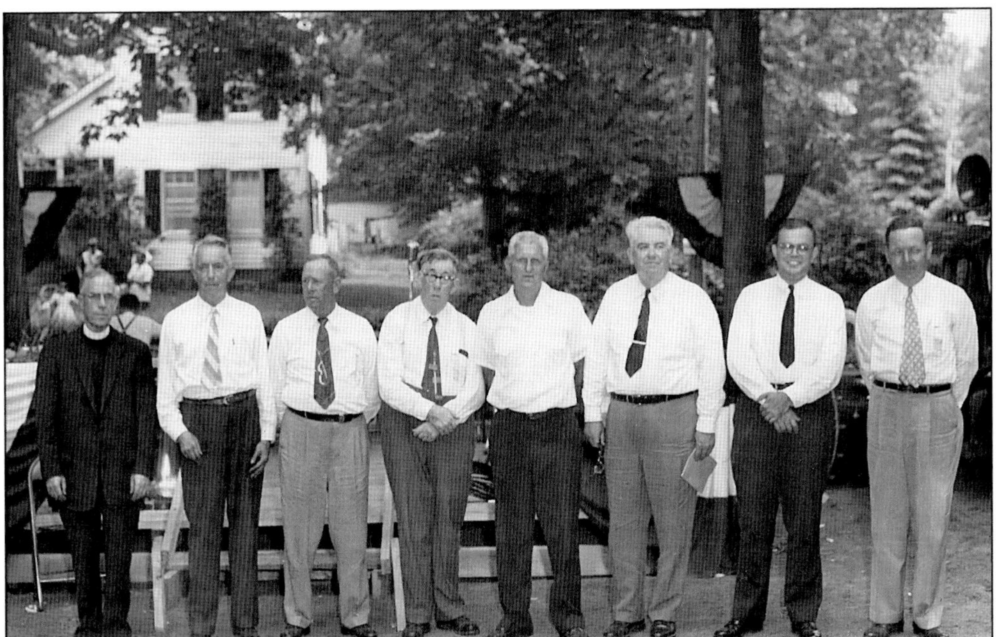

THE DIGNITARIES OF THE SESQUICENTENNIAL CELEBRATION. Seven of the eight are identified. They are, from left to right, as follows: Rev. John J. Sullivan, George W. Hull, Morris Hogan, Merton W. Hodge, Frank Pavlik, Rev. Wilfred LaPoint, Rev. Nelson Cheney, and unidentified. (BPL.)

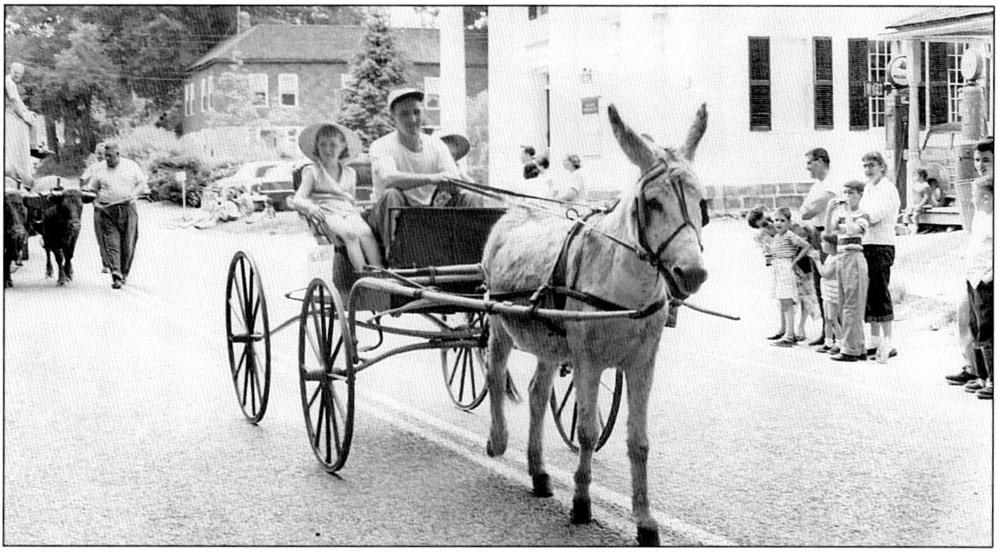

A DONKEY CART FROM WHIGVILLE, 1956. One of the 41 units in the parade was this entry by Army veteran of World War II, John F. Hynds, from West Chippens Hill Road. Hynds and two of his three daughters, Carla on the left and Lynda on the right, rode the parade route in the cart. The program says, "This parade will depict organizations and people who have contributed to the advancement and growth of our country from 1806 to 1956. It will demonstrate the way in which our democracy has provided opportunities for all, and how, in turn, this democracy has flourished because of the efforts of all kinds of people from every walk of life." (BPL.)

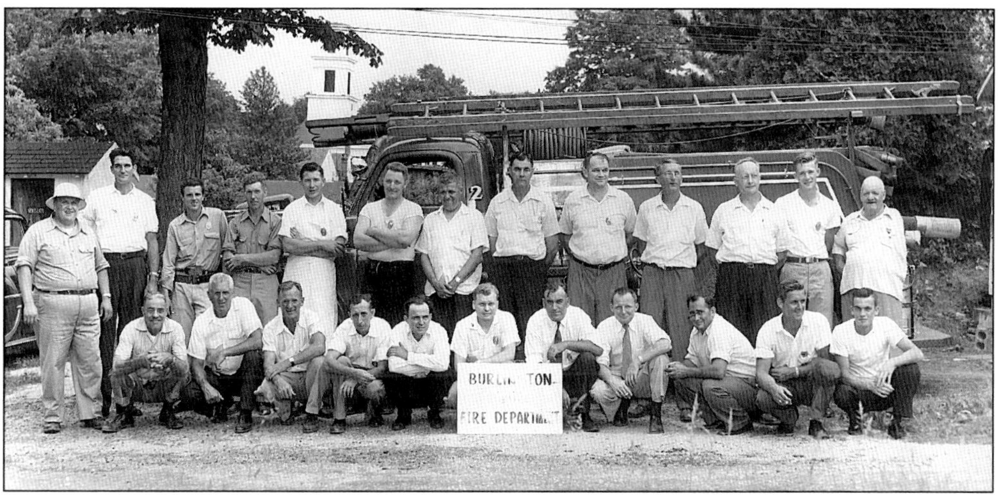

THE BURLINGTON FIRE DEPARTMENT. There were between 50 and 60 members of the volunteer fire department in 1956. The most active of them are seen with the hook-and-ladder truck at the parade to celebrate the sesquicentennial on June 16. They are, from left to right, as follows: (front row) Rudolph Bodamer, Clifford Lyons, Frank Pavlik, Ralph Carlson, George Amelotte, John Tibbetts, Joseph Dlubac, Francis Scheidel, John Daniels, Carroll Turner, Laverne Goodwin, and Ernest Wollman; (back row) Chief Clarence Spielman, Reinhardt Bodamer, Wilbur Goodwin, Robert Adams, Paul Coleman, Edward Trapp, William Robinson, William Speilman, George Pavlik, William Reeve, Frederick Wollmann, and John Larson. Tadeusz Szydlo and Erick Tharau were also active but are missing from this picture. (BPL.)

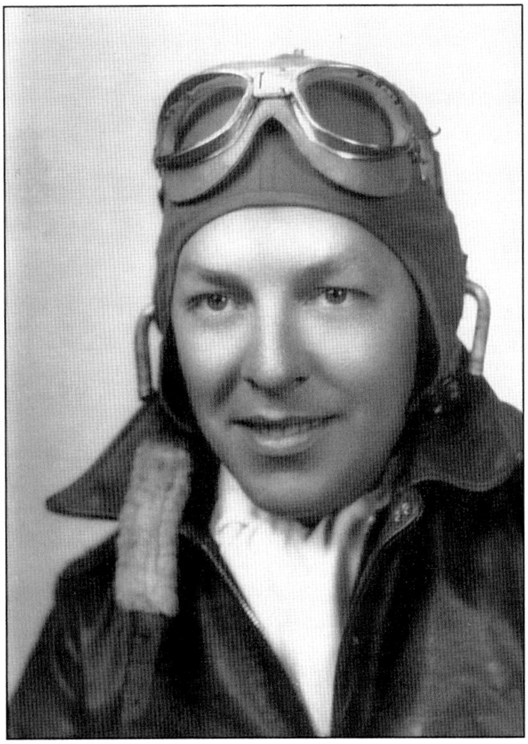

JOHN HINMAN AS A PILOT. A teacher before World War II, John Hinman returned not to teach but to work with his brother at the family lumberyard on Milford Street. The brothers worked together during the day and sang and made music together at evening social events in town. (BHD.)

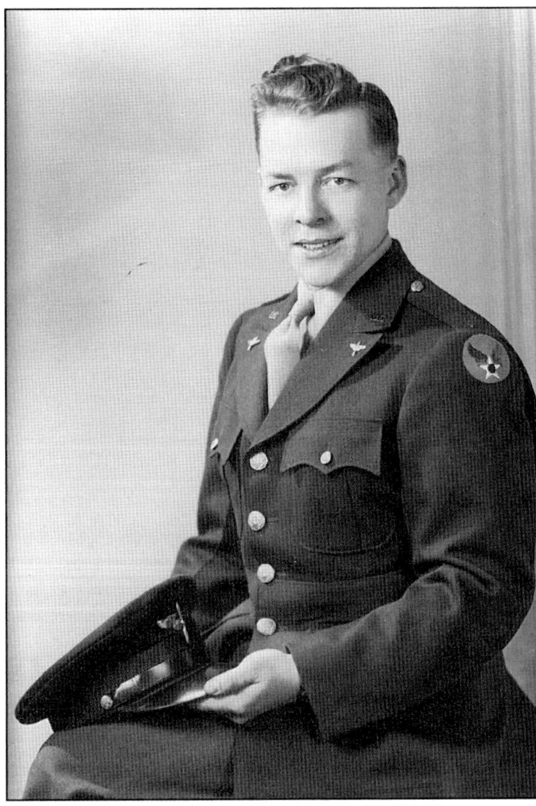

Three

A Water Pail and Dipper

By 1800, the red schoolhouse in the center of Burlington was already serving children, ages four to sixteen, from the first to the eighth grade. This and most of the later one-room schoolhouses had an entryway where children left their lunch pails, overshoes, coats, and hats. Here was also kept the bucket of water brought from a nearby home, spring, or well, and its dipper was used by all. Stories tell of the children having to crack the ice on top of the water with the dipper before getting a drink on very cold days. Wood to heat the classroom was kept in piles or sheds outside and was brought in by the students for the large stove in the schoolroom. Lucky were the pupils who did not sit too close or too far from that hot stove. Administered by committee and supported by taxes, this local school and up to eight other one-room district schools educated the children. In 1909, a superintendent was hired and, in 1919, free textbooks enhanced the schools. In 1924, one electric light was added to the ceiling of each school. The schools were consolidated in 1949, and a new six-classroom building was completed for the first eight grades. Until the Lewis S. Mills High School was built in 1956, students who continued their education attended high schools in neighboring towns.

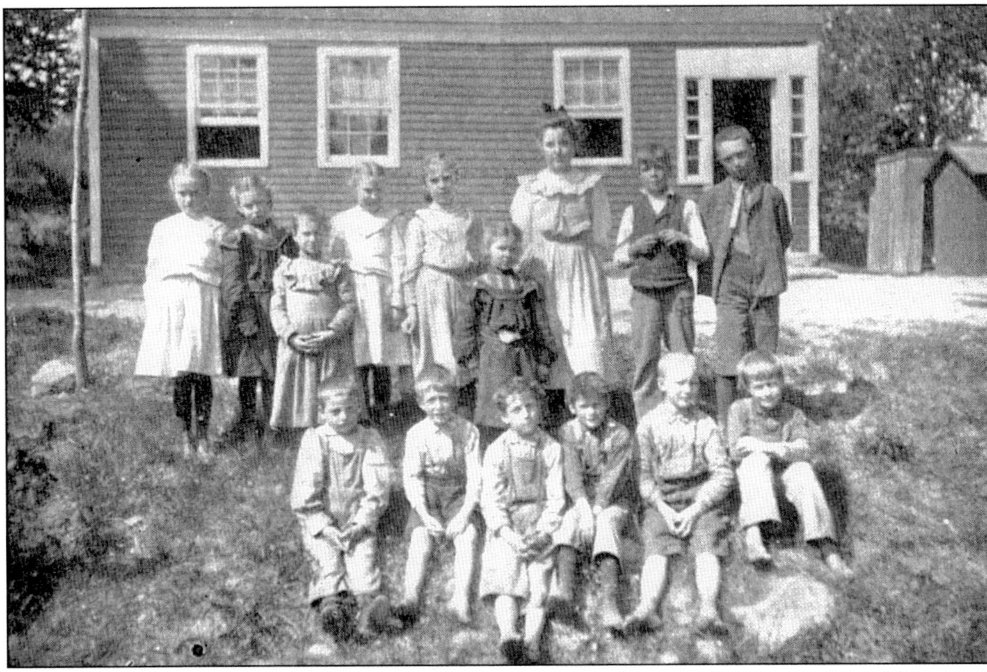

THE RISING GENERATION. This is No. 3 in the centennial postcard series made in 1906. Each school district was responsible for the teacher's salary and other costs until 1909, when the superintendent was hired. These students are unidentified. (BPL.)

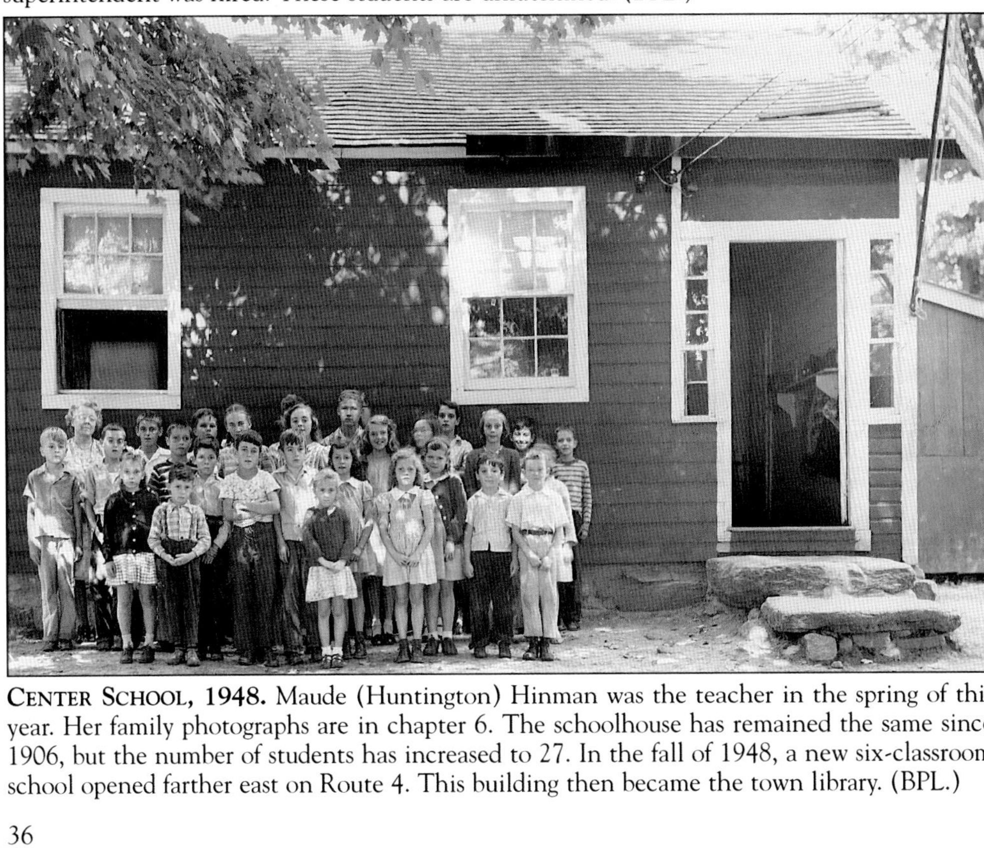

CENTER SCHOOL, 1948. Maude (Huntington) Hinman was the teacher in the spring of this year. Her family photographs are in chapter 6. The schoolhouse has remained the same since 1906, but the number of students has increased to 27. In the fall of 1948, a new six-classroom school opened farther east on Route 4. This building then became the town library. (BPL.)

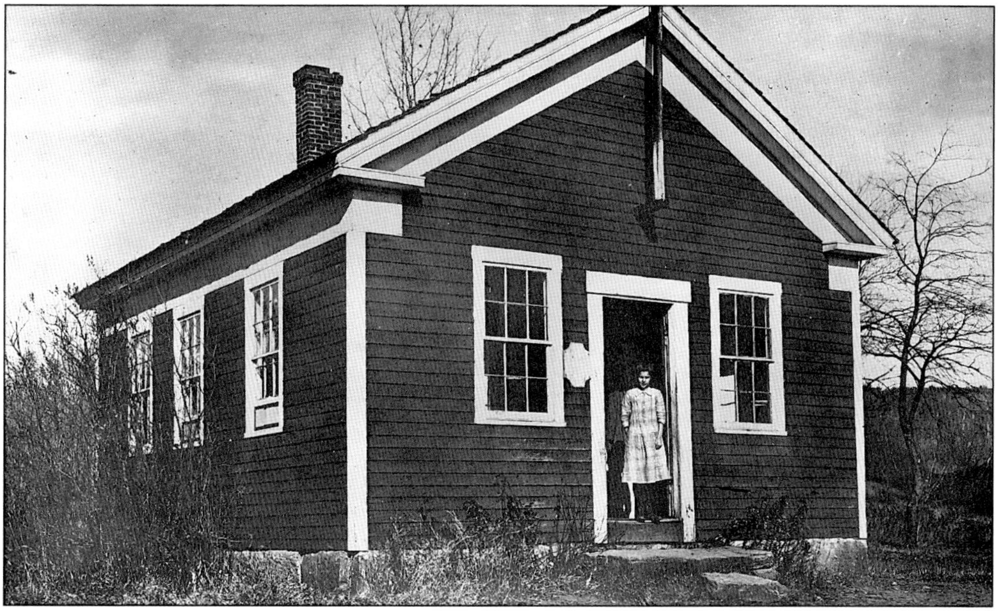

THE MILFORD STREET SCHOOL, DISTRICT NO. 2. This photograph of the school, located on the dirt road east of Lamson Corner Cemetery, was probably taken c. 1879, when Lt. Thomas Brooks was a committee member. The school was closed in 1921, moved to West Chippens Hill, and renamed White Oak School. There, it was closed in 1933, sold in 1946, and converted to a private residence. (BPL.)

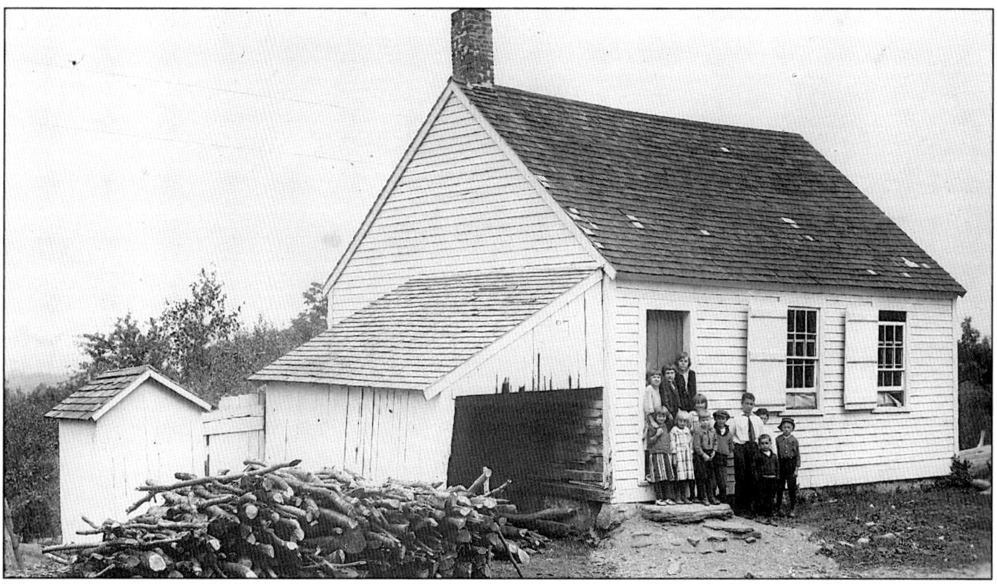

THE HOLCOMB SCHOOL, DISTRICT NO. 3. In the northern part of the town near the New Hartford line, this school was built about 1800 on land donated by Milo Holcomb at the end of Lyon Road, between Covey and Davis Road. The children and teacher are clustered in the doorway. To their left is the woodshed and a pile of logs or fence posts. Behind the logs is the privy. There was very little play area here, so the children spent recess in the road. Benjamin Hinman taught here before 1900 and Laura (Raynor) Barnes taught between 1912 and 1914. Holcomb School was moved to Covey Road, where it is now a private residence. (BPL.)

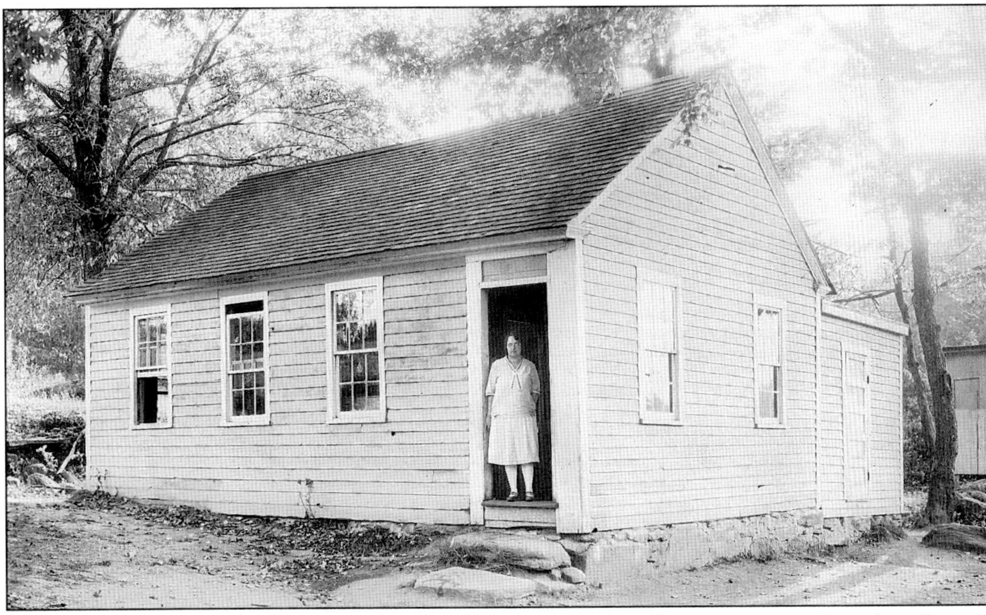

The District No. 4 Schoolhouse, Fall of 1928. Helen Hartigan remembers that she and her brother Carl studied under their teacher Lessie I. Zimmerman for the eight years they each spent at this school. The Town School Committee renovated the school in 1929, painting the interior and exterior, laying a new floor, and installing shelves, bulletin boards, and new tables and chairs. The school was moved from here *c.* 1954 by John Tibbetts, who lived in it with his family. (BPL.)

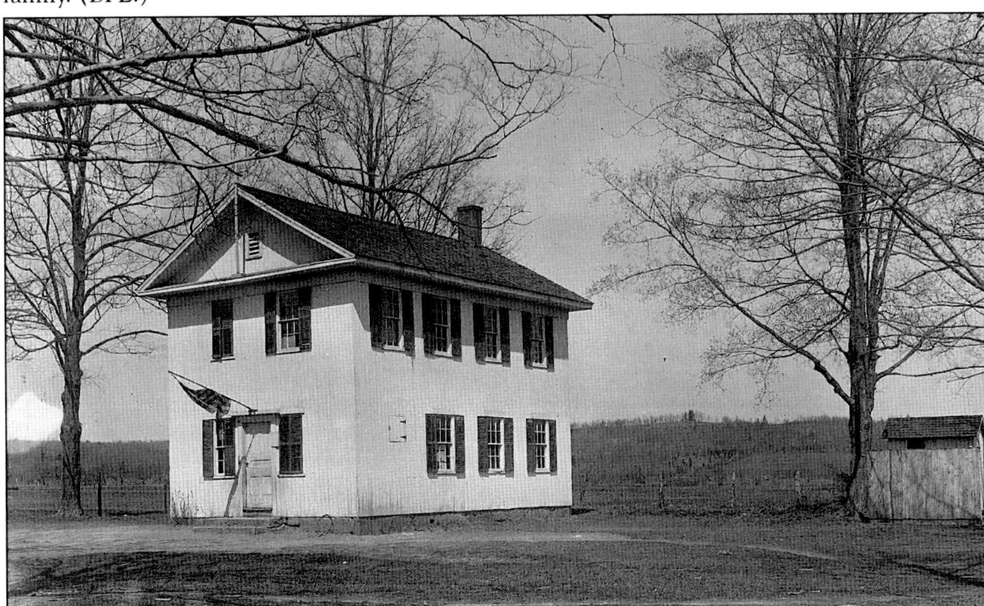

The District No. 5 Schoolhouse, Spring, 1928. This was the Whigville School, with the flag flying out front and the privy on the right. The 8-foot-by-12-foot privy was built in 1875 with an oak partition 2 inches thick. In 1879, the committee decided to have the roof shingled, have the blinds fixed, and have M. Gaylord "get one coat of paint put on the cheapest way he can." The school closed in 1948 and is now a private residence. (BPL.)

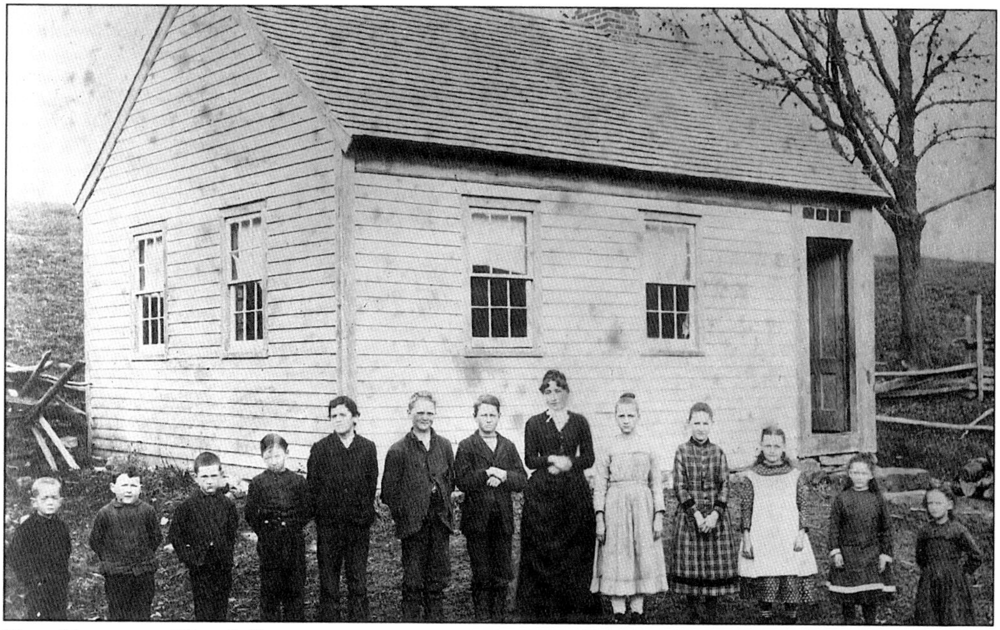

THE DISTRICT NO. 8 SCHOOLHOUSE, C.1889. Russell School was located on Punch Brook Road near Taine Mountain Road. It opened in 1884 and closed in 1902. Some of these students have been identified, and numbering from left to right, they are (1) Albert Case, (3) Maurice Russell, (6) Hubert Alderman, (7) Clifford Alderman, (8) Louisa Alderman, and (12) Clara Case. (BPL.)

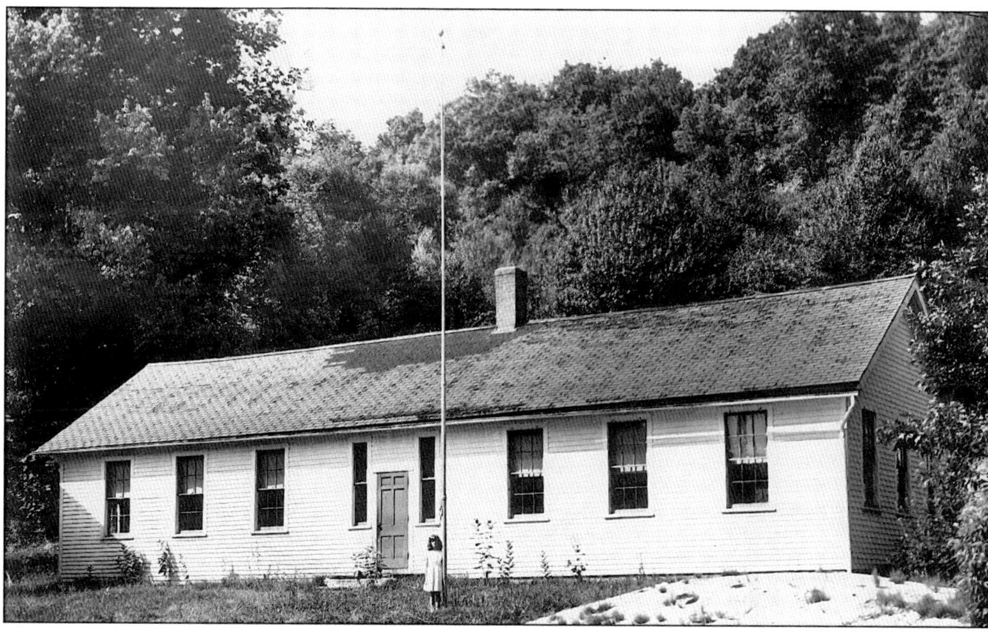

THE DISTRICT NO. 9 SCHOOLHOUSE, 1928. Sand Bank School, built in 1853, was one of the schools that was enlarged in 1911 to accommodate over 100 students and 4 teachers. A second building was added in back for the lower grades. To raise morale the name was changed to Riverside School in 1912. Now shortened and a private residence, the building is on Claire Hill Road at the end of Riverside Avenue. (BPL.)

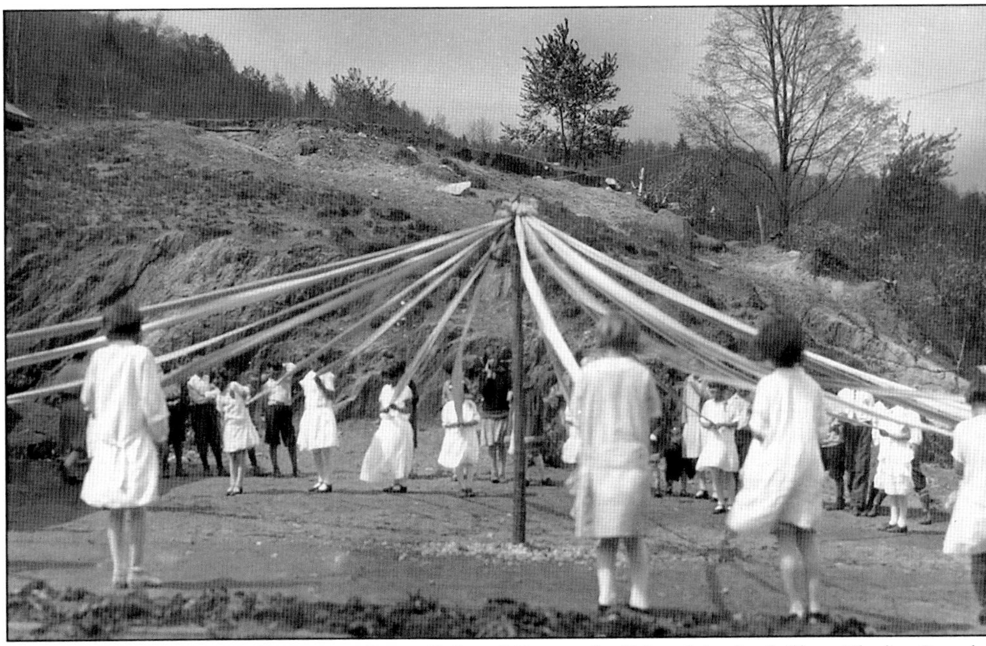

THE MAYPOLE DANCE, RIBBONS OUT. Behind Riverside School is the hill to Phelps Brooke Dam. In 1915, Elizabeth Klatte, an eighth-grade student, wrote an essay about the building of Nepaug Reservoir to hold reserve water for the city of Hartford. In 1943, the Holcomb School pupils came to Riverside School. After June 1948, they all went to the new consolidated school at Burlington Center. (BPL.)

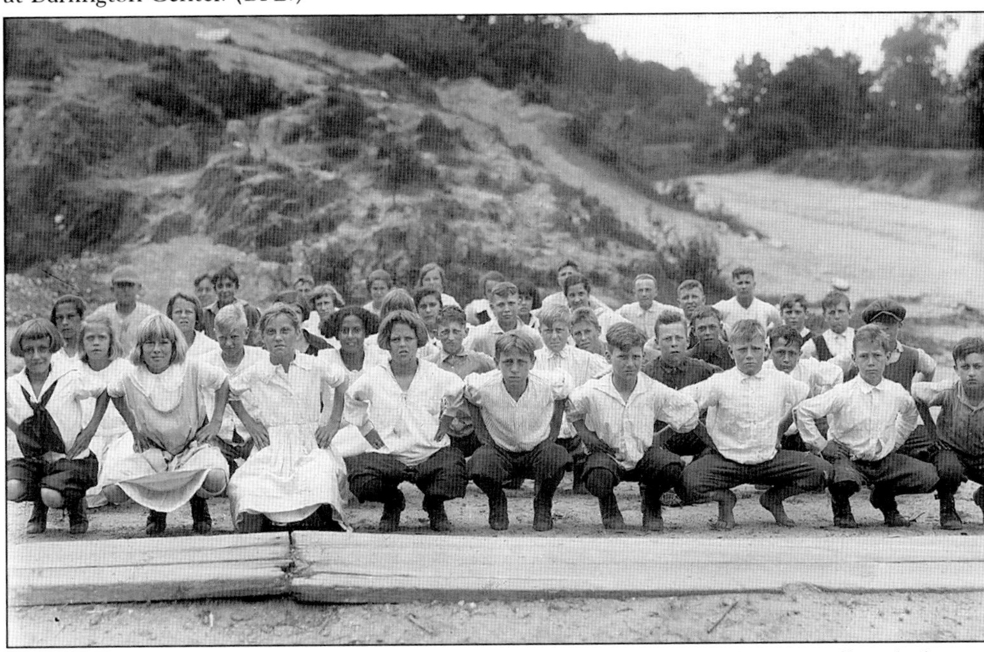

ATHLETIC GROUP SQUATTING. At Riverside School the playground was small and close to the road. Physical exercise was important since the students were in school for many hours at a time. Older students exercised together and the younger students at a different time to make the best use of this small space. (BPL.)

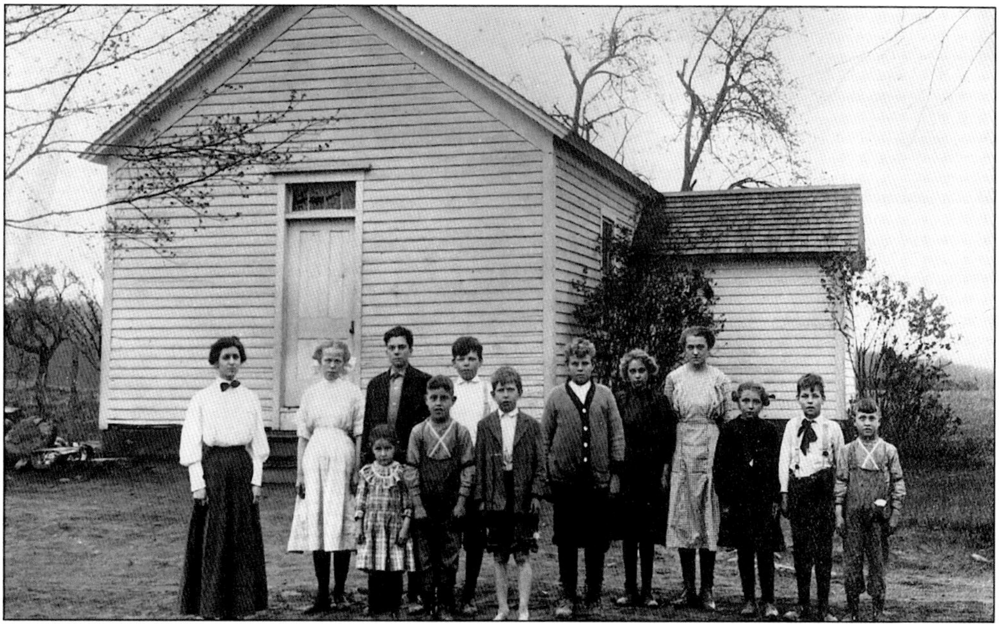

The Old Moses School, c. 1908. Mrs. Pond was the teacher when the students posed for this photograph. Emerson Moses, Robert Moses, Little Hale, Arthur Johnson, Frank Johnson, Calkin and Gregory are suggested names for some of these students. Robert and Emerson Moses operated the Moses Brothers Fruit Farm in the early 1930s. (BPL.)

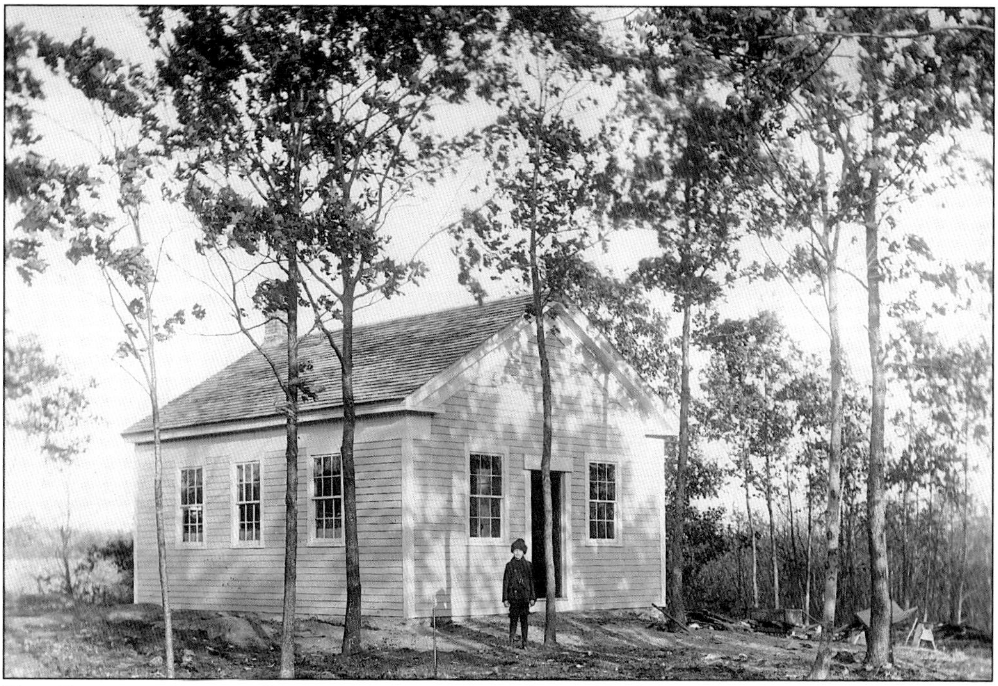

The District No. 10 Schoolhouse, 1927. The Milford Street Schoolhouse was built on the dirt road east of Lamson Corner Cemetery *c.* 1800. It closed in 1921, was moved to West Chippens Hill, and renamed White Oak School. The scholar is unidentified. Closed in 1933 and sold by the town in 1946, the school is now a private residence. (BPL.)

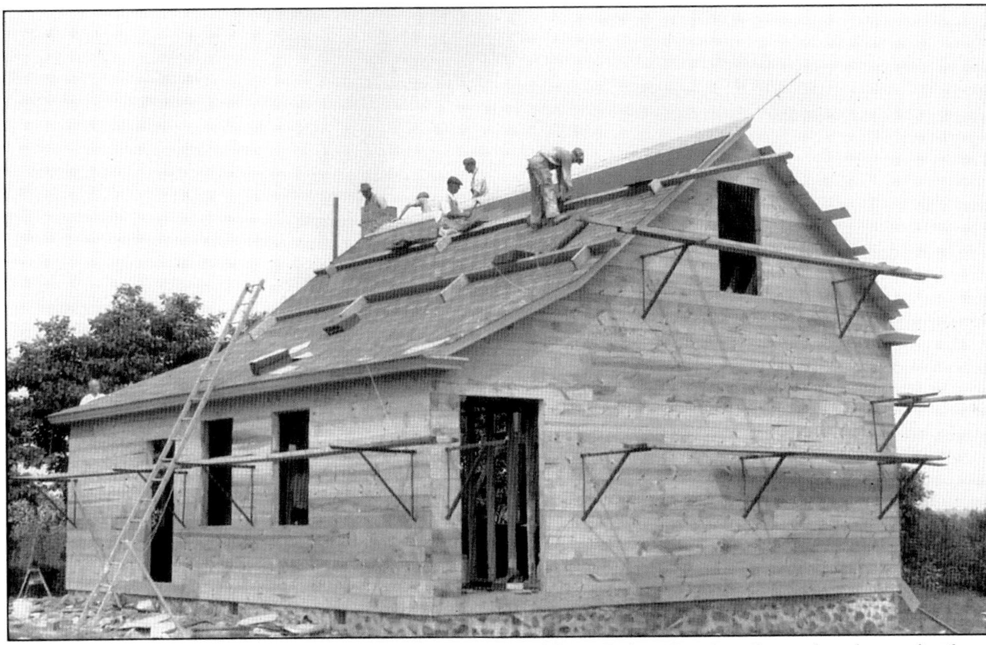

BUILDING THE DISTRICT NO. 7 SCHOOLHOUSE. Near Lake Garda, this school was built to accommodate a growing population. It was named in honor of L.S. Mills, school supervisor from 1916 to 1929. When a high school for Burlington was built in 1956, the town named it Lewis Mills High School. A new Lake Garda Elementary School was built in 1965. (BPL.)

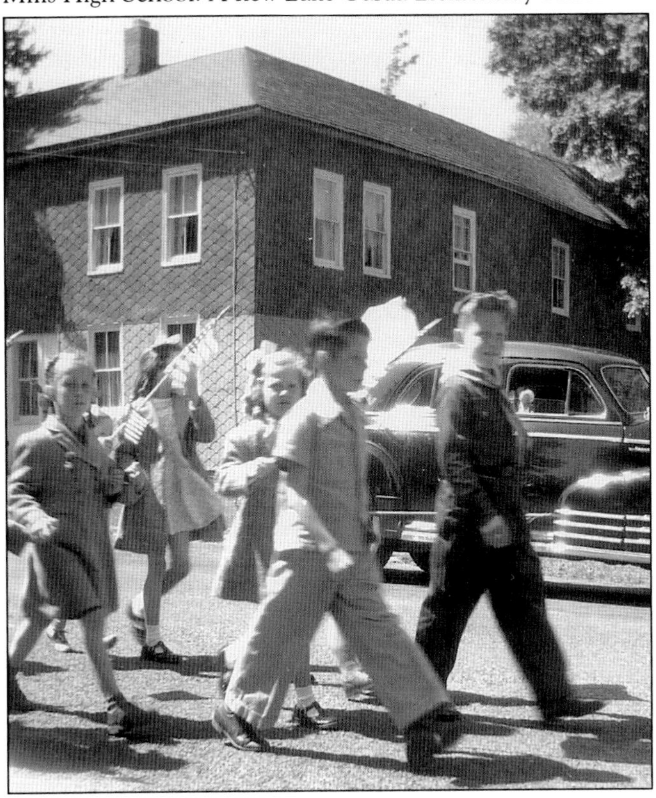

FLAG DAY, C. 1940. Leading the parade through the town center on Flag Day are, from left to right, Judy Reeve, Hazel Tharau, and Joyce, George, and James Reeve. This annual event allowed each of the schools to perform for all of the other schools, with songs, essays, and poetry. The Ladies Aid Society provided a grand feast, complete with ham sandwiches and cakes, and it was all washed down with fresh lemonade. (LA.)

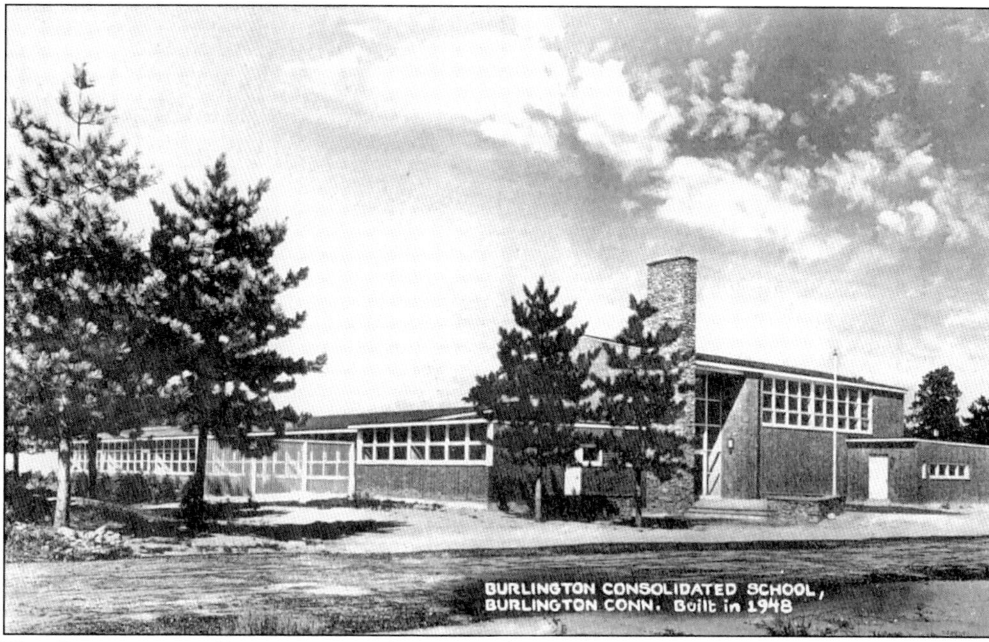

THE BURLINGTON CONSOLIDATED SCHOOL. This 1948 postcard shows the new consolidated school. After this building opened, all of the district schools were closed and education became more interactive and more uniform in terms of quality. The school cost $150,000 and opened on September 8, 1948, with five teachers and a principal. (CA.)

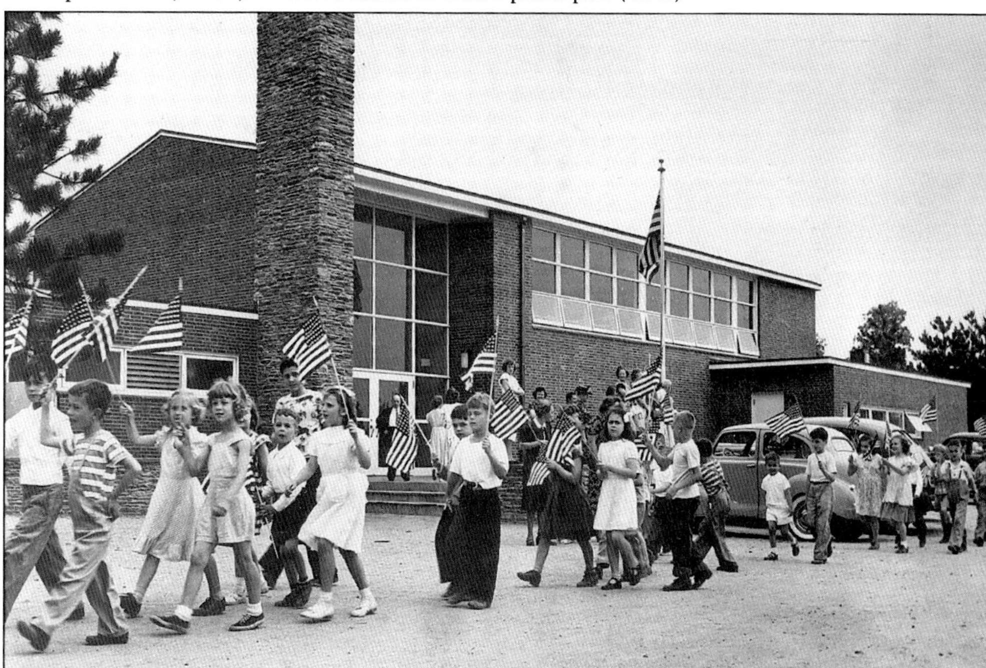

FLAG DAY, THE CONSOLIDATED SCHOOL, 1949. This was the first parade of flags at the new school. Traditionally eighth-grade diplomas were awarded on Flag Day as well. June 14 is the anniversary of the day in 1777 when the design of the American flag was adopted. (BPL.)

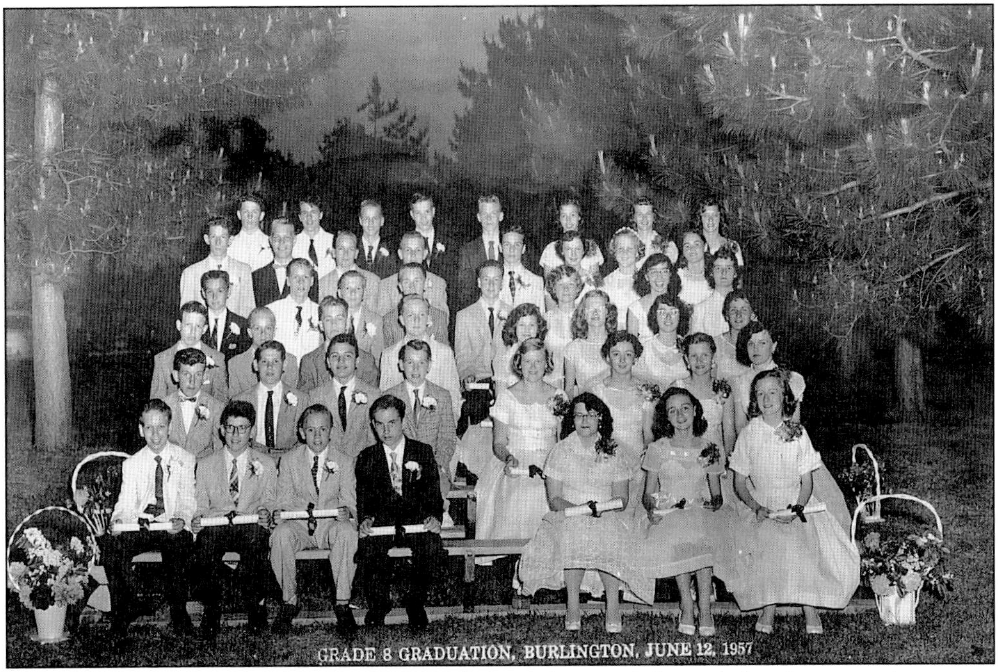

EIGHTH-GRADE GRADUATION, 1957. Graduation from eighth grade has been a milestone in Burlington since schools first started. For many students it was as much formal education as they got. To continue meant going to another town, until the high school was built in 1956. (BPL.)

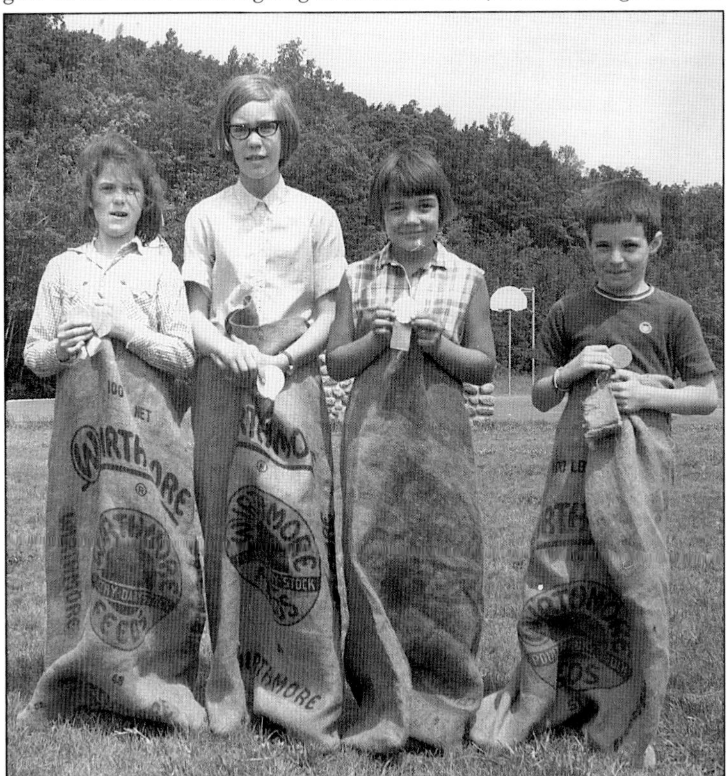

FIELD DAY, 1965. Potato-sack races are always fun, but especially when it means time off from school. Several people have identified one of these winners as Irene Kellerstedt, third from the left. (BPL.)

Four

JOHNNYCAKE MOUNTAIN

The highest point in Burlington, at 1,150 feet above sea level, is the peak of Johnnycake Mountain. Located near the western town line and about equally distant from the north and south boundaries, this spot was for many years crowned with a fire tower. The Tunxis Trail enters Burlington near the southwest corner and winds northerly to the top of this mountain before making a sharp turn to the east, dipping across Route 69 south of Hinman Lumber Company and then up Wildcat Mountain, down to cross George Washington Turnpike, and up again to cross into Unionville at the top of Taine Mountain. The only airport in Burlington is the Johnny Cake Mountain Meadows Airport near Speilman Highway (Route 4), close to the Harwinton town line. Electricity came to Johnnycake Mountain in 1941. The Hogan Farm is at the intersection of Johnnycake Mountain Road and Route 4. It is one of the few farms to retain most of its early outbuildings. Today, these buildings are used to store and sell produce and to house facilities for a golf course, laid out on the early pastures and cornfields. South of Hogan's Farm was the largest farm in Burlington in 1960, owned by John and Jane (Weeks) Martin. Martin was the great-grandson of Andrew Heublein, founder of the spirits company in Hartford. The Martins established other farms and residences in the Ozarks, Florida, Canada, and Arkansas, giving them all the Johnnycake name.

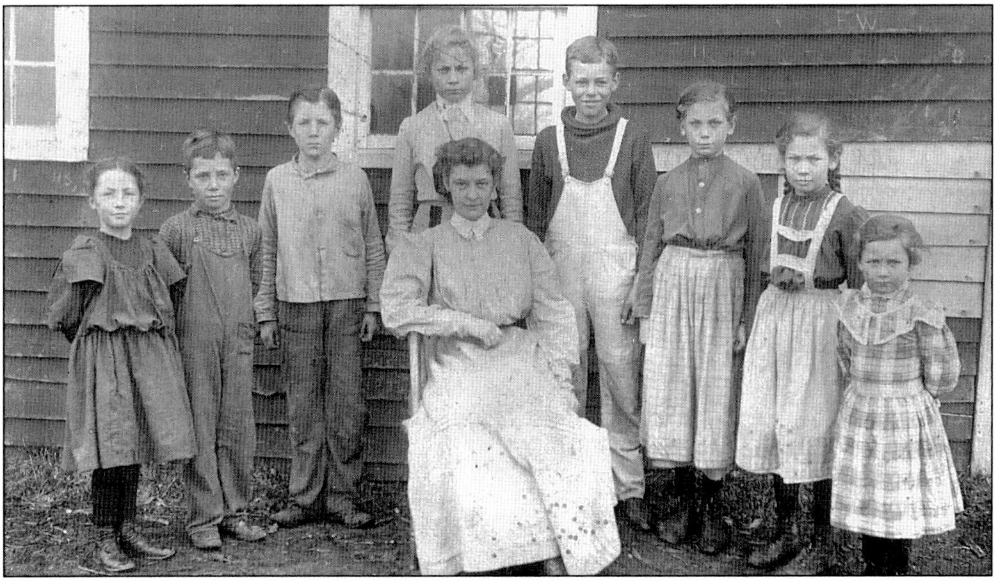

THE JOHNNYCAKE SCHOOL. This school was built in 1825 or earlier on land donated by Joel Bunnell and family. Hortense Case French wrote a poem entitled "Johnny Cake Mountain School." It begins: "The old red school house was the crown that capped the highest hill in town." In 1908, Gertrude Wollmann was the teacher at "the crown." Eight students in this photograph flank her. The only ones identified are the two on the left, Elsie and Daniel Edwards. (BPL.)

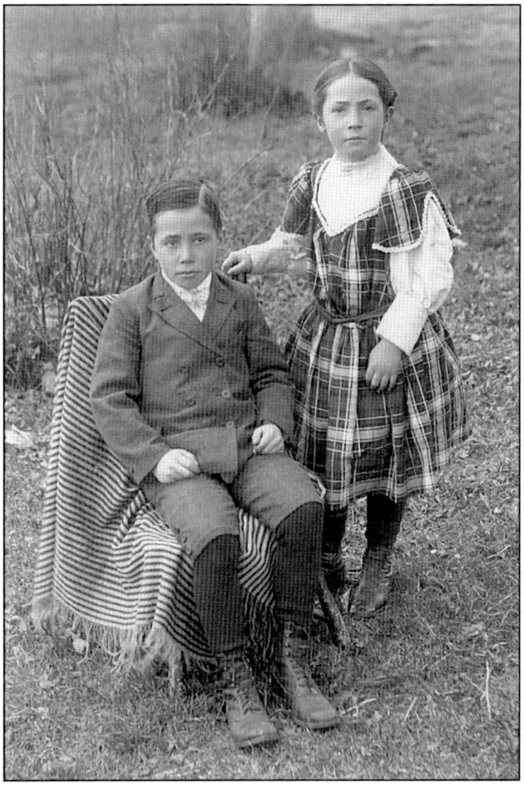

ELSIE AND DANIEL EDWARDS, 1910. Carrie Woodruff and Milton Edwards were married in 1896. Edwards worked on the family farm on Johnnycake Mountain. His parents, Louisa and Jerome S. Edwards, took charge of some of the poor of Burlington for 51 years. In 1916, Milton and Carrie Edwards and their two children moved to Avon. Across the road from this scene is where Katherine Gaylord lived after returning from Wyoming. (BPL.)

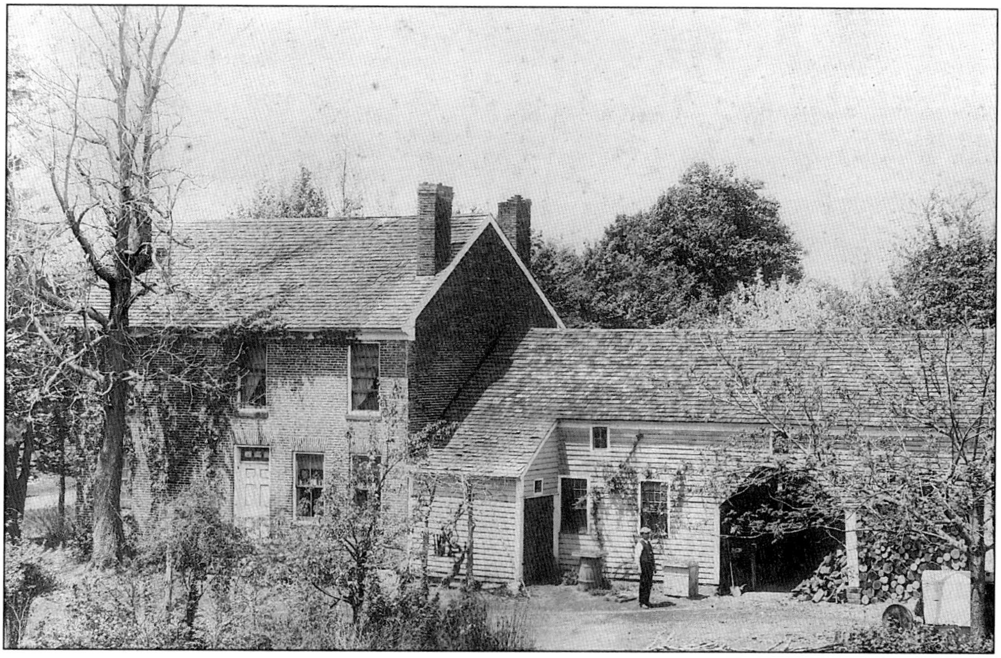

The Bride's House. A newspaper clipping from 1928 said, "The Edwards' House is a handsome old brick house below the hill to the northeast, with a trumpet vine, sheltered by trees, and there is a barn across the road." If one could get from West Chippens Hill to Johnnycake Mountain Road, this would be the first old house to be seen. Built in 1823, it still stands. These photographs, one from the south (side view) (BPL) and the other from the southwest (LA.) show the original brick house and its long attached workrooms and sheds. Bee boxes, wells, woodpiles, and tools give evidence that this is a busy dooryard. The four chimneys serve fireplaces in each room.

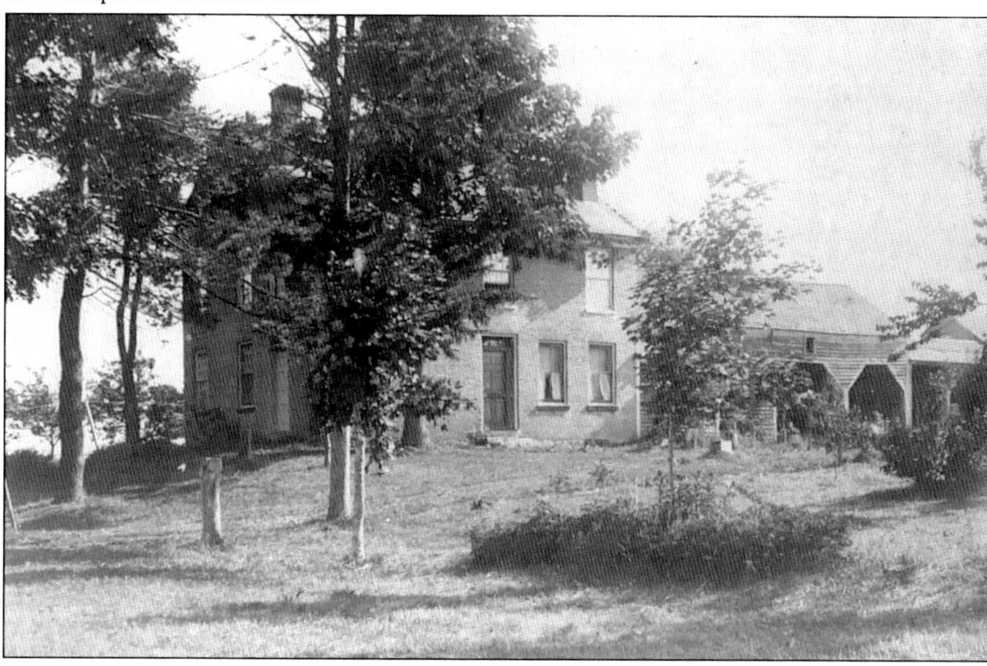

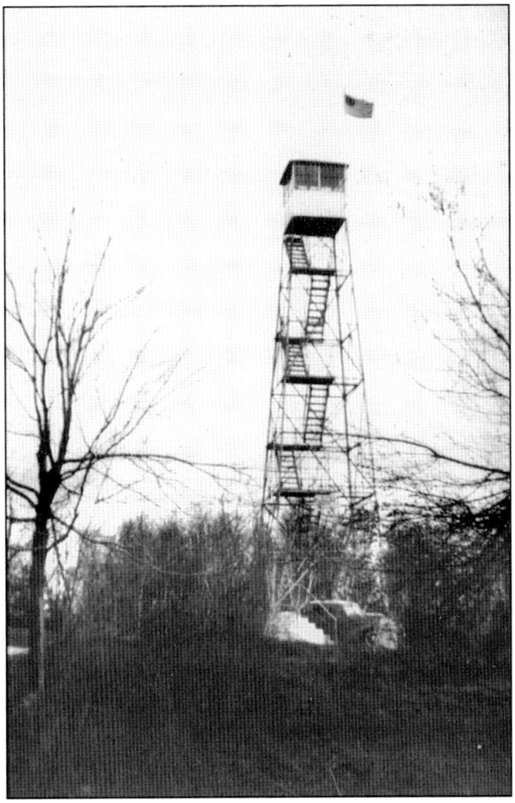

The Fire Tower, c. 1940. The 50-foot steel tower atop Johnnycake Mountain was built by Mr. Lathrop in 1929 at an elevation of 1,155 feet to provide a lookout for forest fires. Henry Ney of Farmington donated a quarter of an acre of land to the state to protect the 1,180 acres of Nassahegon Forest and the springs which feed the state fish hatchery. In 1919–1920 Augustina Backes kept a Citizenship Journal for sixth grade in which she wrote: "The last forest fire in Burlington was near Whigville. It was on the Wild Cat Mountain. It burned over about twenty acres of woodland. There were about thirty men fighting the fire. They came from most every house in the southern part of town. This fire was in June 1919." (LA.)

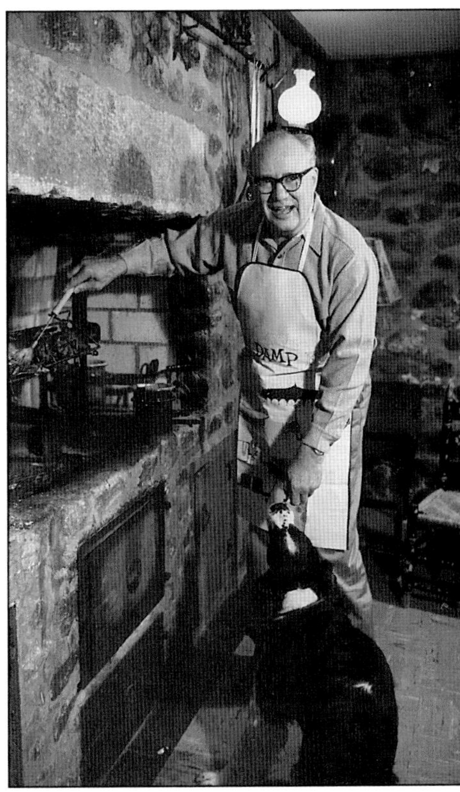

John Martin, 1961. This photograph of John Martin and his dog Poky was taken by Larry Fried, of PIX Inc., New York. It shows Martin at the grill in the home that he and his wife, Jane, built on Johnnycake Mountain. They brought celebrities and neighbors together for their parties at and around their rustic house at Johnnycake Ranch. They raised peacocks, pheasants, quail, Aracuna chickens, dogs, and the beautiful white French cattle, Charolais. (BPL.)

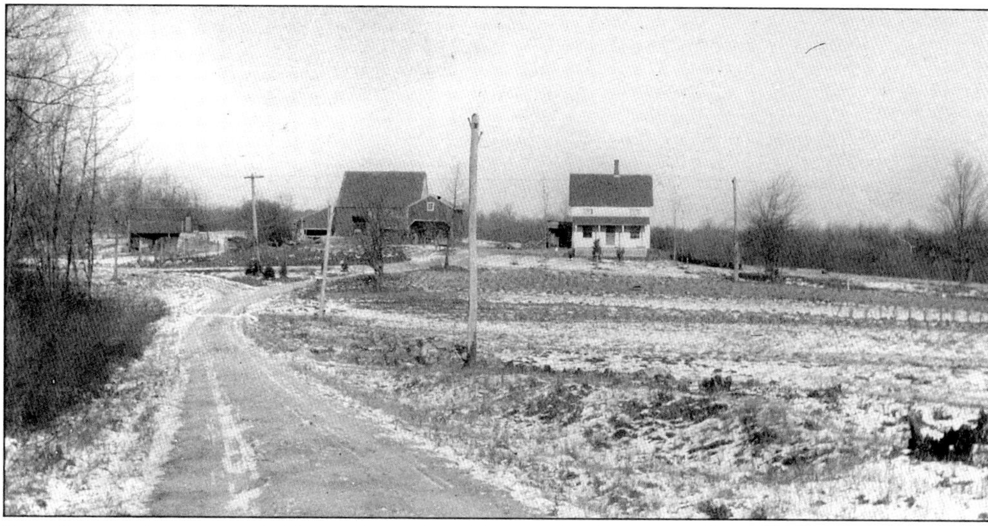

THE HOGAN FARM, C. 1915. At the end of Johnnycake Mountain Road on Speilman Highway is the old Hogan Homestead. This view shows the sheds, cider mill, barns, and the house where Patrick and Marion (Morris) Hogan lived on the second largest farm on Johnnycake Mountain. The land was ideal for growing strawberries and blueberries. The Hogans also had a large cider business. This and the following photographs of the Hogan Farm were taken by Richard Hogan. He and his brother Morris Hogan remained on the farm after their parents died. They grew fruit, raised animals, harvested logs, made charcoal, cut ice, and graded roads. On days when the weather was not nice, they went hunting, according to Alice (Brown) and Waldemar Szczesniak, who worked on the farm with them and inherited these photographs. (WABS.)

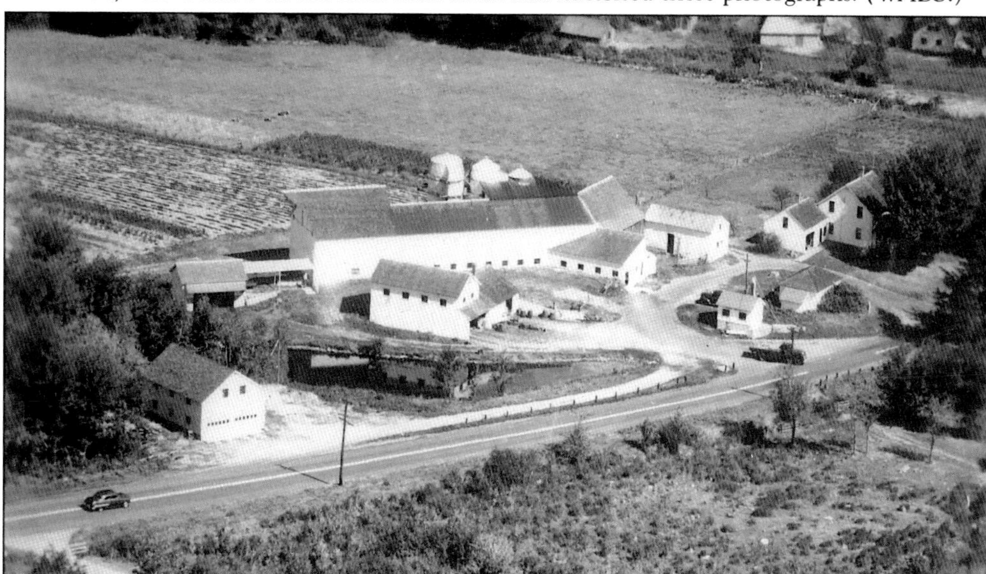

THE HOGAN GREETING CARD. By 1950, the Hogan Farm buildings had grown to better fit their large acreage; this card was mailed to all their friends. Richard Hogan, aged 56, and Morris Hogan, aged 48, with his wife, Mabel, enjoyed life on the farm. The barns had expanded and three silos are visible in the card; the cider mill and pond were the same, but everything else had grown. The brothers were partners on the farm for 74 years. Morris Hogan also served on the Burlington Board of Finance for 29 years and in the state legislature for 32 years. (HHM.)

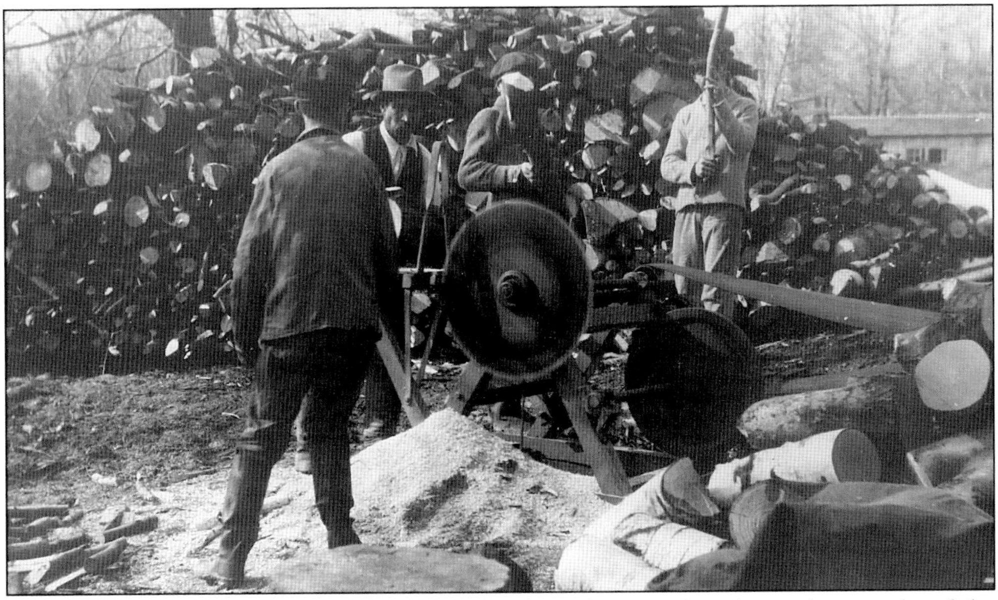

The Sawmill in the Field. In the 1920s, wood was harvested in the cooler months of the year. It made sense to set up the saw where the logs were stacked, especially if the end product was to be charcoal. To make charcoal the trees had to be cut into suitable lengths. Most were longer than those in the foreground, typically six feet. To build a charcoal mound, one first digs a pit and then begins with a center stake, around and toward which all the logs are laid. Each charcoal man had his own idea of what made the best mound and he determined the length of the logs. (WABS.)

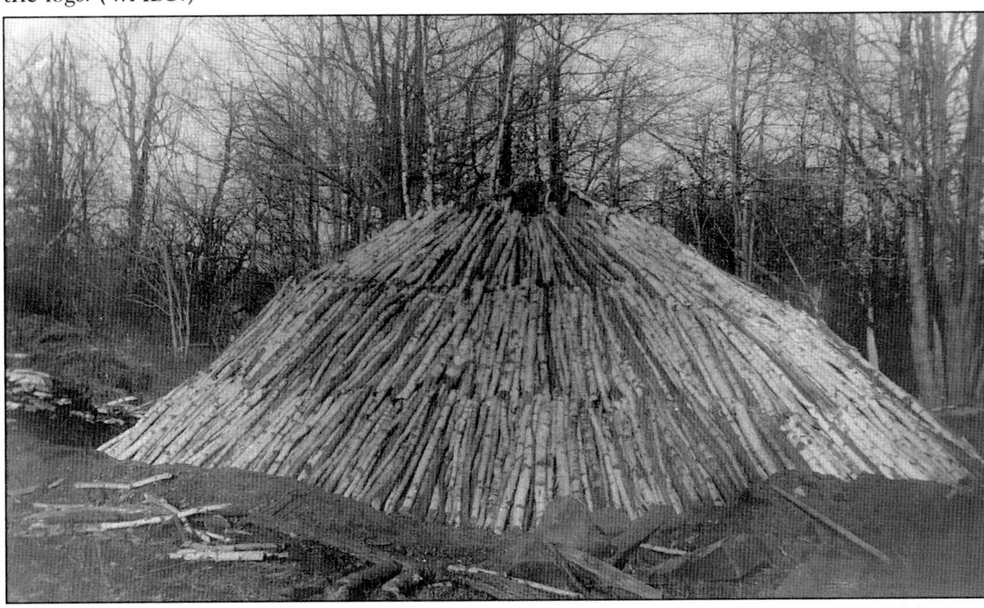

Making the Mound. A plank base was laid around the center stake. Mounds varied from 12 to 30 feet around. The time it took to char the wood depended on the size of the mound and how tightly it was stacked; a month of burning was average for a mound of 30 to 40 cords of wood. During that time the charcoal man dared not leave his mound for fear it would explode into a full fire and consume the mound. (WABS.)

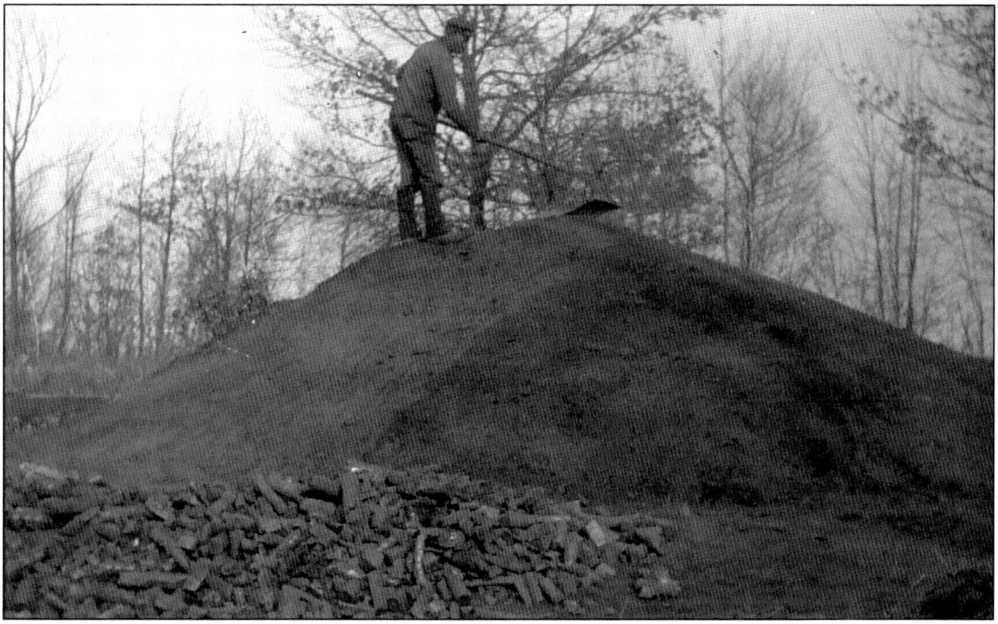

COVERING THE MOUND. The pile of wood was covered with dirt and charcoal dust; some charcoal men also used wet leaves, fern and/or sod instead of loose dirt. The key was to pack it tightly so it could be walked on to tend all parts of the mound. (WABS.)

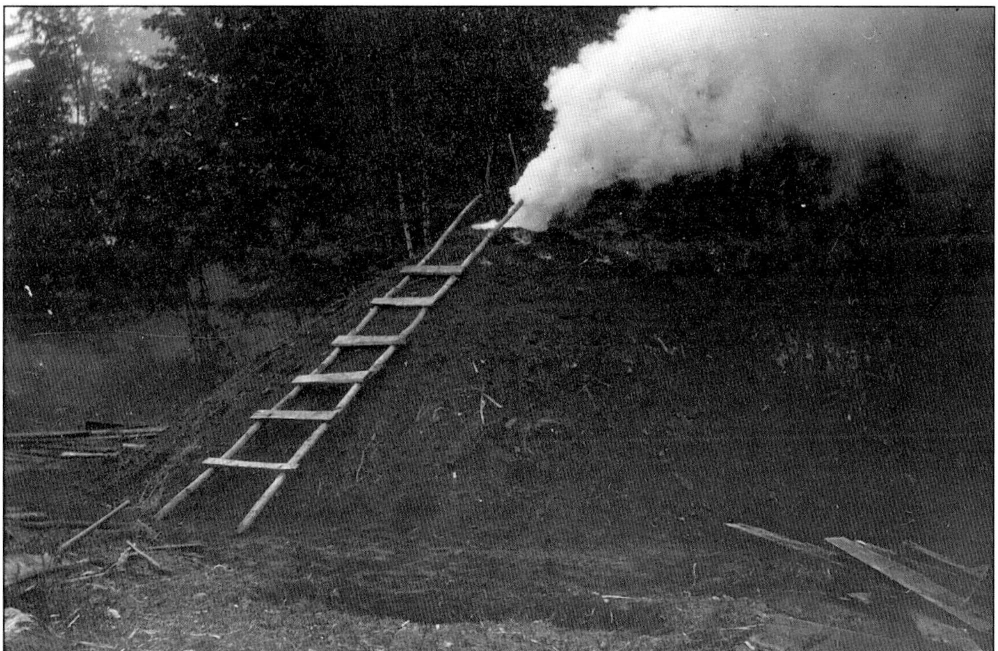

THE SMOKING MOUND. When the mound was first lighted, a black smoke would pour from the central holes. This would smother into a blue haze, which would continue until a "sweating period" arrived and yellow smoke arose; then, moist charcoal or mud would be applied until a gray smoke arose. The mound continued working until all of the logs had charred; the charcoal man used the ladder to check near the center. (WABS.)

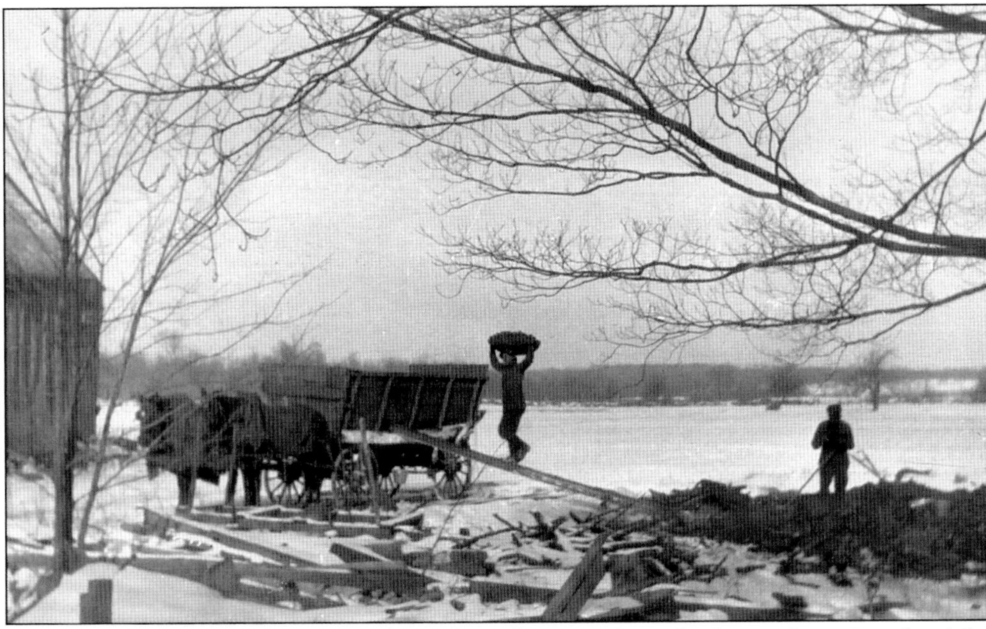

WALKING THE PLANK. The charcoal pit where the mound was fired is on the right side of this photograph. Two planks are laid up to the wagon and the baskets of charcoal were carried up and emptied into the wagon. The wagons had removable sides and a bottom that dropped down to unload the charcoal. (WABS.)

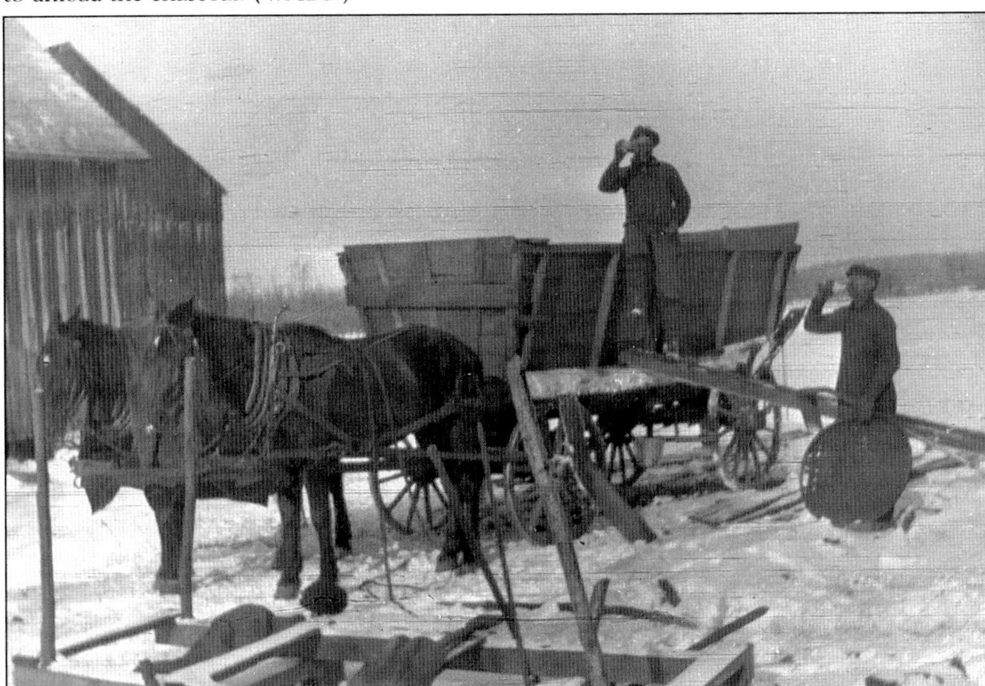

A REFRESHING DRINK. Even on a cool snowy day this was hard work, and the Morris brothers enjoy a short break. In the foreground is a stone boat, or sled, and on top of that is a shovel used to scoop the charcoal into the baskets. (WABS.)

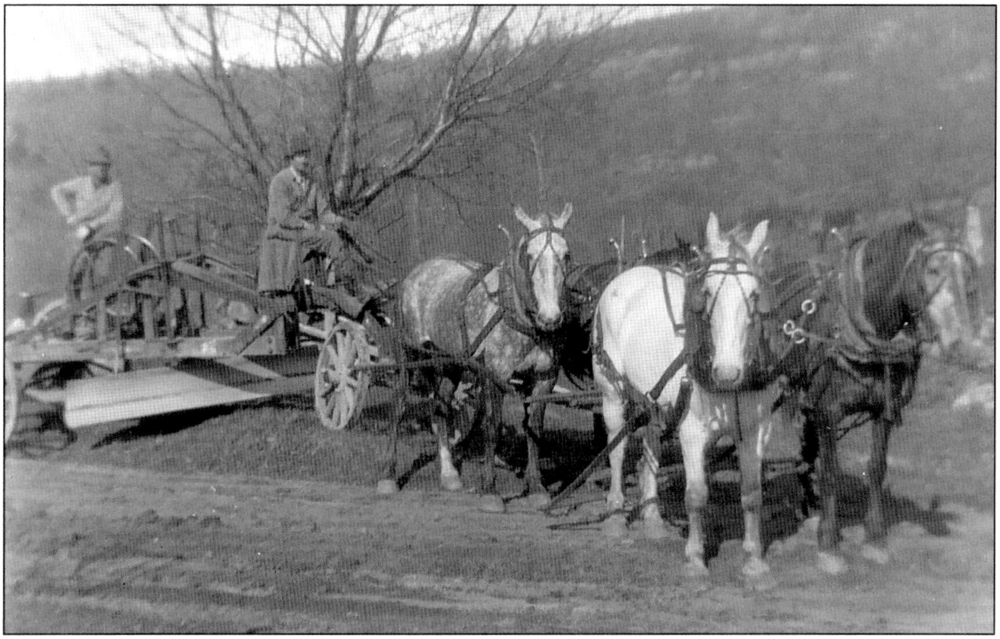

GRADING THE ROADS. The Morris Brothers and their teams of horses were not idle long. In the spring after the heavy rains, the dirt roads all over town had deep ruts, so they went out and dragged these blades across them to make them level again. The man in the front drove the horses. The one in back raised and lowered the blade by turning the two large wheels. (LA.)

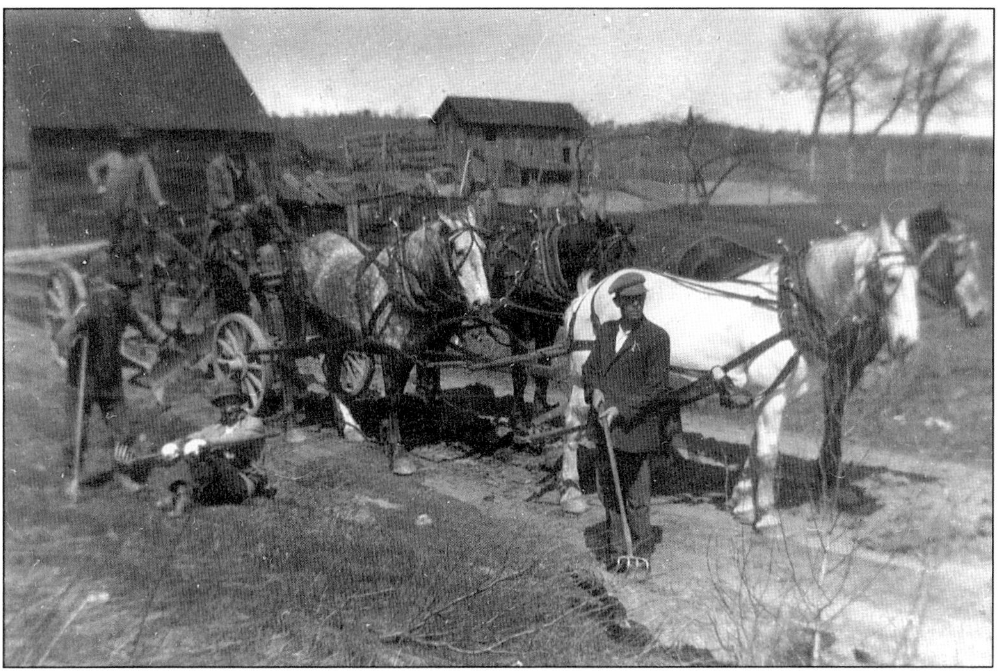

A ROAD GRADING POSTCARD. There are five men and four horses here. The man in front, near the white horse, has a four-tined fork to loosen mounds of dirt and weeds from the edge of the road. A second man is resting and listening to the third man; both have a long-handled tool. Two other men are at the wheels on the grader. (WABS.)

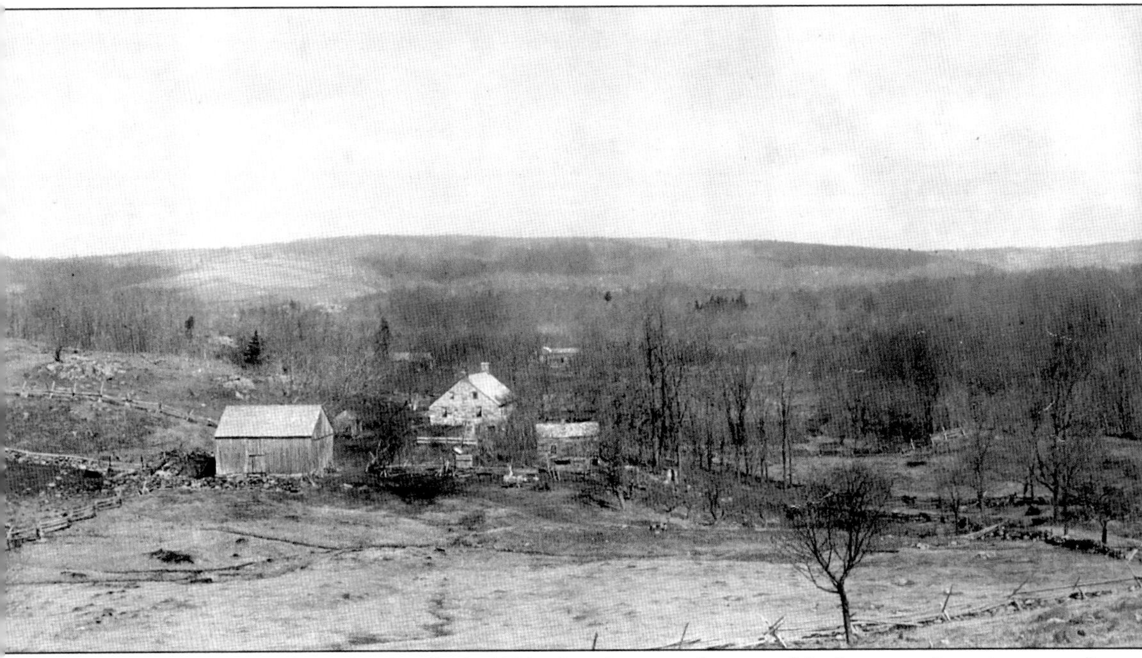

East Chippens Hill. On April 19, 1889, the photographer stood looking north and captured the old stone house and its outbuildings, pastures, and barnyard with the mountain in the background. The road runs on a diagonal, starting in the front right and going up beyond the house to the left. (BPL.)

Five

Three Stone Houses and More

In the southwest corner of Burlington is a natural rocky ledge backed by a tall cliff that forms a cave where large rocks reach up and support each other. This stone room with an entrance at each end has provided shelter for countless travelers along the trails. The Tunxis Indians, the earliest residents, surely used it on cold and rainy nights. During the American Revolution, the British sympathizers in the West Woods scrambled over stone fences, through the marsh, and along ditches to hide themselves in what has come to be called Tory's Den, while the "Sons of Liberty" searched for them. Steven Graves, Ebenezer Johnson, and Chauncey Jerome escaped detection, but Moses Dunbar and Joel Tuttle, both of Chippens Hill, were captured elsewhere and hung. Tuttle did not die and returned to the cave. John Fuller built a second house made of stone before 1800, on East Chippens Hill. This old Colonial house was home to the Curtis family for many years and is in a fine state of restoration today. The third house in this chapter is a wood-frame house, home to the Stone family during the early 20th century; it is on West Chippens Hill. When Elbert Stone wanted to retire in 1946, he advertised Pleasant Valley Farm, his 169-acre dairy farm, with the potential to be a truck farm, a maple sugar business, a cordwood farm, or all four. The farm, complete with animals and equipment, was on the market for $27,000. Other early homes, many of them no longer standing, make up the rest of this chapter.

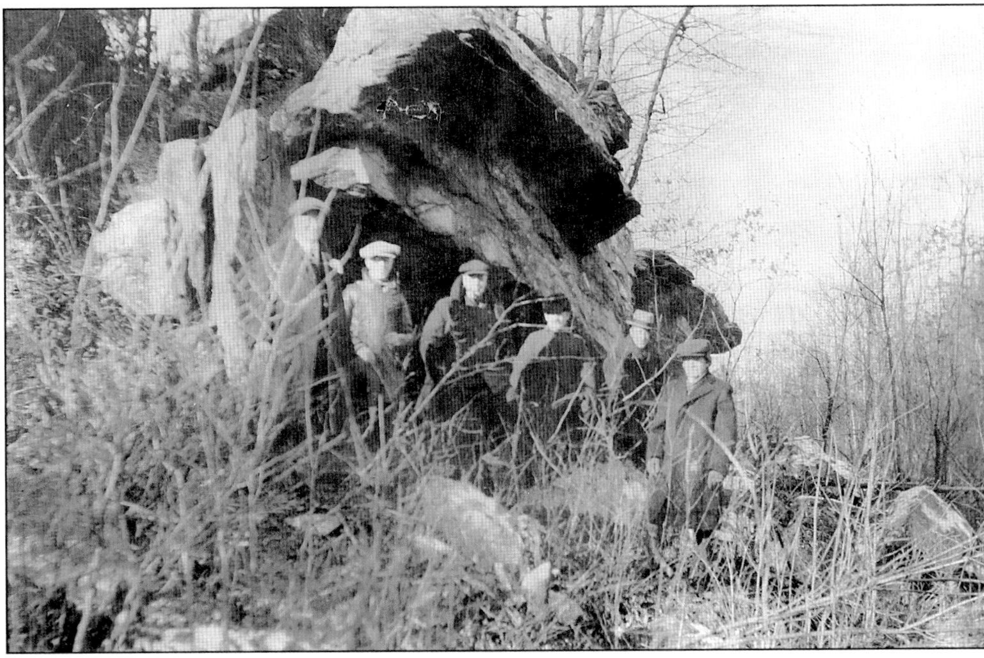

TORY'S DEN. Six hearty men stand in the lower entrance of the cave. The den goes into the mountain, and has a second entrance at the top of the chamber. Due to the many ledges and rocky outcroppings on the mountain, finding either entrance is difficult unless you know the way. (BPL.)

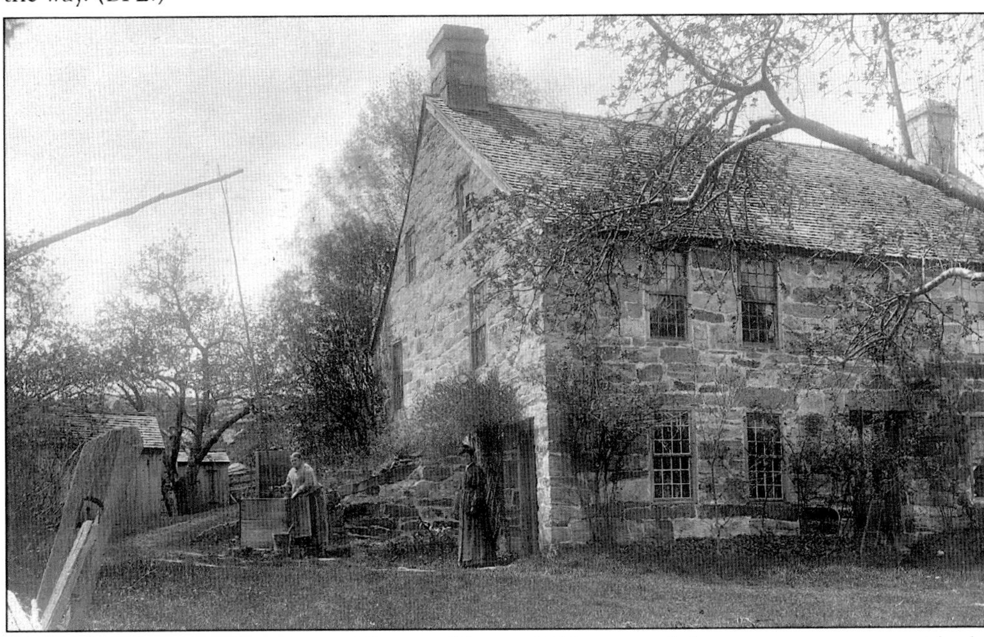

THE SPRING AT THE OLD STONE HOUSE. This *c.* 1890 postcard shows two women outside the door near the well. Beyond the well is a shed, with the privy beyond that. Elmira Curtis is in working clothes while her sister, Caroline Curtis, appears dressed to go out. They shared the house with their brother, Cyrus Curtis. All three were the three children of Salmon and Nancy (Gaylord) Curtis. (CA.)

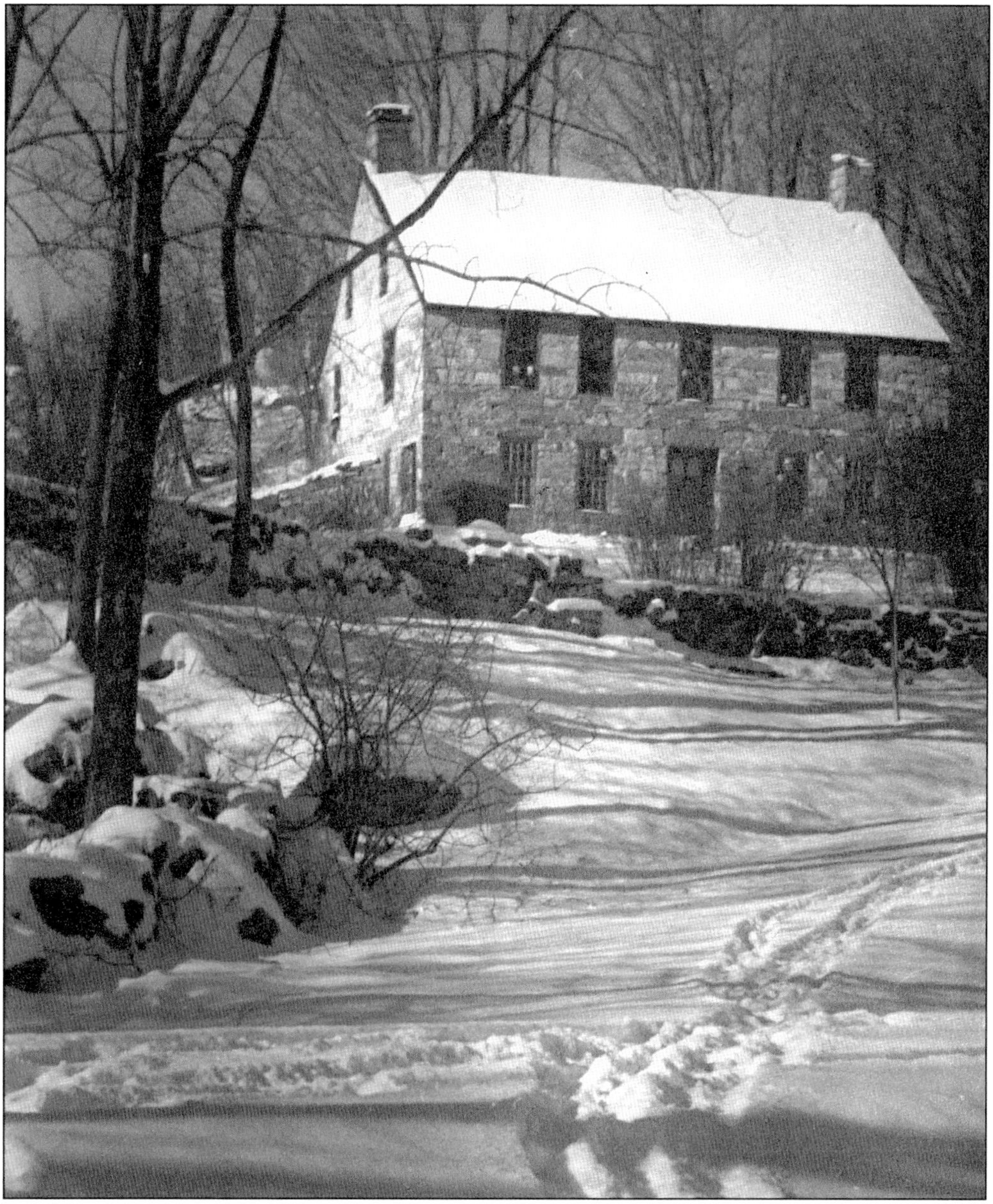

Winter at the Old Stone House. W.L. Gillette took this snow scene; the tracks in the snow may be those of the photographer. On the left is a steep and rocky corner between the photographer and the drive up to the house. The stone retaining wall, straight ahead, was not in view from the other vantage points. (BPL.)

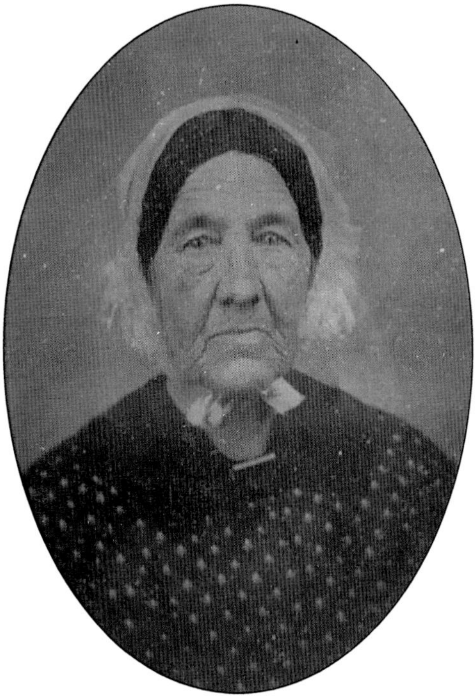

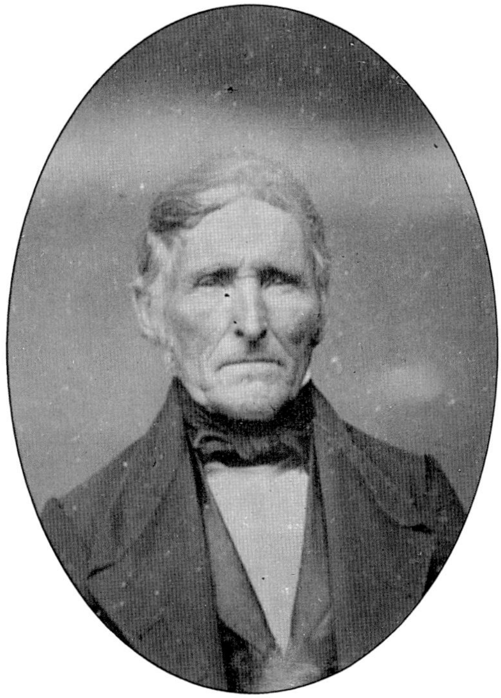

GREAT GRANDMA AND GREAT GRANDPA. Nancy Gaylord and Salmon Curtis were born in 1786 and 1787, respectively. They bought the stone house in 1819 and lived there for the rest of their lives—she until 1856 and he until 1840. (BPL.)

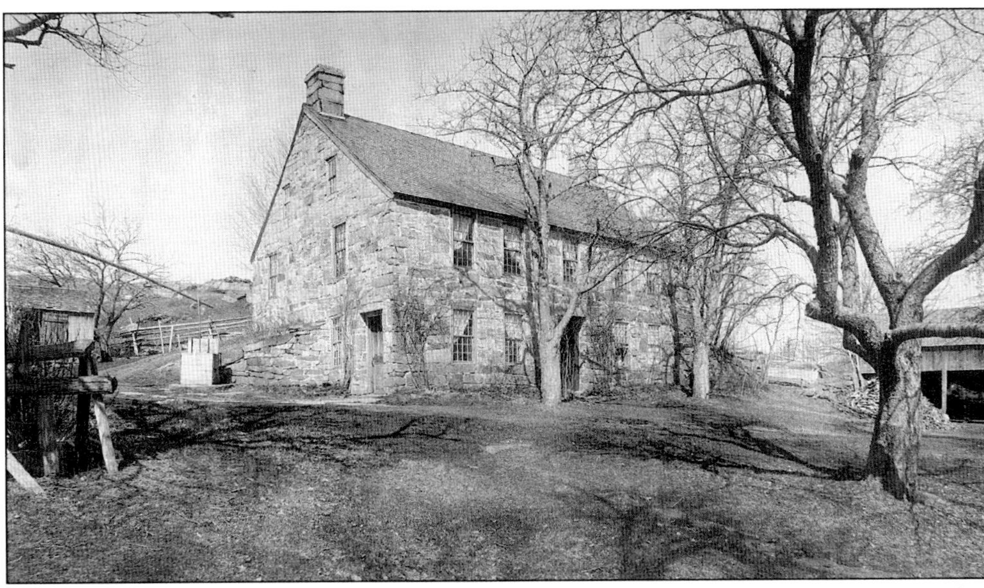

EARLY SPRING AT THE OLD STONE HOUSE. On April 19, 1889, W.L. Gillette photographed the house. This perspective shows not the privy but the carriage shed on the right, where a patient horse in harness is hitched to a cart. The long well sweep and the well are also shown. (MFD.)

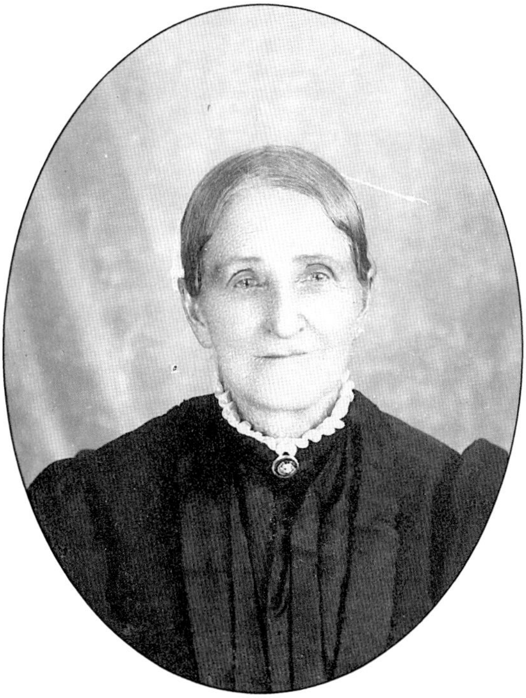
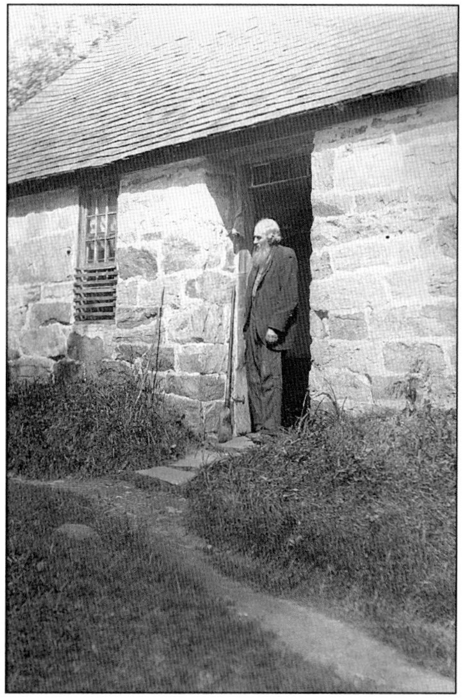

GRANDMA EMILY AND GRANDPA CYRUS. Emily and Cyrus Curtis lived on the second floor of the house with their two children, Nancy and Henry. The Curtis sisters, Caroline and Elmira, lived on the lower level. Cyrus Curtis is shown at the door to the upper level, or second floor, facing the back of the house. The well-worn path leads down to the well and to the privy. (MFD.)

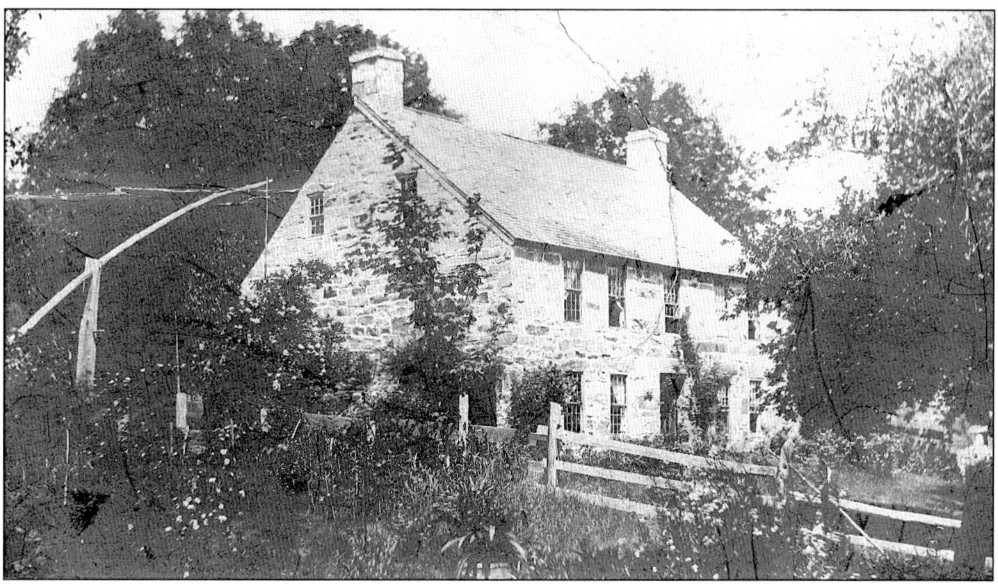

SUMMER AT THE OLD STONE HOUSE. In 1900, the stonewall and rail fence enclosed a thriving flower garden. The roses were in bloom and the windows of the house open to let in the fragrance. On the back is written: "Taken by W.L. Gillette with an 'Anthony 5 X 8 camara [sic].'" (BPL.)

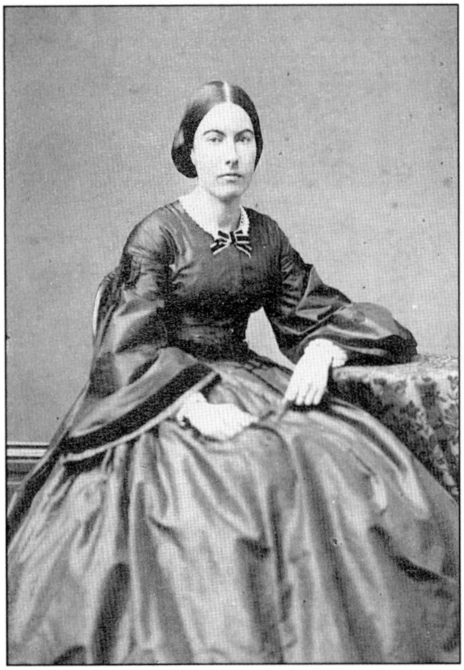

AUNT CAROLINE. Caroline Curtis sat for Prescott & Gage in Hartford for this portrait. She was born in 1826 and died in 1898. In the late 1940s, her nephew Henry, son of Cyrus Curtis, was the last member of the Curtis family to live in this house. (MFD.)

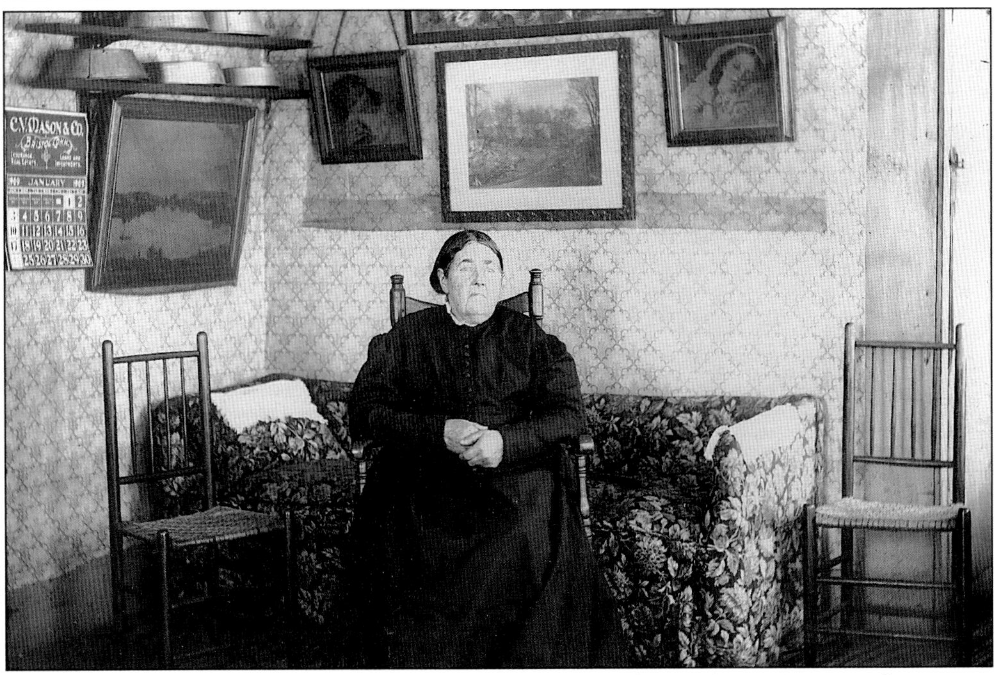

AUNT ELMIRA. Taken on January 31, 1909, this portrait shows Elmira Curtis in her sitting room on the lower level. She sits in an armchair in front of a daybed. Above the daybed are framed prints and photographs, a calendar, and shelves with tin milk pans upside down on them. Perhaps she made cheese or butter in the pans. According to her diary, she sold both cheese and butter to the neighbors when they came to call. She also sold rugs, which she wove on a loom in the attic. Her diary for 1894 is in the Burlington Room; it has many drawings of people, animals, birds, and landscapes. (MFD.)

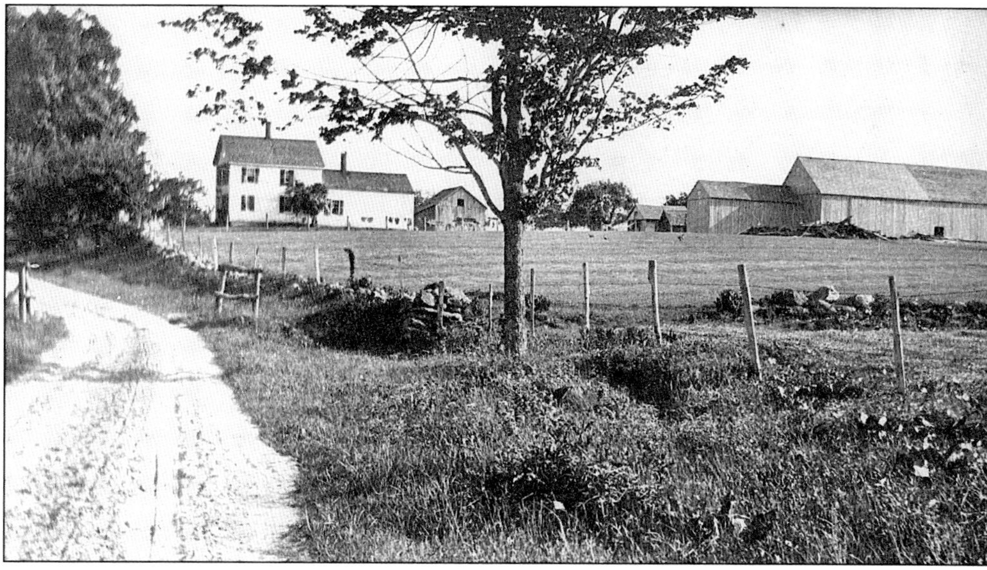

THE STONE FAMILY, CHIPPENS HILL. This third stone house is not made of stone but was lived in by the Stone family. The Stones were related to the Gaylords and the Curtises. Elbert J. Stone was born in 1897, son of Harry L. and Ina (Curtis) Stone. He and his wife, Eva (Olson) Stone, operated a dairy farm in town until they moved to Bristol. His brother Ralph H. Stone was born in 1902 and lived on Milford Street with his wife Florence (Beamish) Stone and one daughter. The above view shows the house, with clothes drying on the line, and five barns. We also see wire fences, stone walls, and chickens in the pasture. The photograph below is the view across from the front yard, showing cornfields and the rocky outcroppings of Chippens Hill. Could this be "Pleasant Valley Farm"? (BPL.)

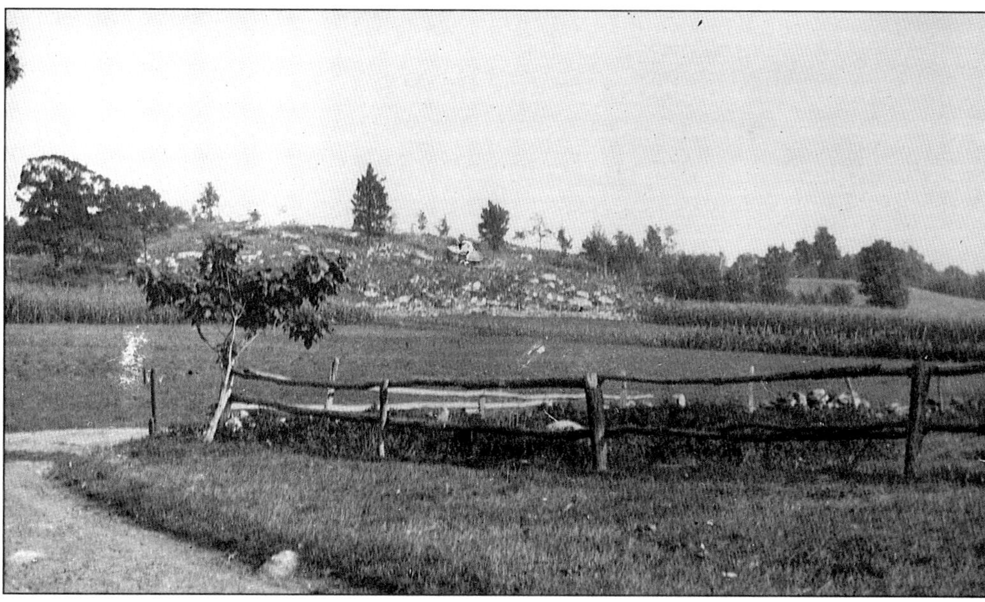

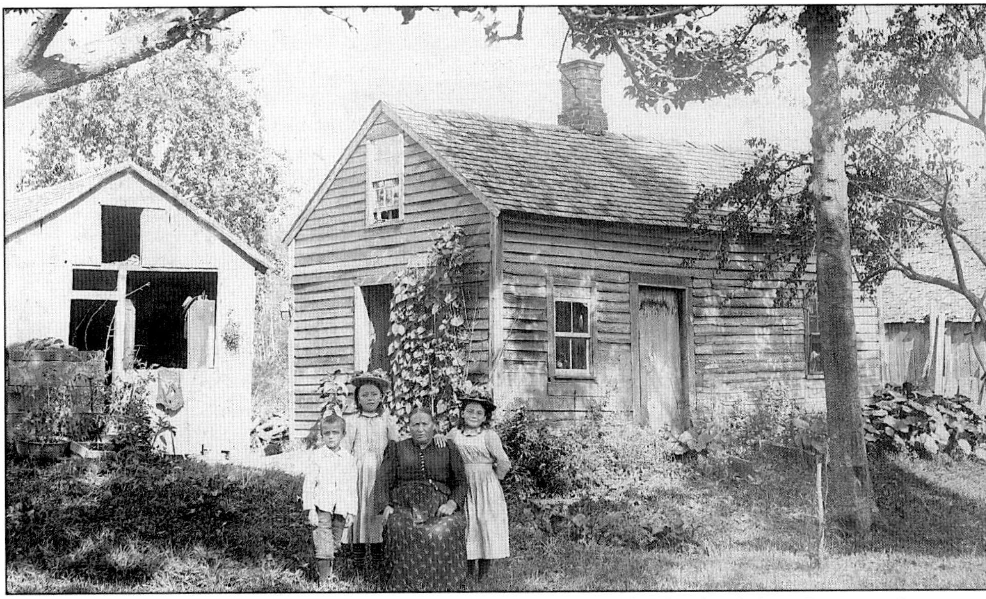

"MY MOTHER'S OLD HOME." So reads the inscription on the back of this photograph, signed by "Guy Stone." Her home was probably beyond the end of Greer Road and is no longer there. The flowers, hats, and sheds are wonderful, though. (BPL.)

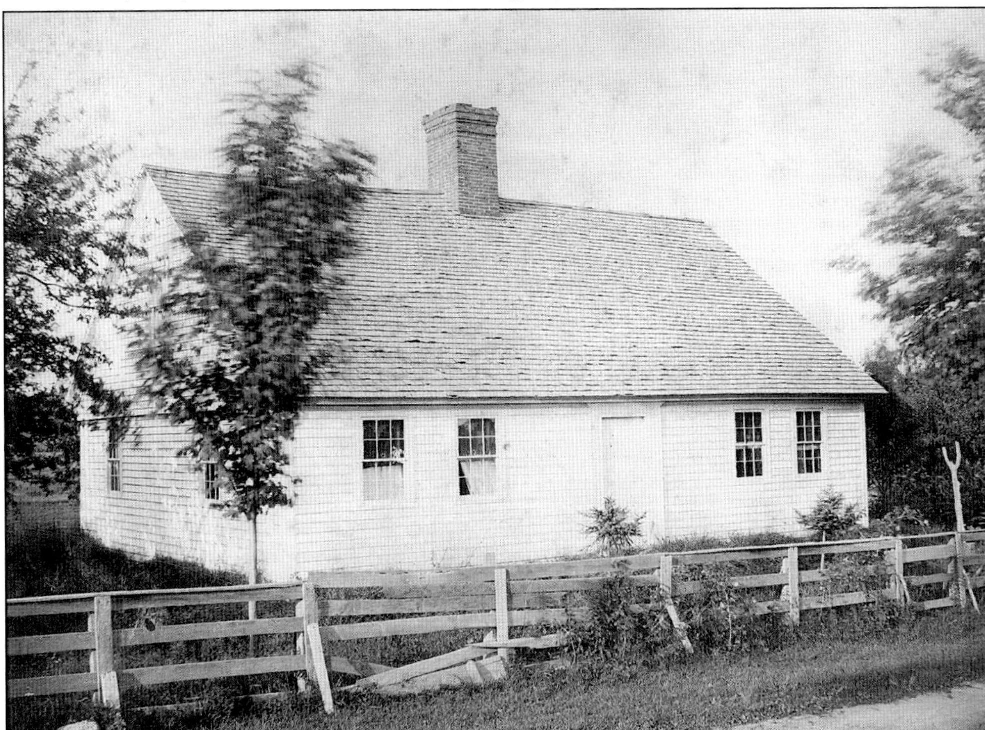

THE WIARD-GILCHRIST HOUSE. Out past the New Burlington Inn, on the right toward Harwinton, is this early center-chimney house. Helen Mullin believes that her grandfather W.R. Hartigan was born here. Still with us, this is representative of the many early houses that are now gone. (HHM.)

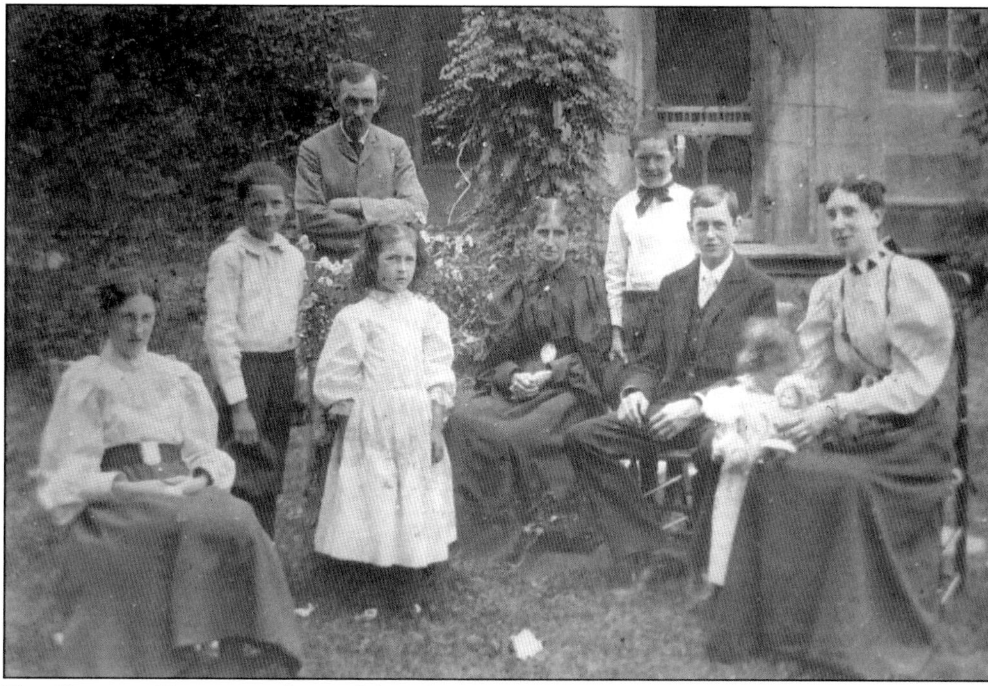

THE RUSSELL FAMILY. In front of their home near the corner of Punch Brook and Case Road are members of the Russell family. From left to right they are: Mary (Humphrey) Russell, Clayton, Frederick Russell, Anna (Grammie), Amy, Arthur, Maurice, Little Lillian (Aunt Nell), and Adele. Three of the children died of diabetes: Adele at age 23, Maurice at 17, and Arthur at 16, one year after this picture was taken. Anna married Russell Wollmann. (RDW.)

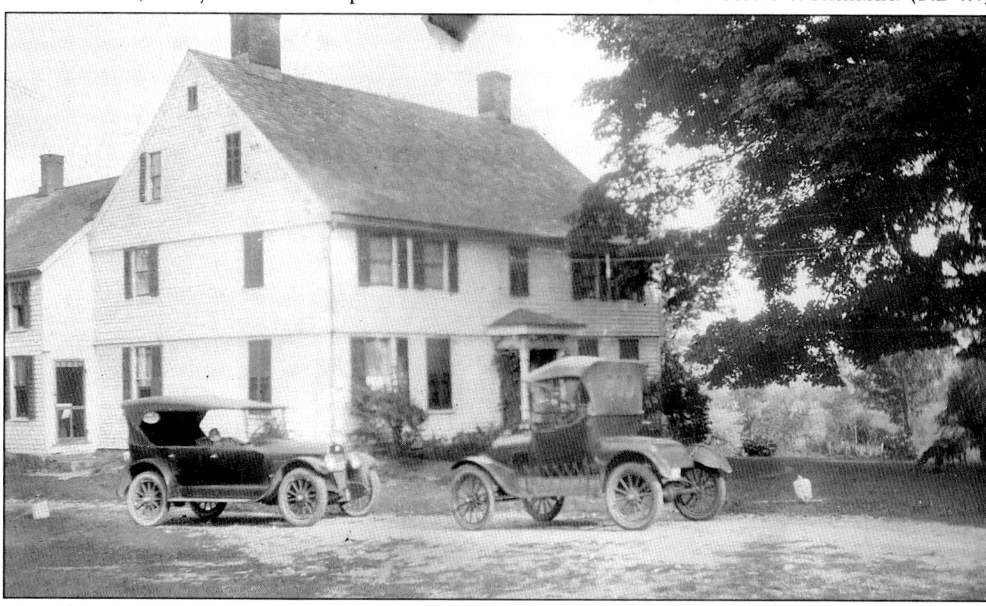

THE OLD MOSES HOMESTEAD. This house is in the southeastern part of town on George Washington Turnpike. In 1932, Arthur Emerson Moses and Arthur A. Moses each had prestigious cars. Their friend Myron Frink of Johnnycake Road lounges in the shade on the right. (VMV.)

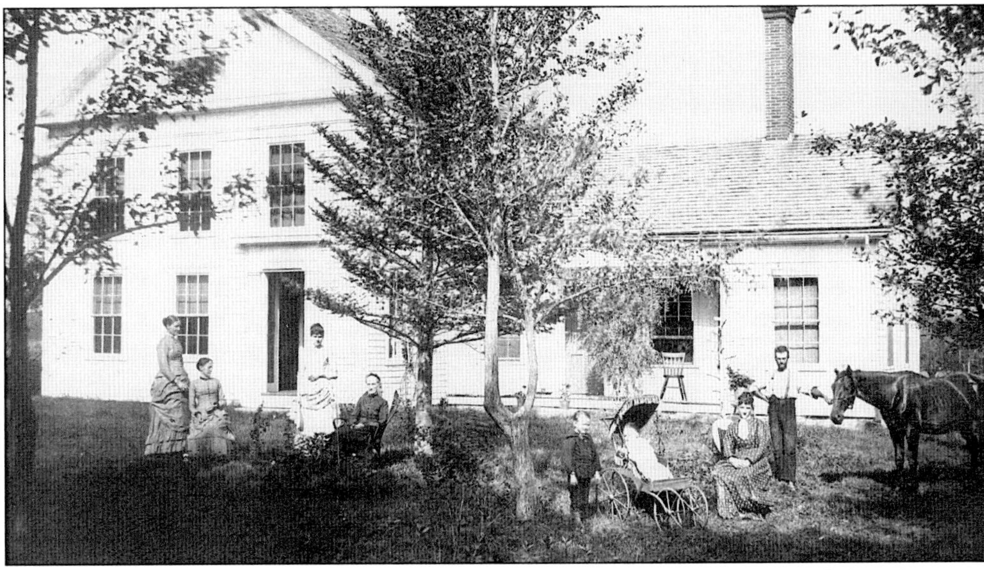

THE UPSON HOUSE AND FAMILY. In 1880, the Upsons gathered in front of their home on Upson Road (between Route 4 and Covey Road). Aunt Delight (Beecher) Upson, the woman in white standing next to the open door, had an apartment in the ell of the house, on the right. Seated second from the left, is Sarah (Foote) the mother of two daughters, who, after the death of her husband, Washington, ran a large farm "with much ability." Anna, standing next to her mother, married Adna North in 1881. Mr. and Mrs. John Horsfall, the other daughter and her family, of Unionville, are beside the horse. Aunt Lula is standing on the left, and Gram Upson is seated by the tree. (LA.)

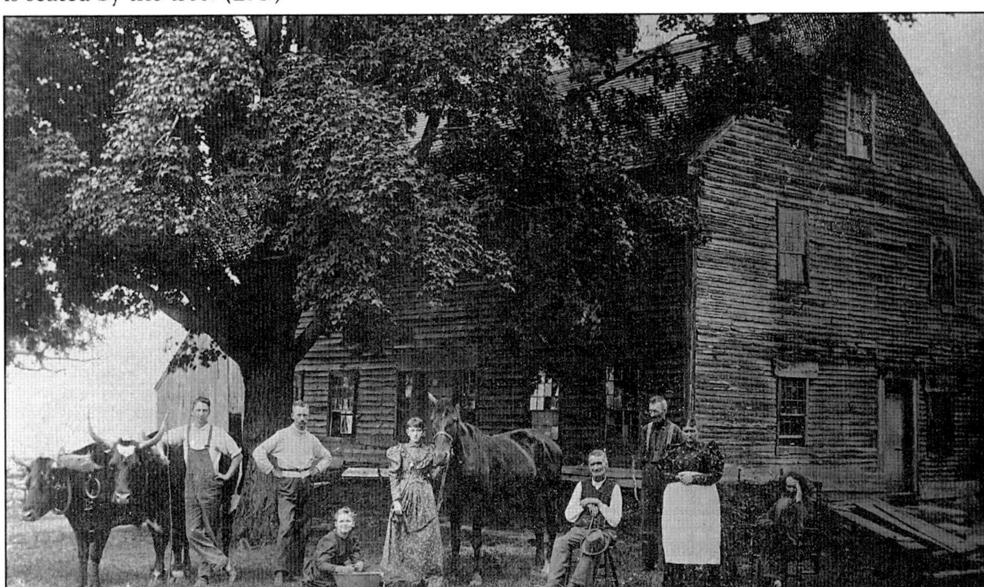

THE CORREL ALDERMAN HOME. On the north side of Punch Brook Road to the west of Case Road once stood this large farmhouse. The family of Mabel and C. Alderman, along with their oxen and horse, were photographed sometime before 1906. Their children were Hubert, who wed Wilhelmina Benecki in 1907; John Correl "J.C.," husband to Inez (Booth); and Carrie Louise, who married Herman Lindquist in 1896. (CA.)

Six

Sawyers and Sawmills

Lumbering and farming were the primary uses of land in early Burlington. With many brooks and streams and the abrupt changes in elevation, harnessing the power of water came about early. The energy powered the lumber, grain, and cider mills. The Grand List for 1798 shows two oil mills, five sawmills, a clover mill, gristmills, a carding mill, tanneries, and distilleries in West Britain (Burlington). Many of those mills are located today by a dot on an old map or by a pile of stones. However, some sites are still in evidence and a few are recognizable. The photographs in this and the following chapter attest to the thriving businesses that were powered by water. The Hitchcock Mill, just north of the center of town, was in operation by 1796. It was a combination grist, cider, and shingle mill. It later became the Foote Mill and finally the Schwarzmann Mill. Towards the northeast corner of town was the Scheidel Saw Mill. South from the center along Milford Street is Saw Mill Road, near the Hinman Saw Mill. Old photographs give us glimpses of the Hinmans, whose family still operates the mill. The foundation for the Alderman Saw Mill can still be seen east of the center along Route 4, where the "Welcome to Burlington" sign has been placed. Arthur Alderman, 19 years old in 1914, described one sawyer's day in his diary: "April 13. Ernest having been nursing the old sawmill into convalescence for the last week, we put the finishing touches on this morning and then went to sawing. Ernest sawing and I taking away. We got along pretty well considering that I had to run up to the house about 20 times to bring down tools to fix up some little defect."

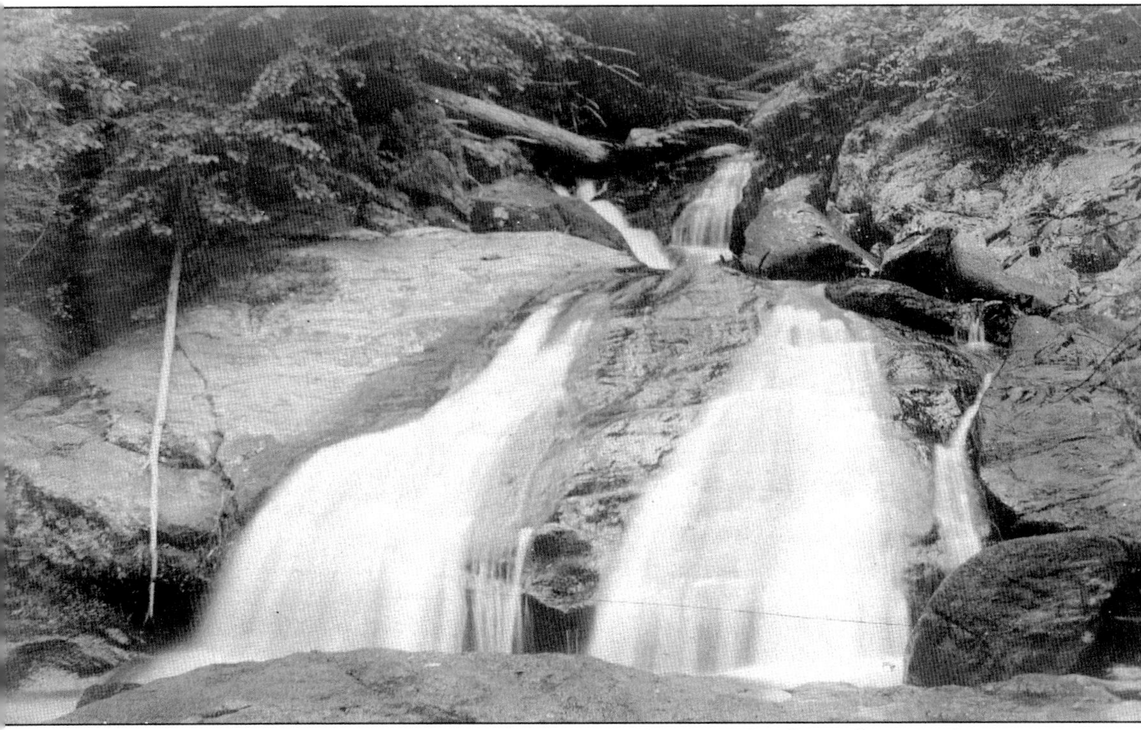

The Falls at Vineyard Postcard, c. 1910. The water for the mills in Burlington came from small brooks and streams. The power was generated by the fast-moving water that dropped from high elevations on the mountains to the level of the Farmington River. This waterfall is not visible from the road but is just a short hike into the woods. (LA.)

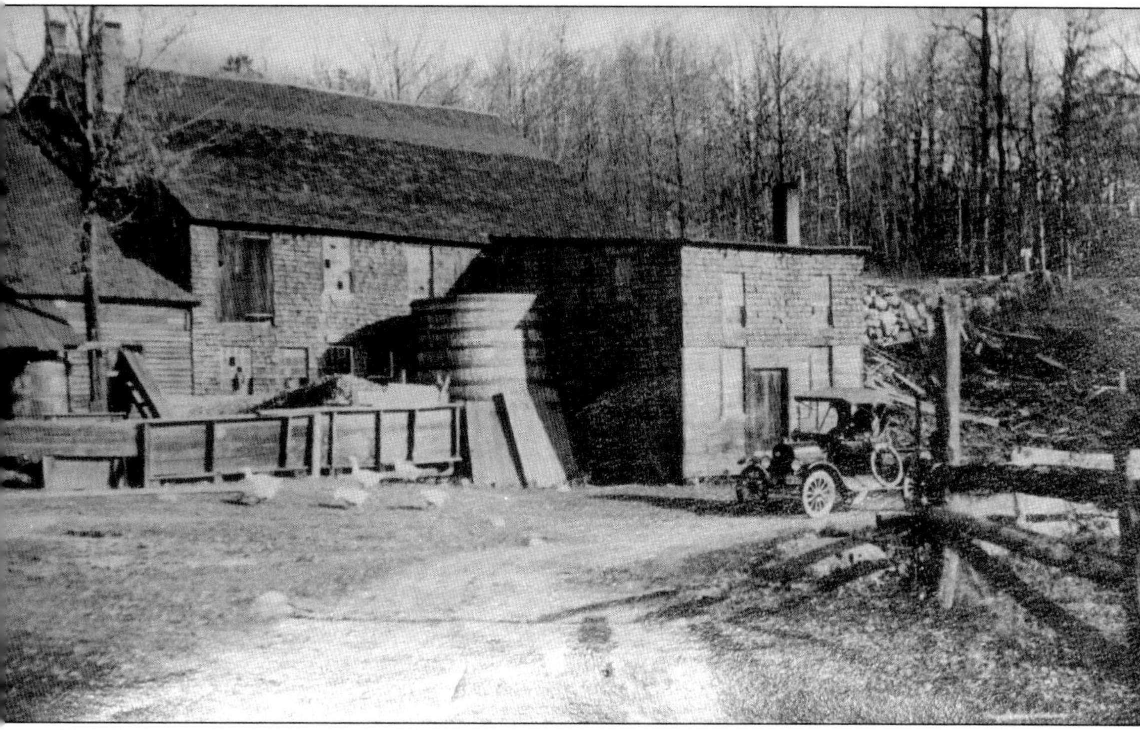

THE SCHWARZMANN MILL WITH GEESE AND AN AUTO, C. 1920. By 1798, Burlington had five sawmills; this one was on Foote Road near Vineyard. Built in 1796 or earlier, this combination grist, cider, and shingle mill was in production until the 1960s. Like most mills, it was framed and shingled with wood and built on a stone foundation near a fast-running stream of water. On May 21, 1914, Arthur Alderman recorded, "Clifford, Ernest and I worked down to the sawmill all day sawing out some logs for the Spencer boys. Right after dinner we received a telephone that Schwarzmann's mill was being cremated alive. We hitched the horse and loaded 5 men and 15 pails in 30 seconds. We almost killed the horse, but we arrived there in time to see the fire before it was put out. It was a small brush fire about 200 feet from the mill. I don't know how many attended the fire, but they were still pouring in when we left." (BPL.)

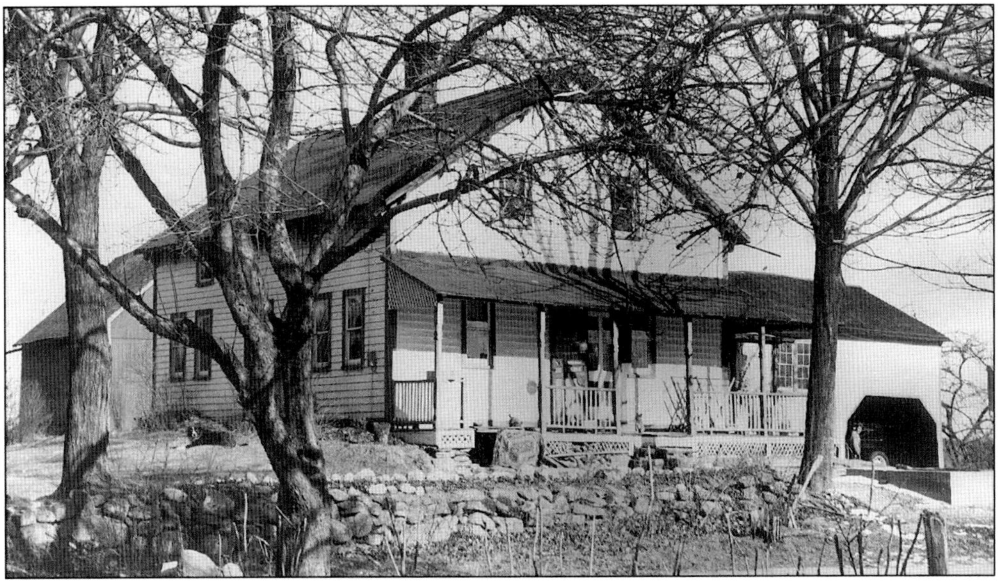

Mother Alice Green's House. Photographed by John Scott c. 1950, this house burned and another now stands at the corner of Covey Road and Foote Road. For the last 45 years of her life, 35 of them as a widow, Mother Green lived in this house, raised her children, and cared for others. One of those she kept in his old age was Silas M. Brooks, a daring and creative man, who died in 1906. He became the first balloonist, with 173 successful ascensions. Brooks also assisted P.T. Barnum with his circus and especially with his Druid Band. (BPL.)

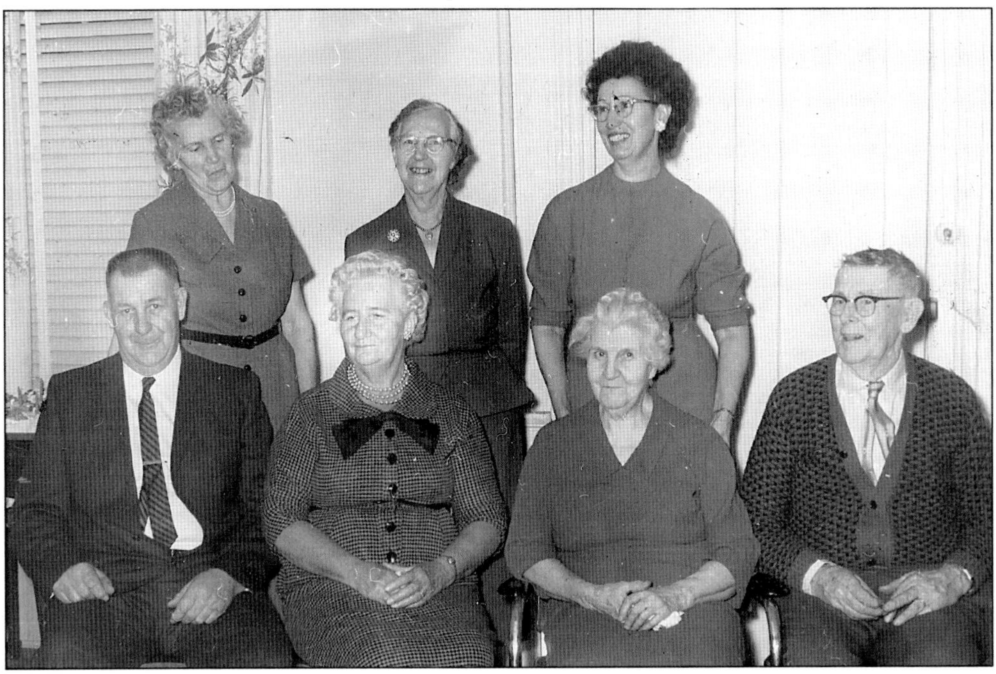

Mother Green's Children, All Grown Up. As children they played and helped at the mill. As adults they are, from left to right, as follows: (front row) Ralph, Georgianna, Floss, and George Green; (back row) Mabel, Maida, and Elizabeth Green. Ralph Green worked for the state fish hatchery for over 45 years. (LA.)

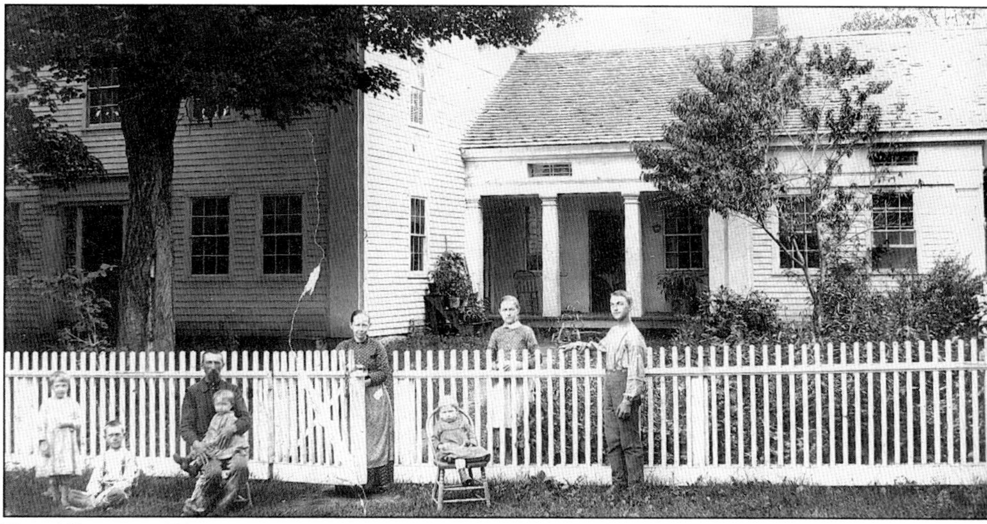

THE HINMAN HOUSE AND FAMILY, C. 1902. Across the street from the Hinman sawmill, on the "Road to Harwinton" was, and still is, this lovely farmhouse with its picket fence and beautifully shingled roof. John Hinman, a church organist, farmer, and sawyer, who died in 1903 at age 56, is seated in the chair holding his youngest son, John. Emma Hinman, his second wife and mother of his younger children Anna, Ernest Ray, and Lillian, is at the gate. The two oldest children are Catherine and Benjamin. Sons Ernest Ray (seated on the ground) and Benjamin operated the water-powered sawmill after their father's death. (LA.)

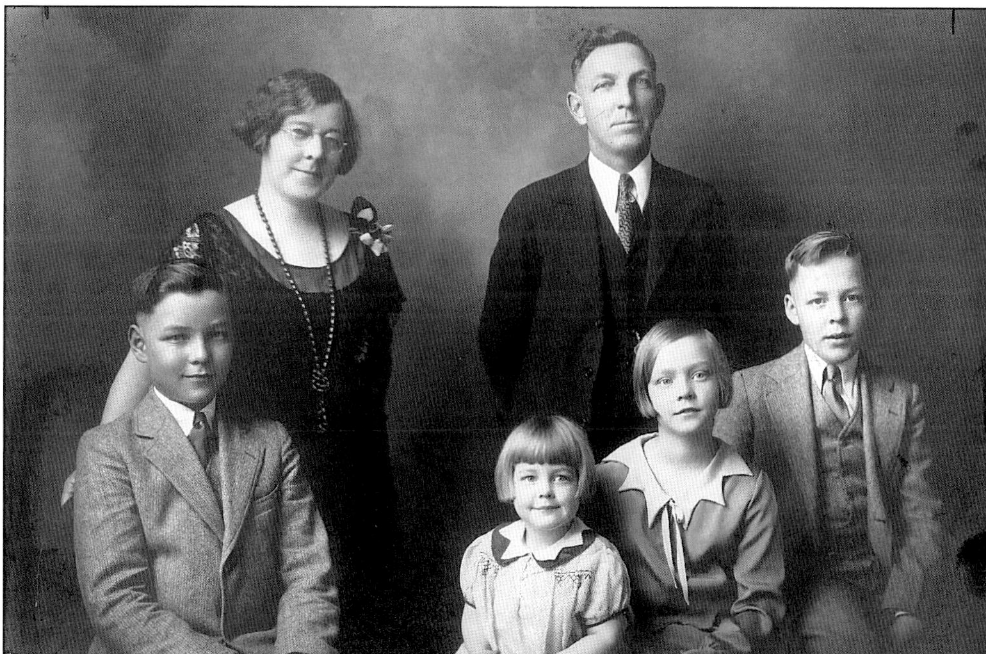

ERNEST RAY "PETE" AND MAUDE HINMAN WITH CHILDREN, 1932. Pete and Maude Huntington were married on July 6, 1910. They are shown with their children, from left to right, Howard Beverly, Helen Lucille, Jeanne Isabelle, and John Douglas. When this picture was taken to celebrate the parents' wedding anniversary, they were living on Milford Street in a new bungalow house on their dairy farm near the new sawmill. (BHD.)

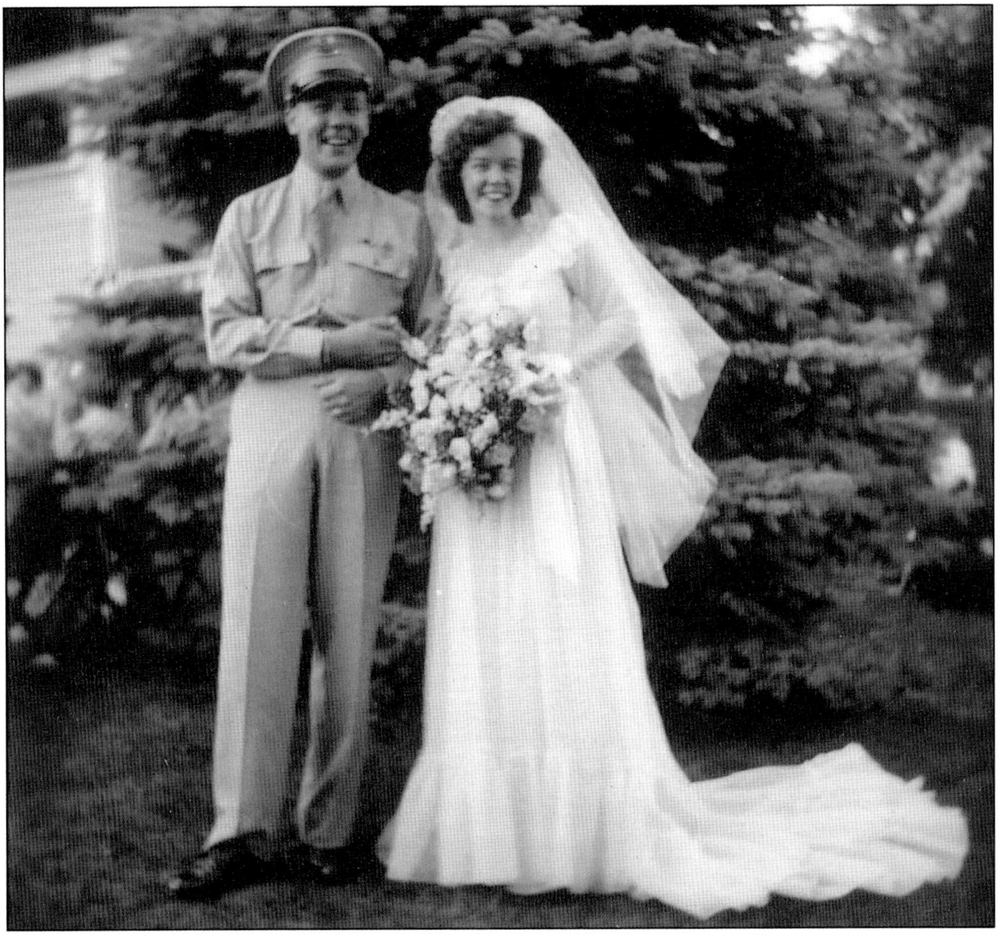

GREETINGS FROM BURLINGTON, 1944. Jean Isabelle married Raymond Bartman Jr. on July 9, 1944, during World War II, and her proud parents sent out the wedding photograph of their daughter to all of their friends. In a 1994 taped conversation, recorded in California and on file at the library, Jean (Hinman) Bartman recalls walking down the red-carpeted aisle at the church that summer day. (BPL.)

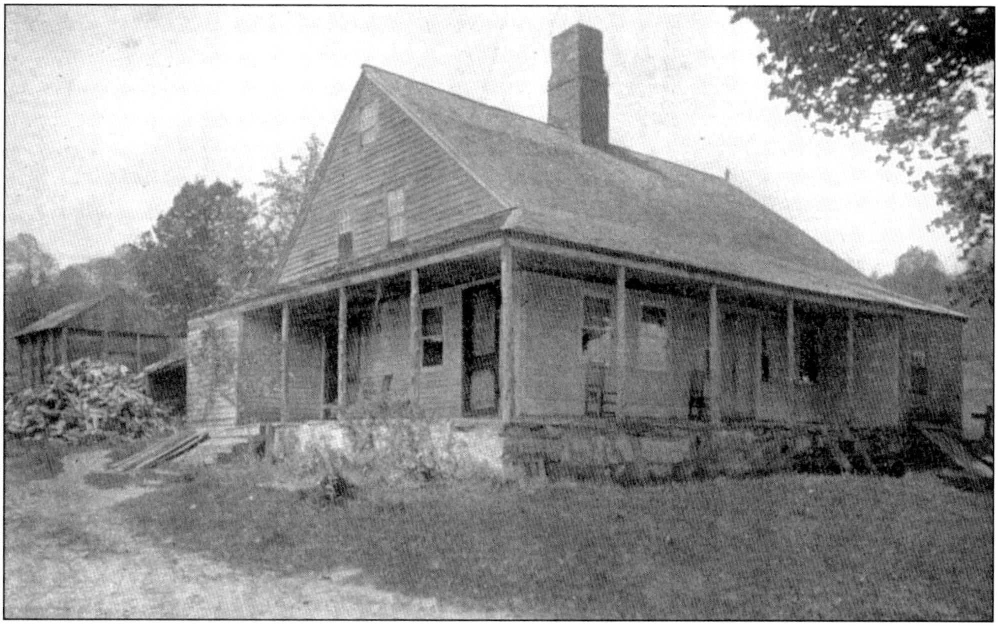

THE OLD WEBSTER HOUSE. The Hinman's built their bungalow and retained the old house for a few years. Then they took it down and built the new sawmill on this site. (BHD.)

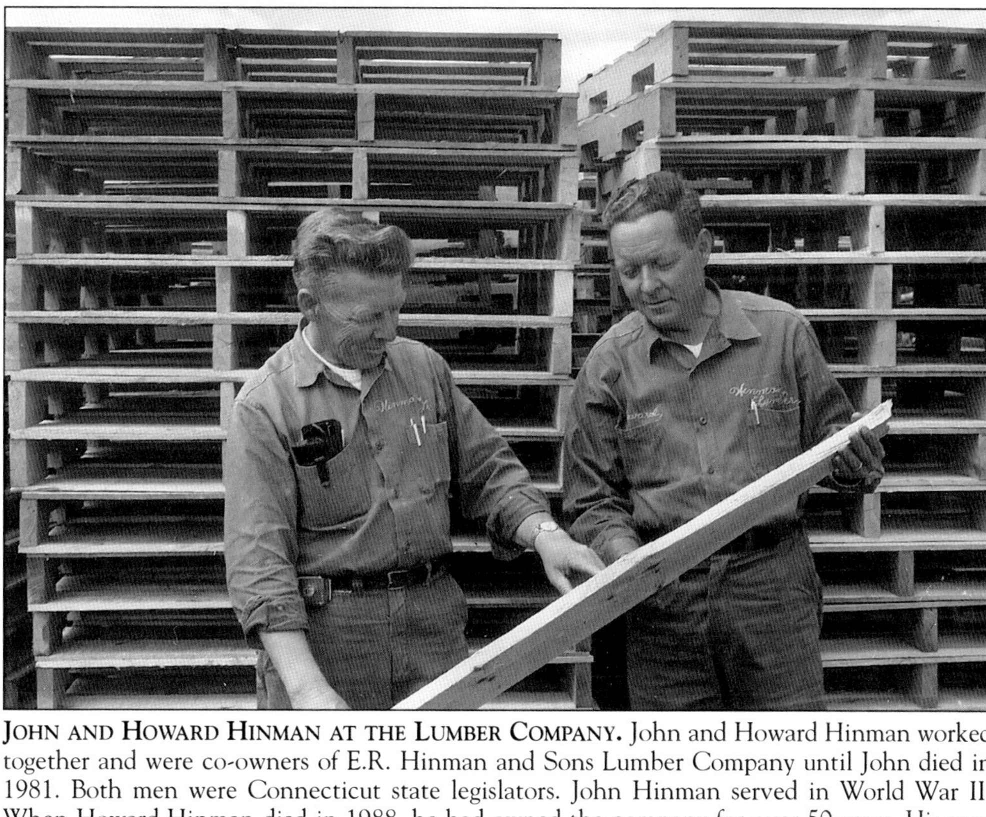

JOHN AND HOWARD HINMAN AT THE LUMBER COMPANY. John and Howard Hinman worked together and were co-owners of E.R. Hinman and Sons Lumber Company until John died in 1981. Both men were Connecticut state legislators. John Hinman served in World War II. When Howard Hinman died in 1988, he had owned the company for over 50 years. His sons Paul and Michael still operate the mill. (BHD.)

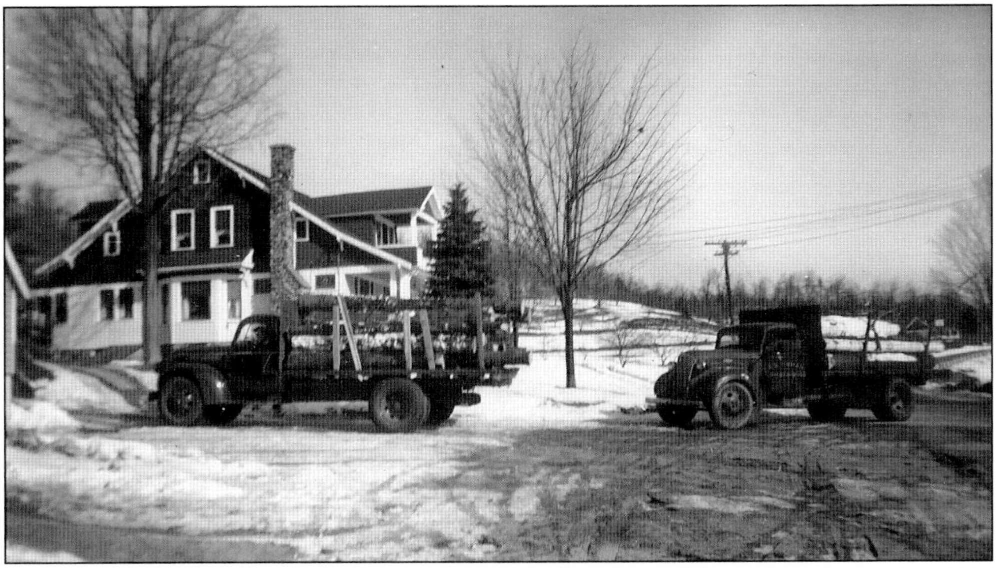

THE BUNGALOW AND THE BARN. This house was built in front of the Webster house. In a 1994 tape recording, Jean (Hinman) Bartman recalled her memories about life on Milford Street and walking to school in the center. "We used to trudge up through the road. I suppose it didn't hurt us too much to walk to school; it was a long walk. Remember that we were down in an area of

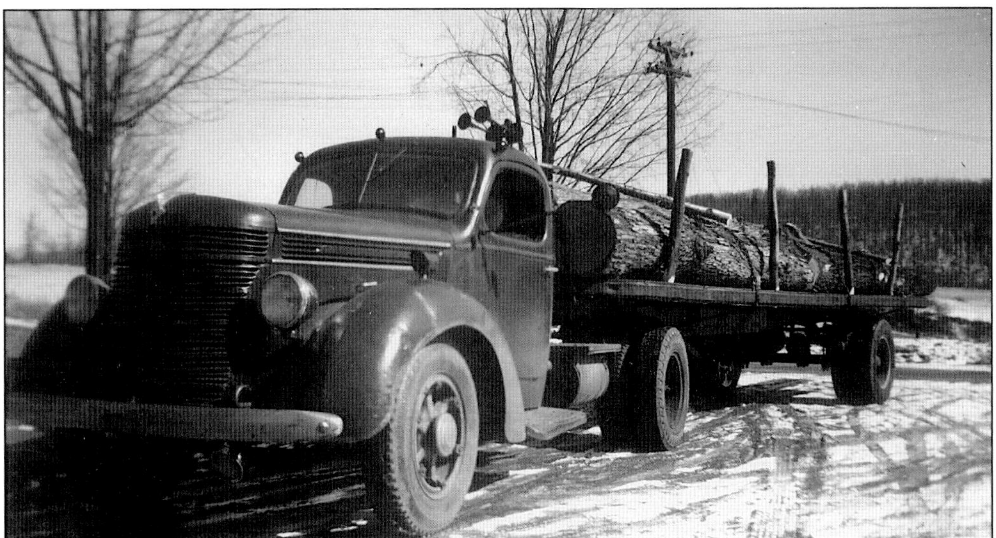

HINMAN LUMBER TRUCKS. Pete Hinman's and his family owned many acres of land and grew much of their own lumber, but they also purchased some. Their trucks to transport the logs were

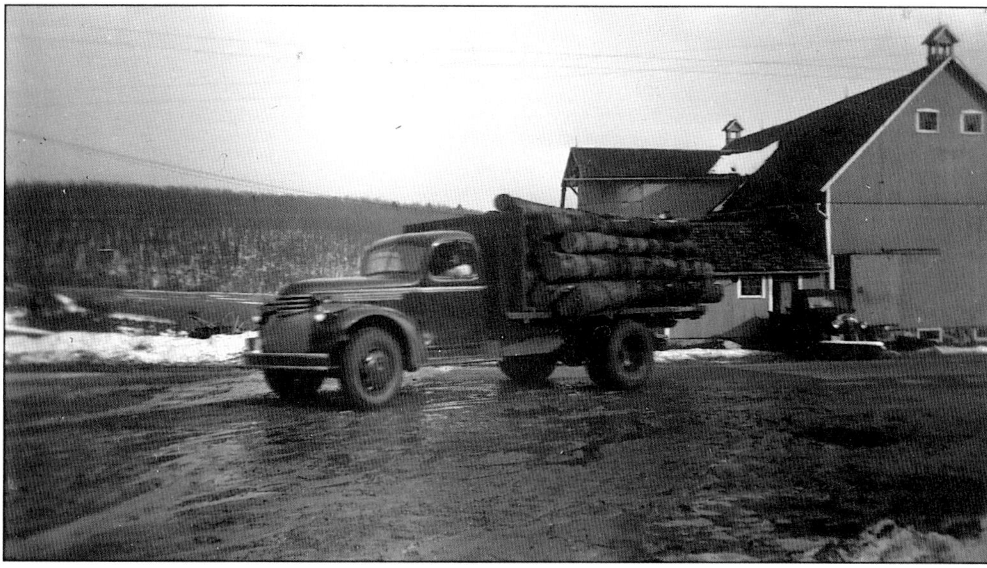

the town where we had nobody—nobody but us to go to school with. For a very brief few years, there were some kids that lived in the old Webster place. They were the Lubys that lived there, where our sawmill is today. But that was very brief, so we girls and my brothers, too, kind of grew up by ourselves." (BHD.)

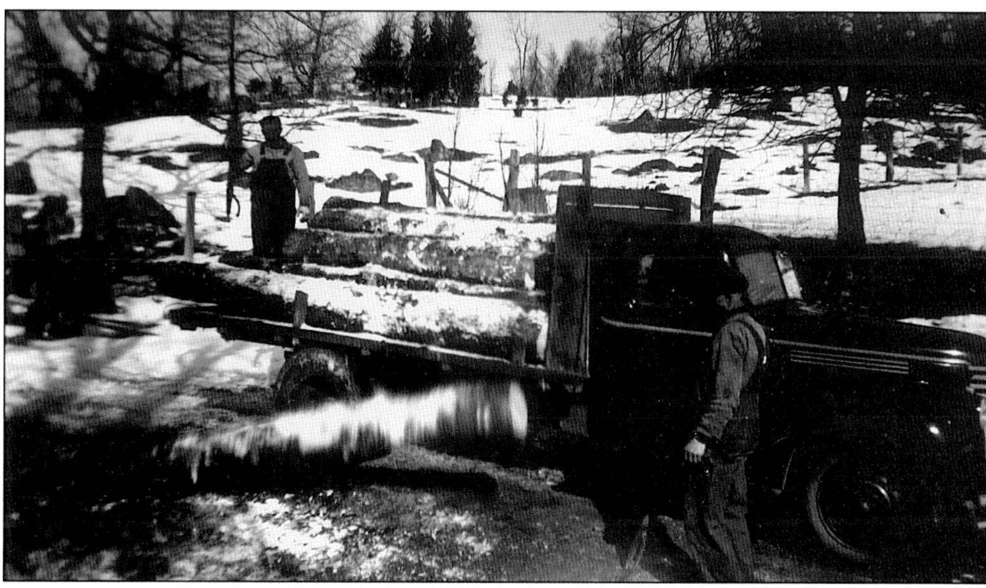

equipped with side poles to keep the logs from rolling off when the trucks were in motion. At the lumberyard, the poles were removed and the logs rolled off of the truck. (BHD.)

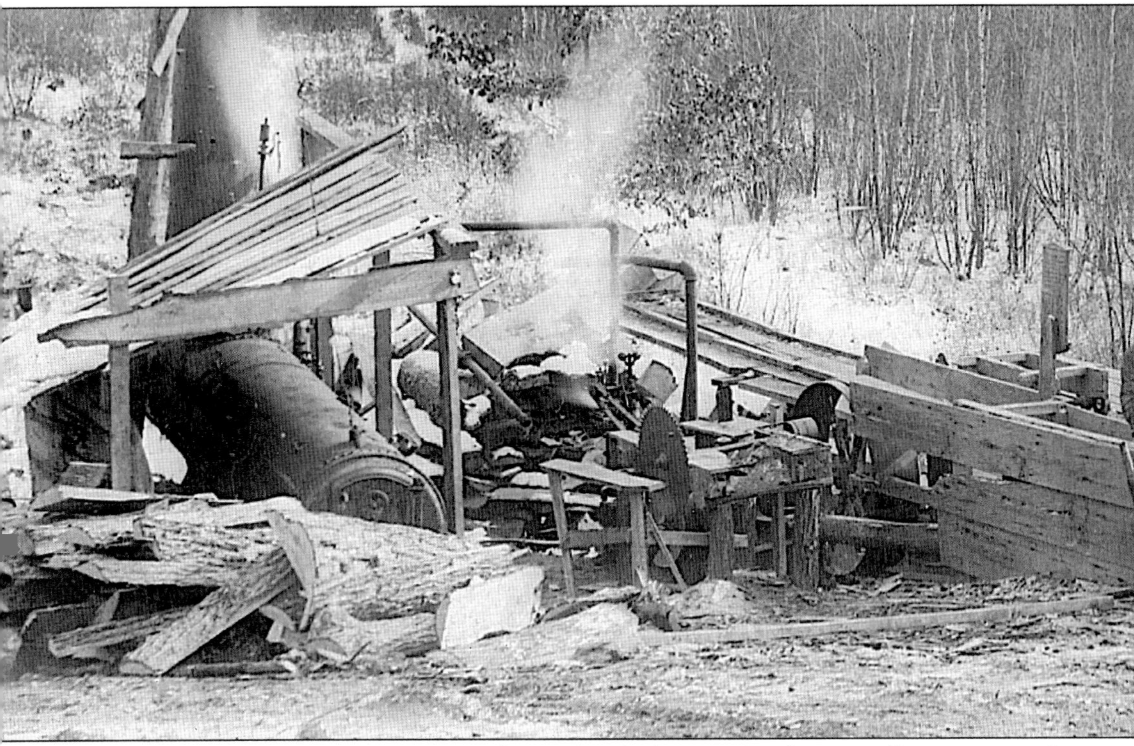

THE OLD BURLINGTON SAWMILL. This undated photograph of a sawmill scene was taken *c.* 1900. On the left is the source of power that turns the belt to the saws. Three lumbermen are in the center near the gears. The large saw is at the left end of the log. Five sawyers and a dog

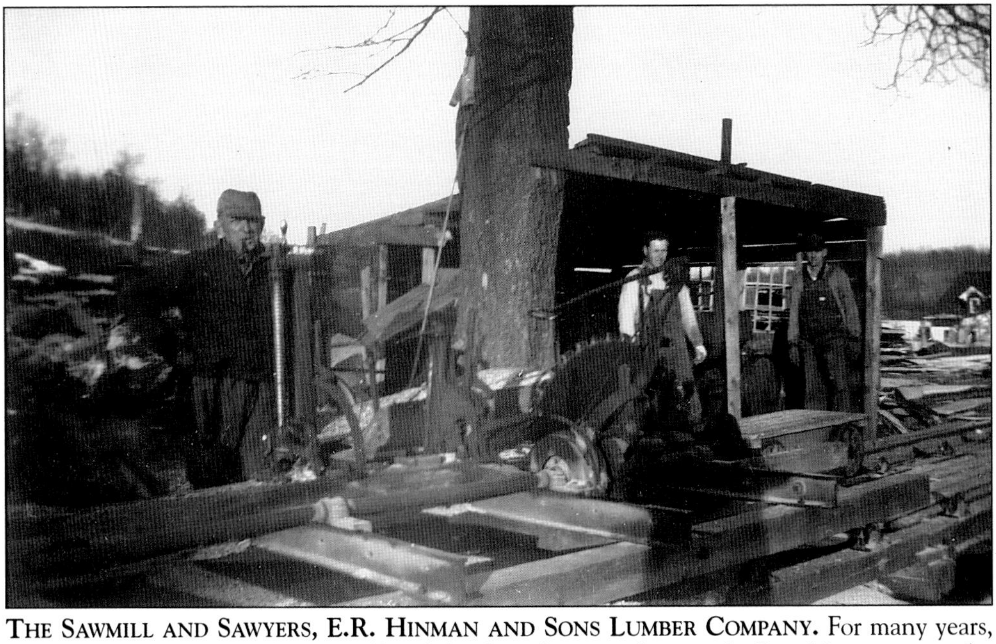

THE SAWMILL AND SAWYERS, E.R. HINMAN AND SONS LUMBER COMPANY. For many years, Ernest Hinman operated the sawmill and the dairy farm simultaneously. Pete Hinman is on the left, holding his pipe. His sons are on the right, and beyond them is the bungalow. (BHD.)

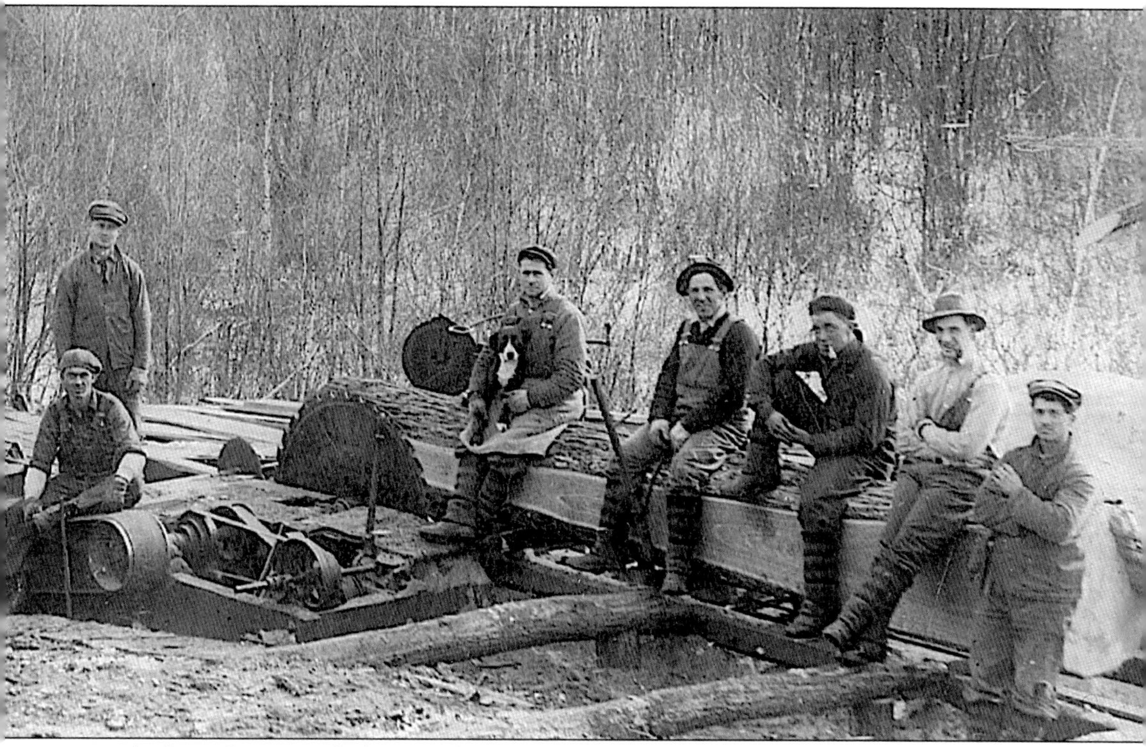

sit on the log. The original photograph is owned by Shirley J. Tibbetts. (BPL.)

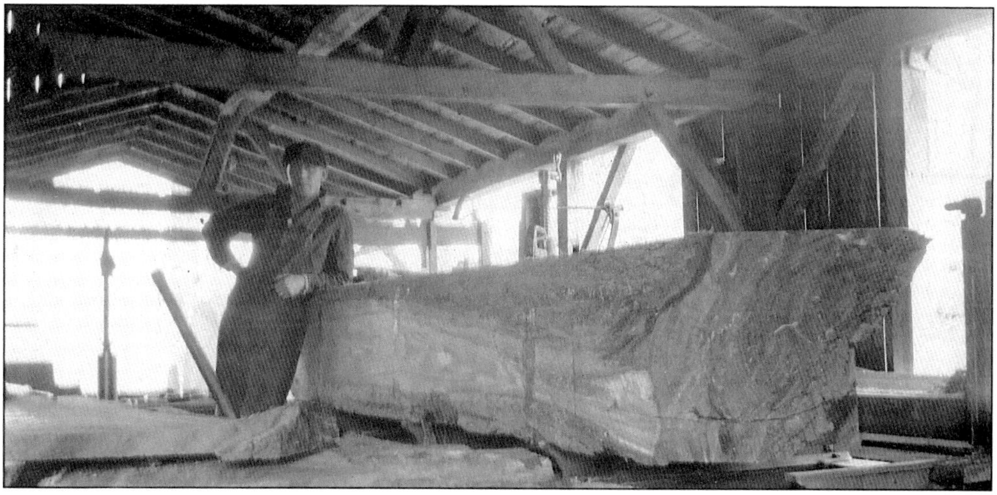

A CHESTNUT LOG AT ALDERMAN'S SAWMILL. On April 29, 1920, Ernest Alderman was the sawyer at the water-powered sawmill. The chestnut trees in Burlington were not horse chestnuts but Castanza Dentitia, which grew to 200 feet tall. This tall straight hardwood was especially well suited for bridge and railroad ties. On March 4, 1914, Arthur Alderman wrote in his diary, "All hands worked down to the sawmill, the same as yesterday. Uncle Philip sawed, I took away and Ernest and Clifford supplied us with logs. We sawed 108 ties and considerable lumber. I worked all day with Uncle Philip. We sawed 700 feet of lumber and 42 ties." (LA.)

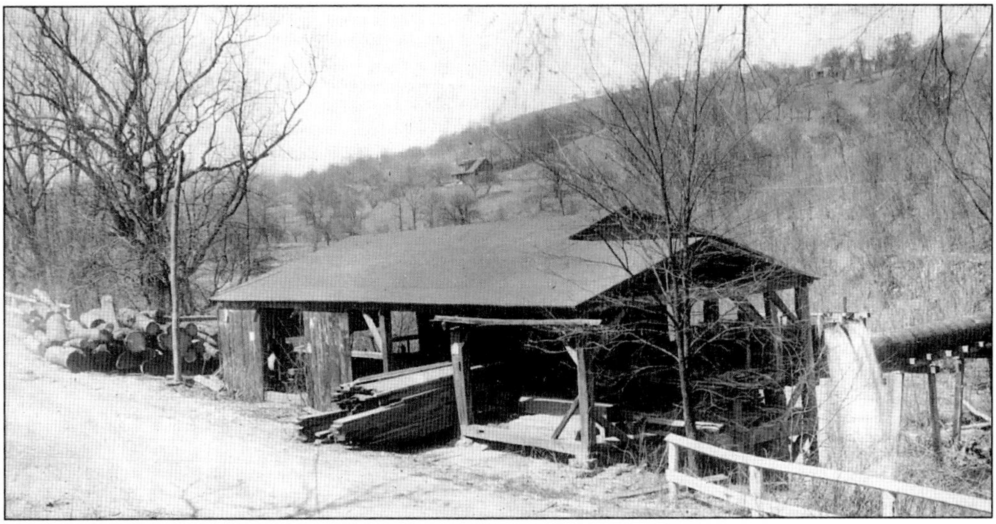

ALDERMAN'S SAWMILL ON ROUTE 4, C. 1920. The water from a dam across Burlington Brook went through the raceway to the cider mill waterwheel and then back to the brook, where there was a second dam and a raceway to the center wheel of the sawmill. The waterwheel powered the saw. The sawmill had a total fall of 31,000 feet and developed about 25 horsepower in 20,000 feet. The water came out the other end of the mill (on the right in this view) and was channeled through the wooden flume, over the brook, and toward the Farmington River. Excess water was released when there was more than needed, and that is what looks like a waterfall at the back of the mill. To the left of the mill are the logs and midway; coming out of the mill and onto the road, are the sawn boards. (LA.)

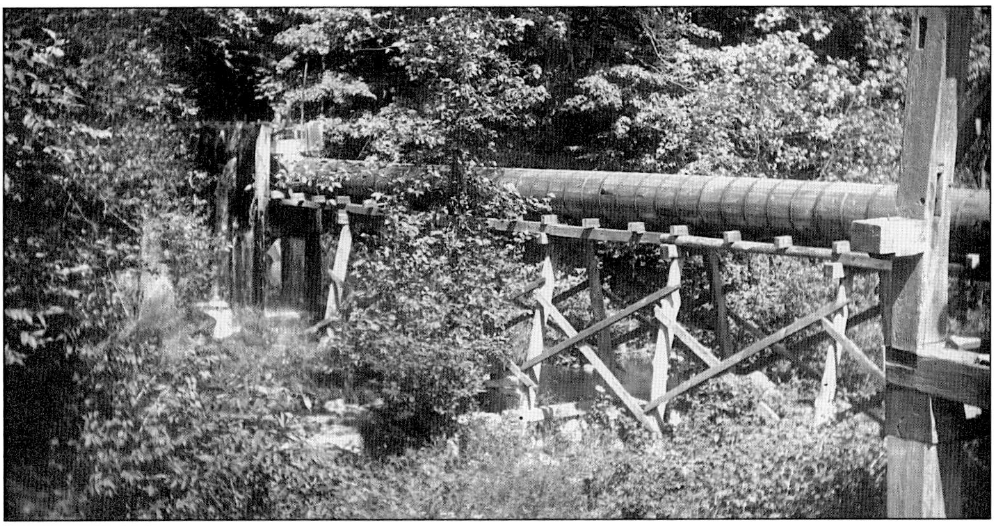

THE FLUME FROM ALDERMAN'S SAWMILL, 1920. On June 24 and 25, 1914, Arthur Alderman recorded his activities: "Today Ernest and I put up the fencing for the new line fence between Szegda's and Grandma's land. Goodwin and Clifford drew logs down off from Uncle Sereno's mountain. These logs are some that Papa has bought. We are going to saw them and use them for repairing the sawmill." . . . "June 25. This morning all hands went up to Uncle Sereno's mountain, and while Ernest and Goodwin drew out the logs, Clifford and I sawed them up. Ernest and I then tinkered up the sawmill while Goodwin and Clifford drew logs to the mill . . . I went swimming in the race then Ernest and I worked down to the sawmill . . ." (LA.)

Seven

Punch Brook and Barnes Hill

Punch Brook Road runs from George Washington Turnpike in an easterly direction, crosses the brook from which it gets its name, and heads north to where it meets Route 4. On the other side, it becomes Barnes Hill Road. Barnes Hill was named for the family who lived in the solitary house at the top of the hill. Today most older folks in town call it Laura Barnes's house. Laura Barnes's photograph appears in the first chapter, in front of the Congregational church. Susan Barnes grew up on Barnes Hill and knew the names given to the fields and lots. When she was young, she wrote them down, which today helps us know how they were used. The Alderman and Barnes families, both early settlers of Burlington, have been close neighbors and friends. There have been a few marriages between the two families. Apple orchards and dairy farming were also a part of the lives of these two families and others, such as the Moses family. The apples were turned into cider and brandy right on the farm. The Alderman cider mill was featured prominently in the news during Prohibition and is in several photographs in this chapter. The sawmill and the cider mill, located a short distance to the north, were both powered by raceways from Burlington Brook.

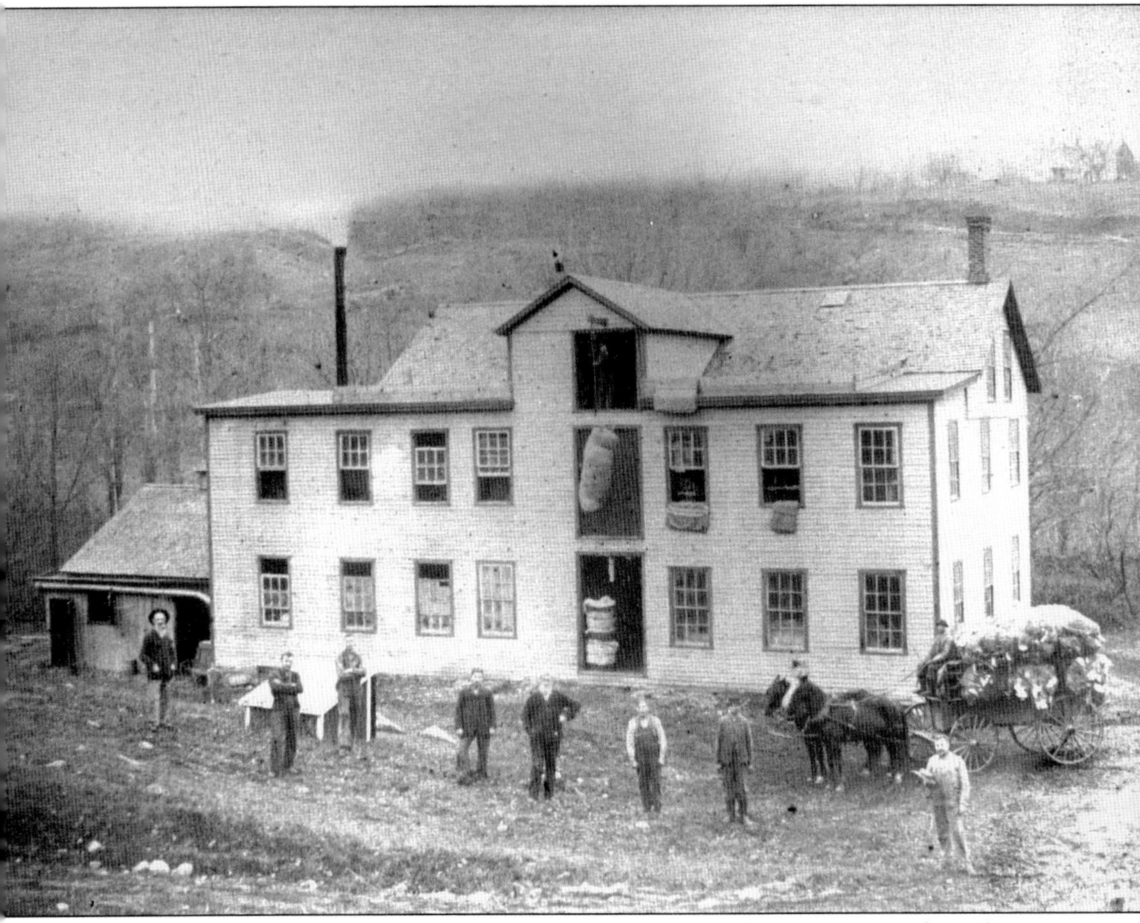

J. BROADBENT & SON INC., LATE 1880S. Cotton yarn and batting were made in this cotton mill by Jesse Broadbent and his son Fred until a fire destroyed the building. The Broadbents and their workers, including a team of horses with a wagon full of cotton, are seen in front of the mill, facing old route 116, now Route 4. The Barnes's house is on the hill, in the upper right. The Alderman Cider mill was later built on this site. (LA.)

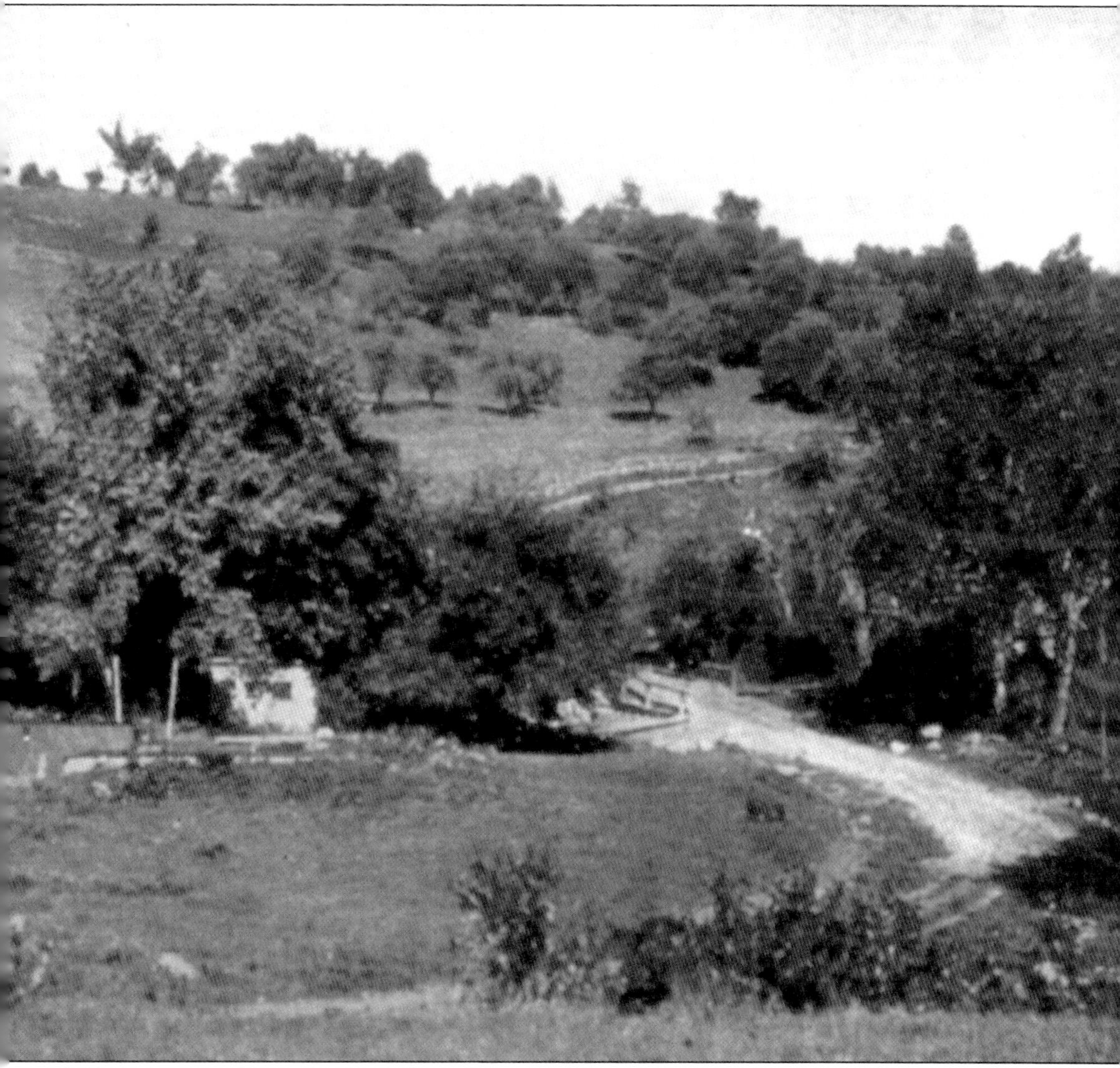

A Postcard of Barnes Hill, Old Home Week, 1906. Postcard No. 4 in the series shows the site of the Broadbent Mill (far left), which burned in 1906; only the storehouse was saved. In 1816, the first Alderman cider mill was built on Punch Brook Road. The distillery in these photographs was built after 1906 on the foundation of the former cotton mill. The cider mill was built on a new foundation dug in front of the still. (BPL.)

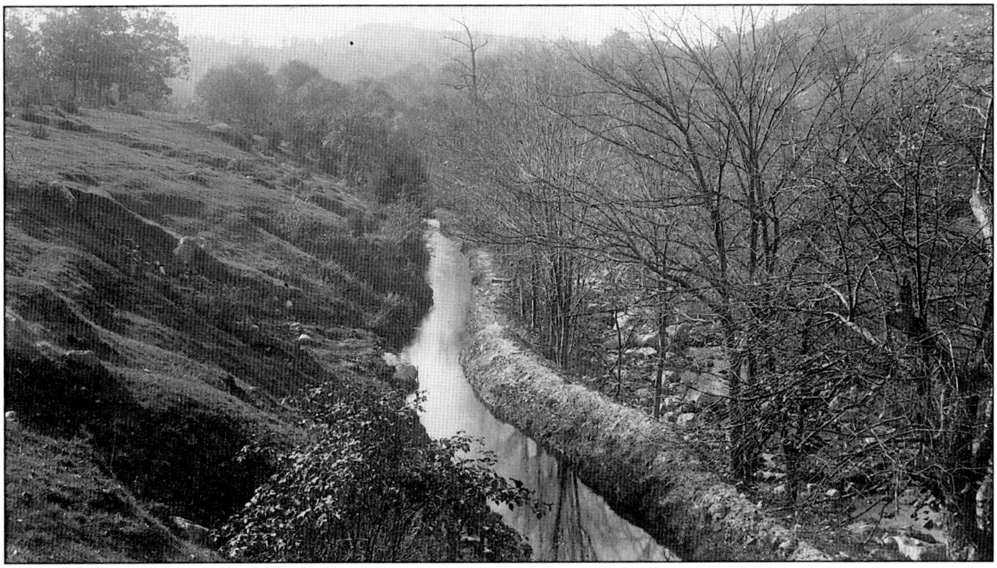

THE RACEWAY FOR ALDERMAN CIDER MILL, 1917. Burlington Brook, to the right in this photograph, was channeled through this raceway to provide power to the cider mill first and then farther downstream to the sawmill. From the sawmill, the water ran down to the Farmington River. This ditch was approximately six feet wide. While it appears calm in this view, it actually drops many feet in a mile and is very cold water. One of the stories Leonard Alderman likes to tell is how he and his friends would jump from one side of the raceway to the other. One time they dared Anna Barnes, who lived at the top of the hill, to jump. She only made it halfway across. Can you picture that sopping-wet little girl trudging up Barnes Hill? (LA.)

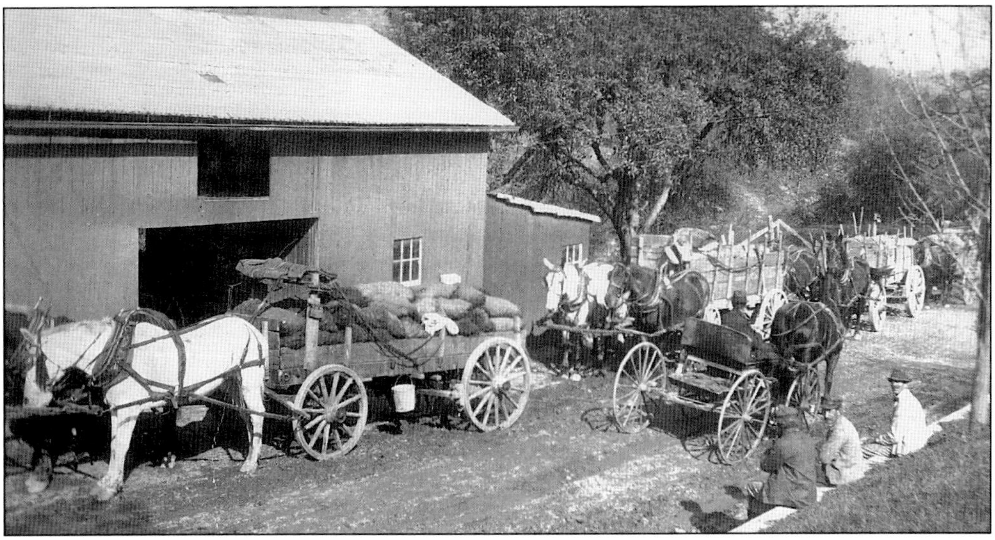

A POSTCARD OF WAGONS LOADED WITH APPLES, C. 1930. Along Route 4 in front of Elliott Alderman's house stood this shed, where the apples were weighed before being unloaded at the cider mill. The drivers sit on a retaining wall as their wagons pulled by horses and one by oxen, await their turn to have the wagons weighed while full, and then again after the apples were unloaded. Locally grown apples made up only a small portion of those processed; the rest came in by trainloads from Maine, New York, and Virginia. (LA.)

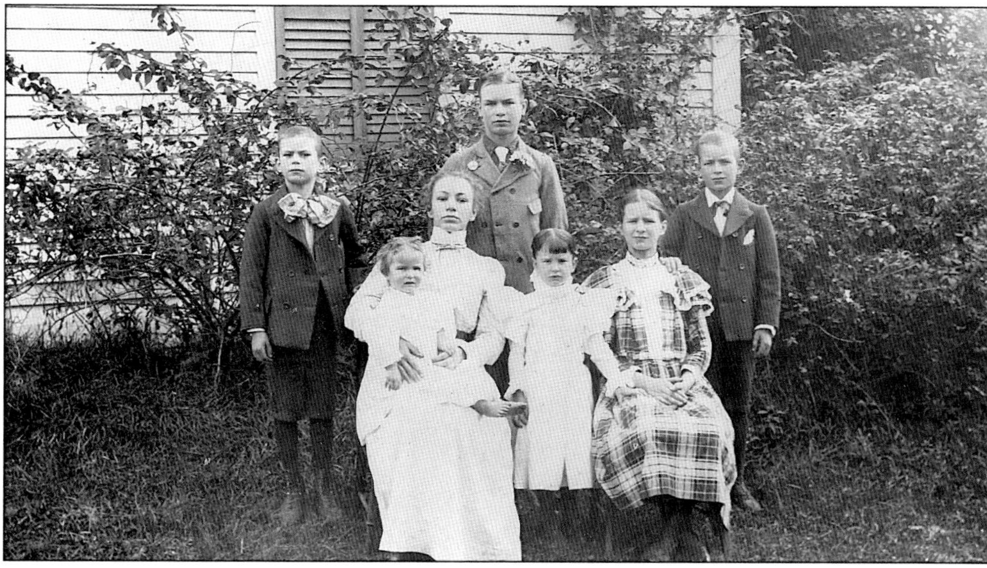

Mother Anna Delight (Upson) Barnes and Children. At the top of Barnes Hill, Anna Barnes poses with her children in front of her home. Shown in this pre-1900 photograph, from left to right, are children Louis, Ula, Winslow, Susan, Rena, and Frank; baby Mildred was not yet born. Their father, Adna Barnes, died in 1911. Louis Barnes lived on Barnes Hill his entire life. He married Laura Raynor and operated Barnes Hill Farm, with up to 50 head of Brown Swiss Cattle, until he retired in 1970. He was a town selectman during the 1920s and fire warden for 40 years. (LA.)

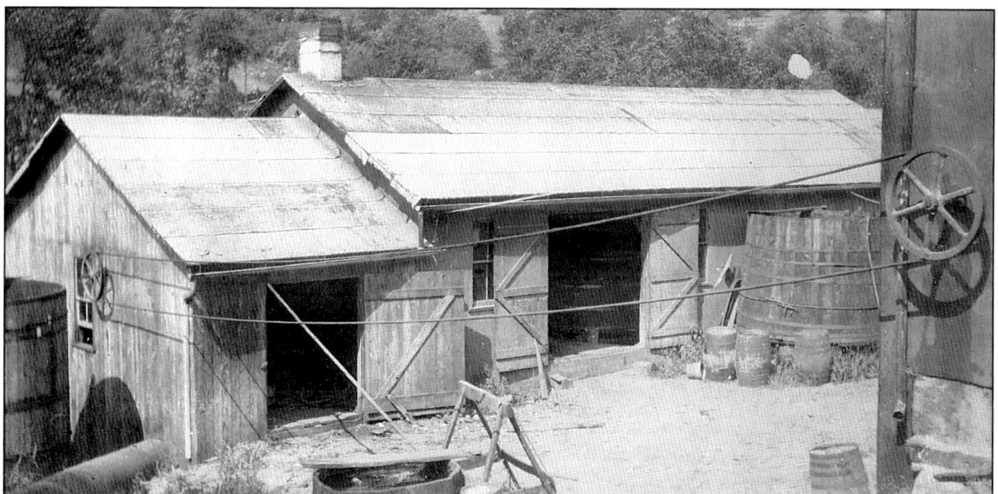

A Postcard of Alderman's Wheelhouse and Still, c. 1930. This card shows the pulleys from the Cider Mill (far right) and the rope to the wheelhouse, which covered the waterwheel that produced the power for the cider mill. The sawmill had a fall of 31 feet and utilized 20 feet to develop 25 horsepower. The strength of a horse equals that of five men. Seen in the lower left corner is the end of the flume, where the water came into the wheelhouse. In the foreground is a tub of water and a drying rack. The cloths that were used to hold the ground apples in place in the cider press were soaked overnight in these tubs of clean water. The cloths were hung on these racks to dry while another set was in use or soaking. The last batch of cider was distilled here in 1942. (LA.)

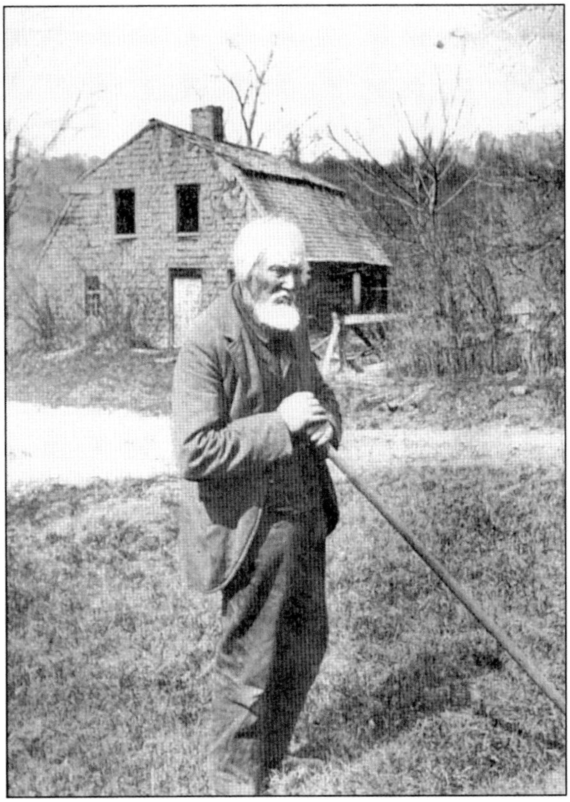

THE OLD CRANE HOMESTEAD, 1906. This hip-roofed house was located near the bridge at the foot of Barnes Hill. Postcard No. 15 is part of the centennial series from 1906 and shows George E. Buck, who had lost the younger of his two sons in 1900. William Buck and a friend were shooting ducks in January from a boat that capsized, and both drowned. (BPL.)

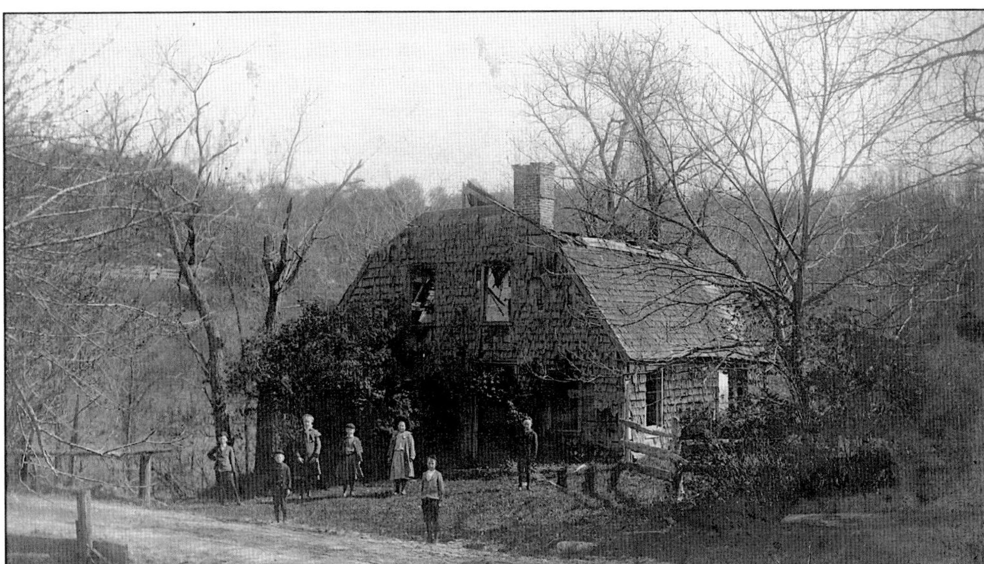

THE OLD HOUSE AT THE FOOT OF BARNES HILL. The children in this 1910 photograph are identified as Charlie Nulty, Walter Erickson, Signe Erickson, Gladys Alderman, Pauline Grops, Willie Nulty, and Carl Erickson. (LA.)

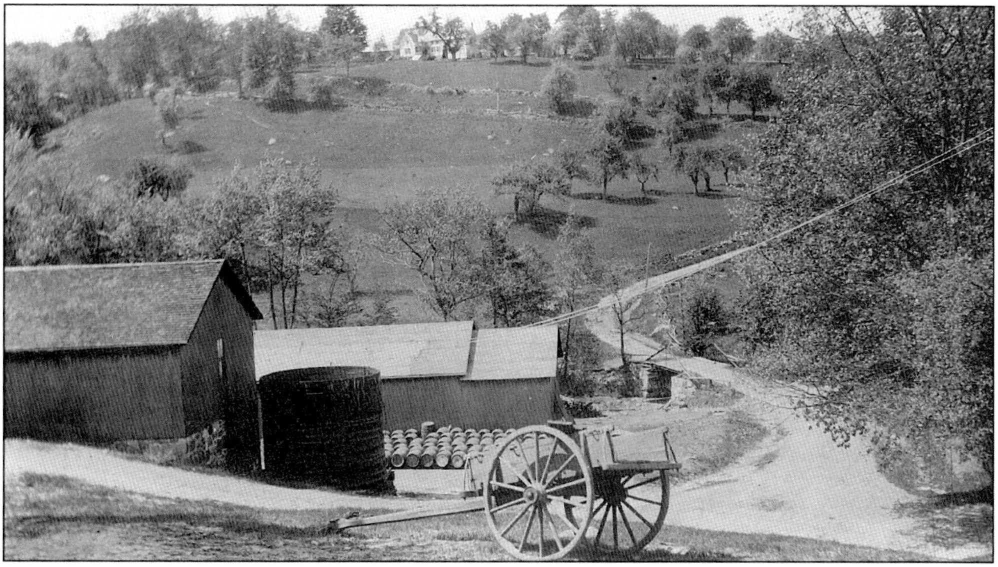

BARNES HILL AND CIDER MILL, WITH A CART, C. 1918. This postcard shows the best view of the cider mill, on the left, and the still behind it. In front of the still are hundreds of barrels used for cider and apple brandy. In the foreground is a cart near Route 4. Barnes Hill Road curves back, crosses the bridge over the brook, and curves to ascend Barnes Hill. The home of the Barnes family is on the crest of the hill near the center of the image. Beneath that house is an open field from which the photographs on pages 86 and 87 were taken. In this field, Ernie Alderman later built his home, which helps date some of these photographs. (CA.)

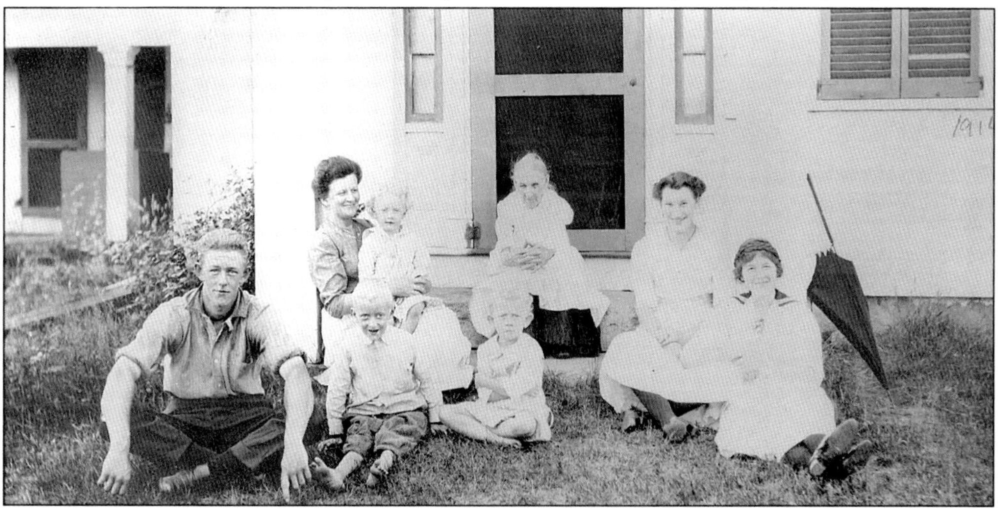

ELLIOTT'S FAMILY IN FRONT OF ARTHUR'S PORCH, 1914. Aunt Marilla Henry, Elliott's sister, watches from in front of the doorway as Elliott Alderman and his second wife, Esther, gather their children, who are, from left to right, Irving Elliott, Alice, and Doris; Hazel was not yet born. On the right are Ethel Hodge and an unidentified young woman. Arthur, an older son, wrote the following in his diary for this day: "We had a good dinner, roast clams, potato, chicken and cucumber salad, cold roast pork, etc. with watermelon dessert. This afternoon I went to Farmington, witnessed the parade and see Farmington defeat Manchester 2-1 at baseball. Tonight Stieg and I set off fireworks, to the wonderment of the admiring thousands gathered on the piazza lawn and steps about our house." (LA.)

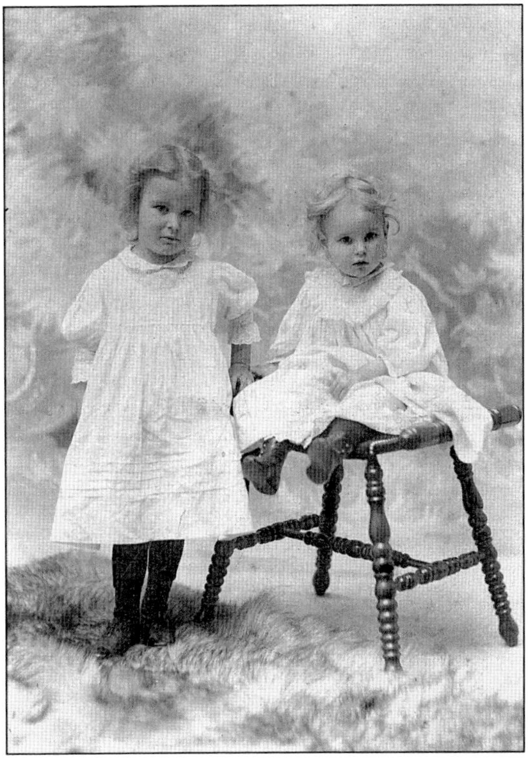

Ula and Mildred Barnes, 1901. Ula Barnes was born in 1897; her sister Mildred was born two years later. The youngest children of Anna and Adner Barnes, they grew up on Barnes Hill. (LA.)

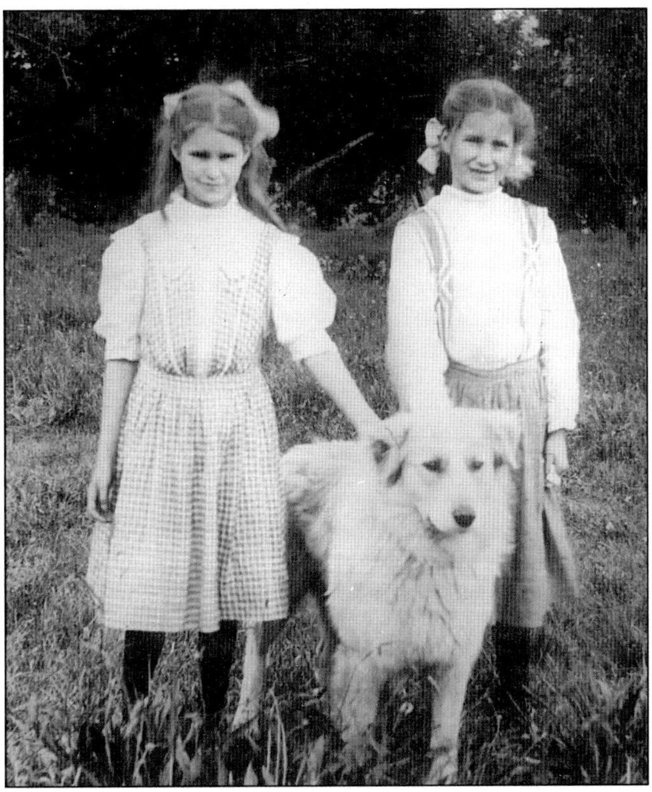

Mildred and Ula Barnes with Uno, Their Dog, 1906. Mildred and Ula Barnes married two of Elliott Alderman's sons. Mildred chose Howard Alderman, who became a civil engineer with Hodge Associates in Unionville. The couple continued to live on Barnes Hill. Ula chose Arthur Alderman, and it is their house we see on Punch Brook Road. Their sons, Leonard and Richard, have supplied many of the photographs for this book. (LA.)

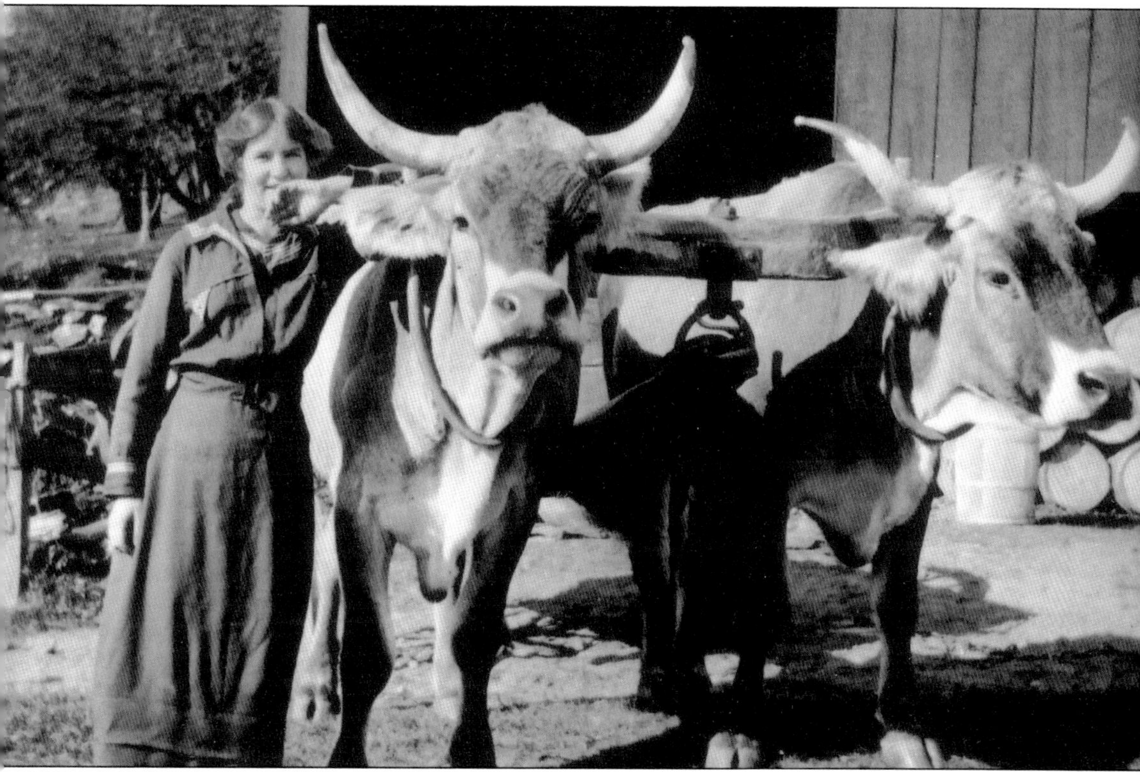

Ula Barnes and the Oxen, 1916. Ula Barnes was 19 when this picture was taken of her with the family oxen in front of the storage barn, which still stands on Barnes Hill Road. Wearing a sailor dress, she leans one elbow on the shoulder of an ox. Over her shoulder is the orchard, and stored beneath the barn are the barrels used to carry the apples to the cider mill. (RA.)

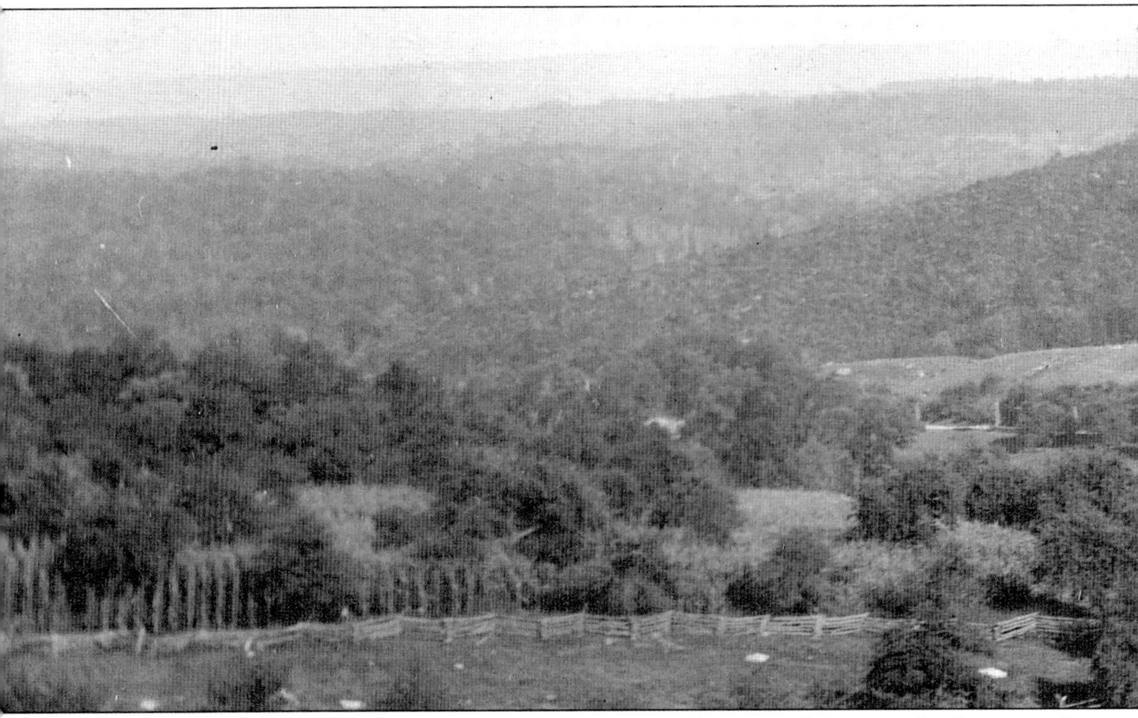

FROM BARNES HILL TO TAINE MOUNTAIN, C. 1920. This pair of photographs shows similar views from slightly different perspectives. Taken from Barnes Hill, both show Route 4 in the middle and Taine Mountain in the background. The upper photograph looks more toward the Farmington River and the lower one more directly at the mountain. The fences in the

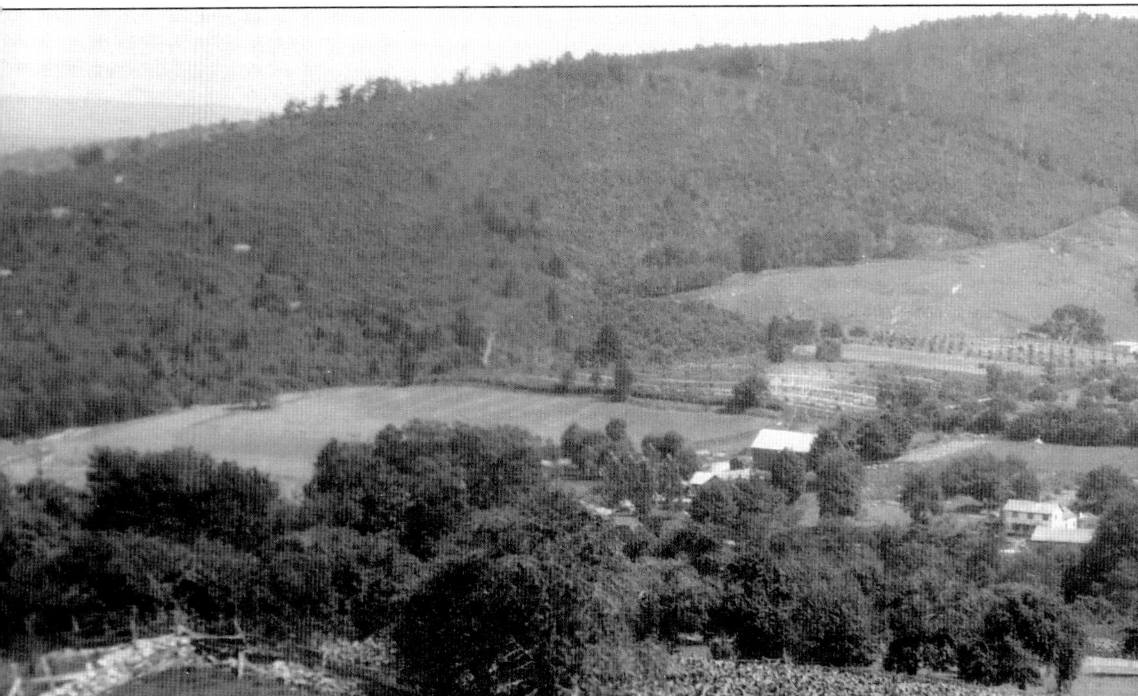

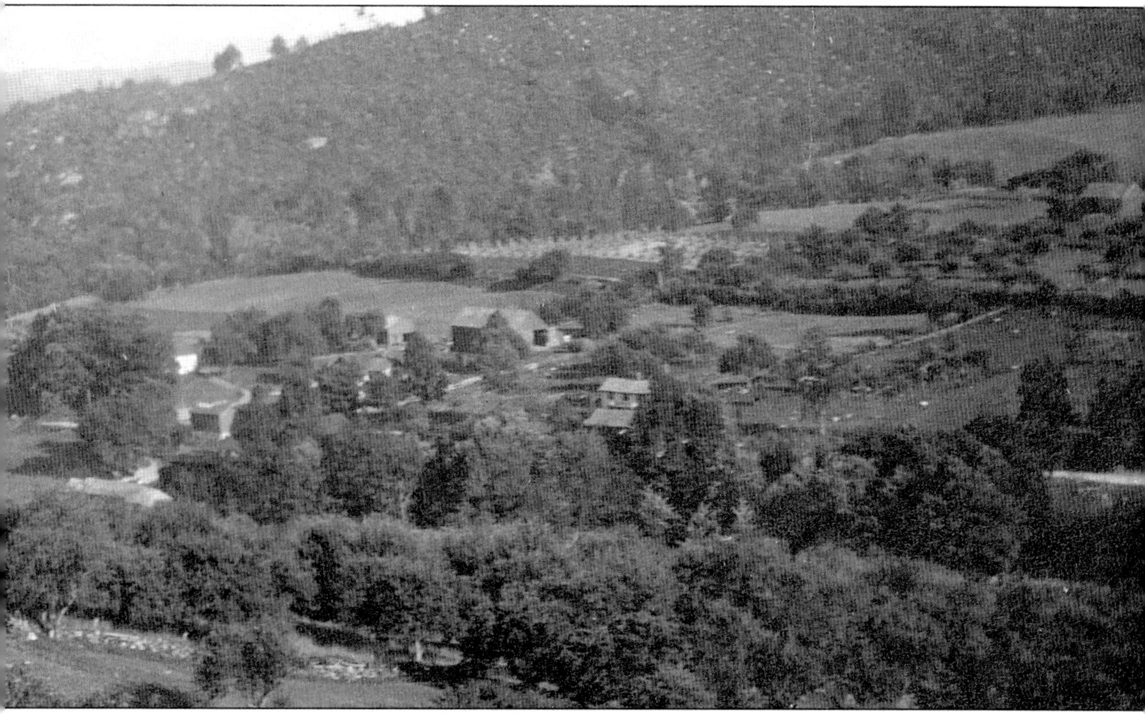

foreground help to orient the viewer. Both views show Punch Brook Road. Arthur Alderman's house and new barn are in both pictures. The lower photograph also shows District No. 4 School to the left of center. (LA.)

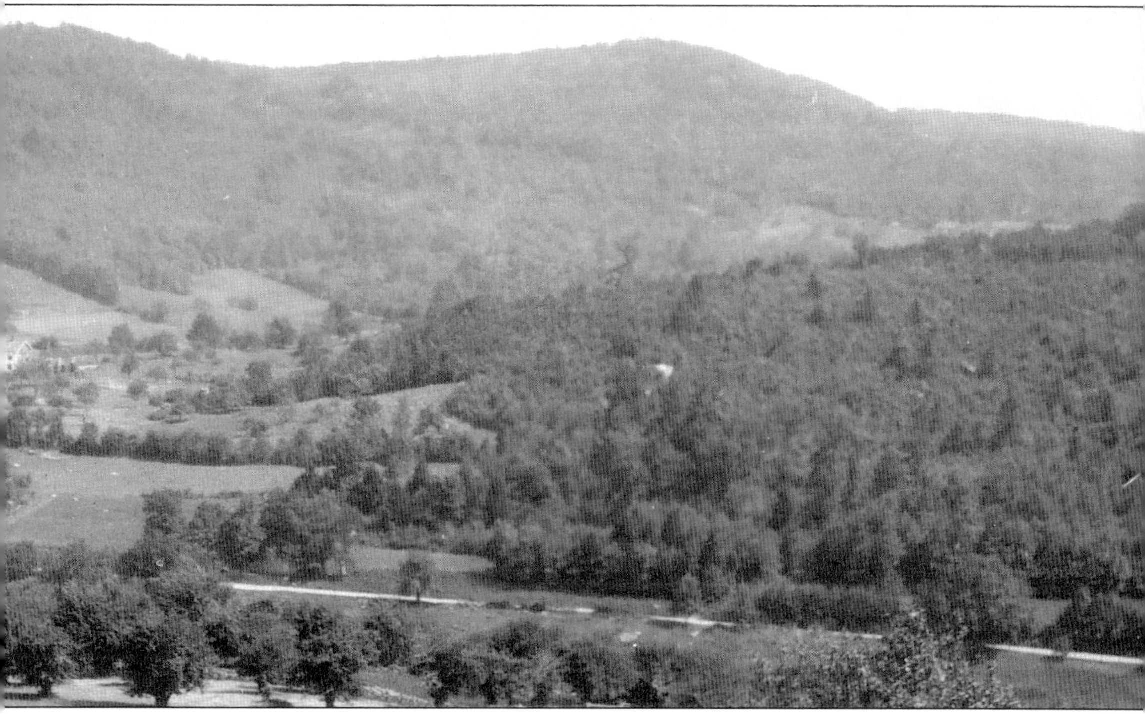

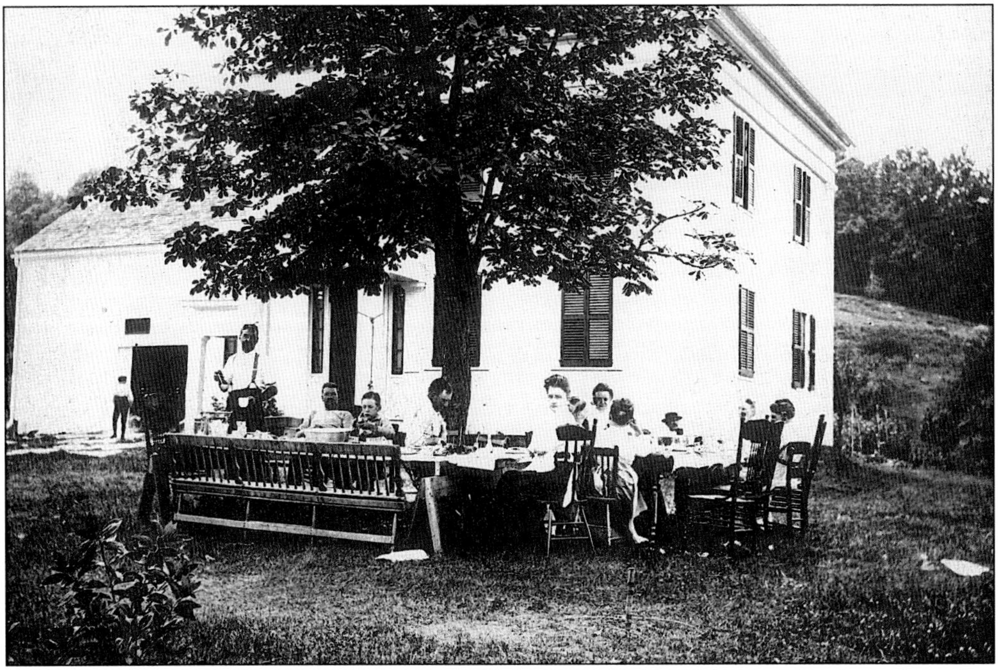

ARTHUR ALDERMAN'S HOUSE AND CHESTNUT TREE. The Alderman family gathered to celebrate the Fourth of July in 1905 under the horse chestnut tree, which still shades this house; picnic tables, benches, and chairs have been set up. Leonard Alderman tells the story of a snake, which was once seen "hanging out" in this tree. Arthur Alderman, who was born in 1895, was a World War I veteran, served in the general assembly in the late 1920s, and was a probate judge in Burlington from 1929 to 1965. The husband of Ula Barnes, he was father of two sons, Leonard and Richard, and a daughter, Nancy. (LA.)

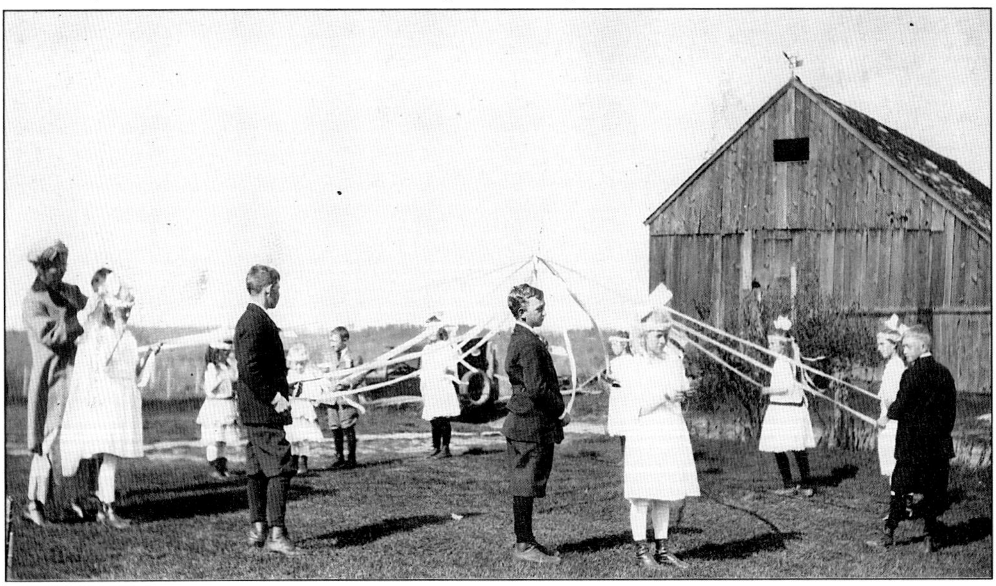

MAY DAY ON THE LAWN AT ARTHUR ALDERMAN'S. While the children wait to dance in celebration of spring, the teacher or a mother repairs the hair ribbon of one of the dancers. Across the road is the old barn, which was replaced in 1929. (LA.)

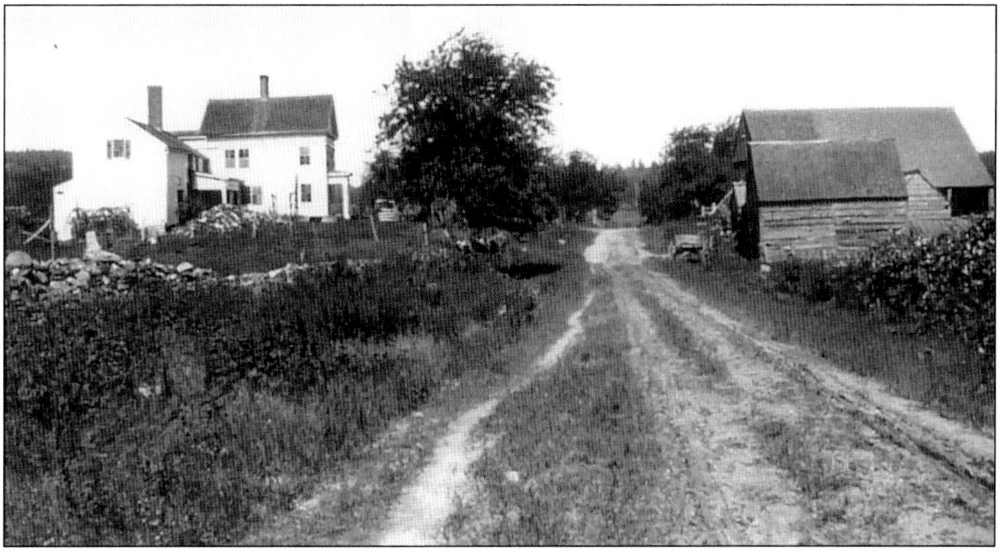

The Arthur Alderman Homestead, Punch Brook Road. In this view, looking south *c.* 1920 along a dirt road with a footpath on the left, are the childhood home of Leonard Alderman and the old barns. Straight ahead in the distance is Barnes Hill. The house and "new" barn are there today, along with a garden, horse, and dog, but the road has been paved. (LA.)

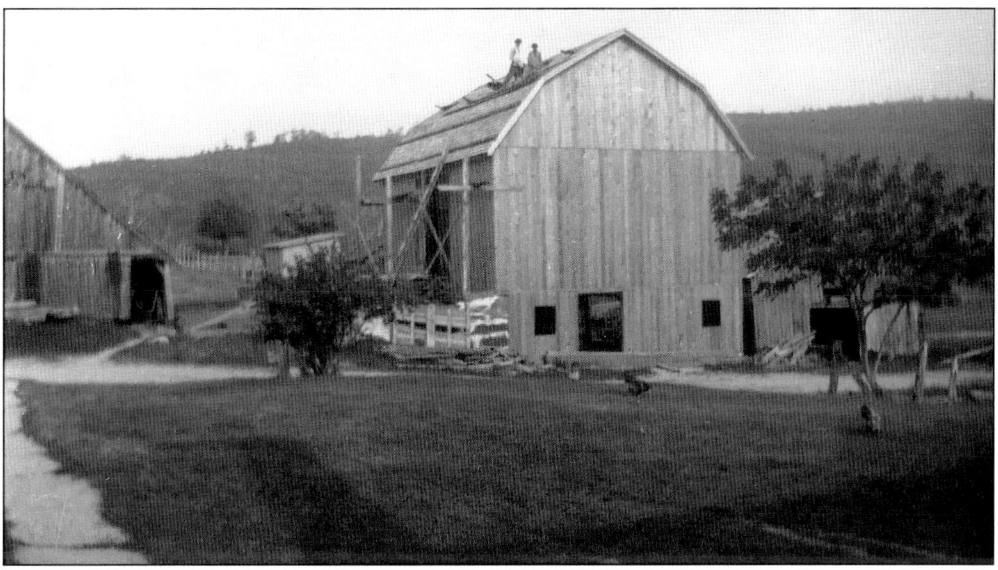

Building Arthur's New Barn, 1929. The old barn is seen on the left as the new barn nears completion. Two men have climbed the scaffolding and are putting shingles on the roof. Two chickens scratch for food on the front lawn of the house from which this picture was taken and where the Fourth of July picnic occurred annually. (LA.)

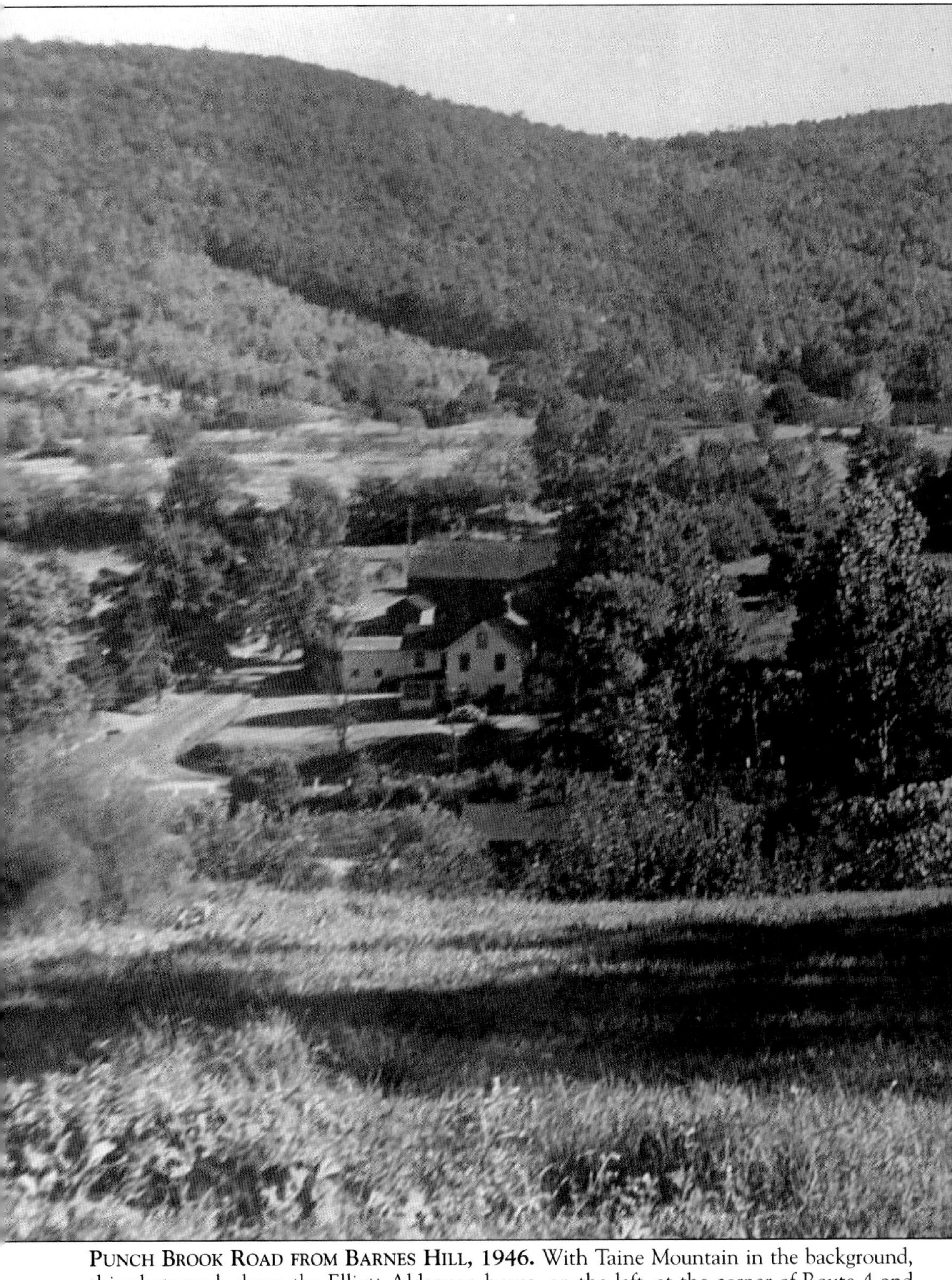

Punch Brook Road from Barnes Hill, 1946. With Taine Mountain in the background, this photograph shows the Elliott Alderman house, on the left, at the corner of Route 4 and

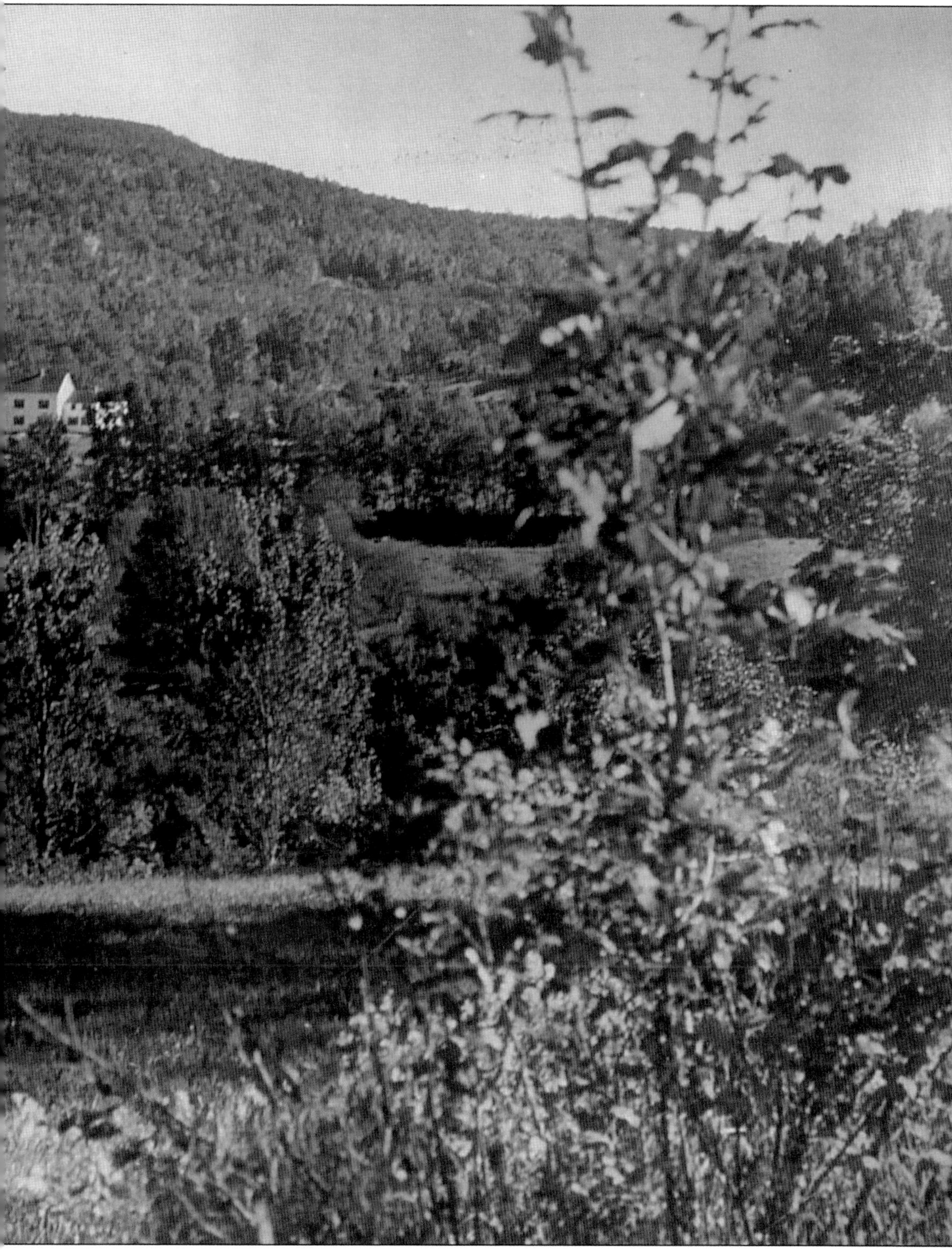

Punch Brook Road. The roof of the cider mill is just visible in front of it, and the Szegda barn and corncrib are behind it. Farther up the road is Arthur Alderman's house and barn. (BPL.)

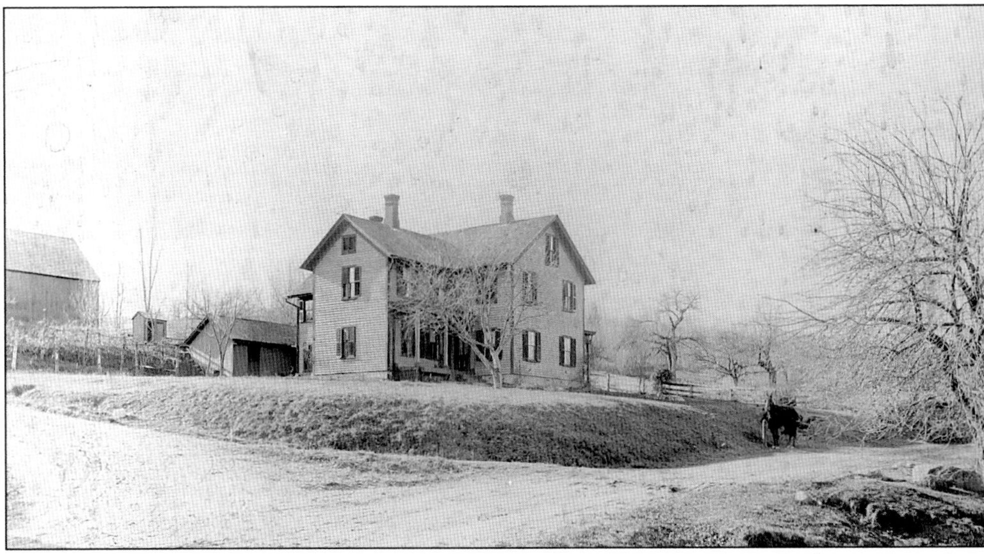

THE HOUSE AT THE CORNER OF PUNCH BROOK AND ROUTE 4, C.1885. The former Broadbent home, like the Cotton Mill property, was purchased by Elliott Alderman. The Szegda barn and outhouse are seen at the far left, above the fence. A horse waits at the hitching post on the right. In 1906, Elliott drove his carriage to the train station to pick up the governor for the Burlington centennial celebration. This is the intersection where Punch Brook comes down from the left and Barnes Hill Road continues downhill to the right. From their front porch, the Aldermans could look across the road to the cider mill. (LA.)

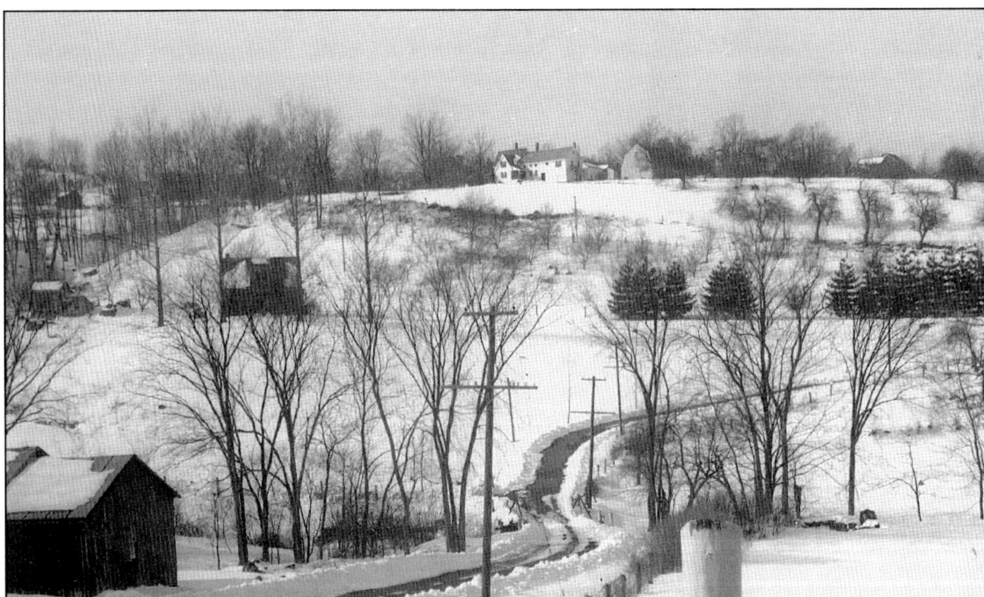

BARNES HILL IN THE SNOW, 1940. Similar to the 1919 postcard, this view shows the cider mill and still after operations ceased. Standing on Route 4 and looking north towards Barnes Hill, there is a clear view of Ernie Alderman's house halfway up the hill, with the poplar trees partially hiding it, and the Barnes house at the top. The world was at war and many of the farmers were overseas. Trucks now plowed roads that had formerly been cleared by men and horses. (LA.)

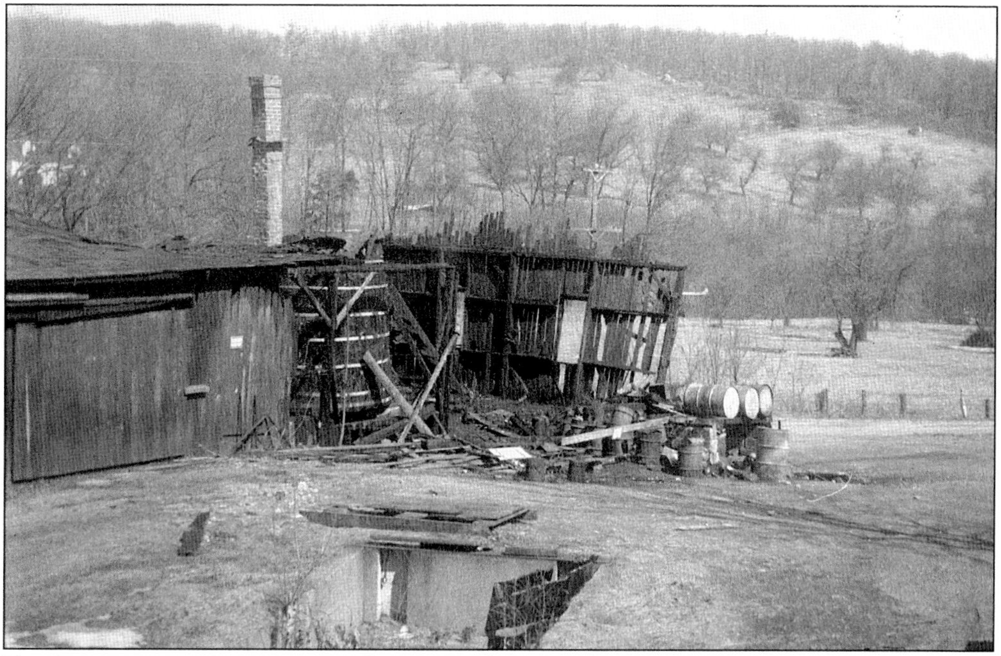

The Fire at the Cider Mill. The state police raided Elliot Alderman's cider mill in 1923; 40,000 gallons of cider were placed under seal as evidence. An additional 20,000 gallons of sweet cider were not sealed. Within days, however, charges were withdrawn and the cider released. After prohibition, cider consumption declined and the mill was sold. It was used with a gas engine for making screws with the Brown and Sharp machines. With an overhead shaft, this "one lunger" gas engine overheated and caught fire. The wooden building burned, leaving the smoke stack in the center, the three gasoline storage barrels, and the cider vats. It was never rebuilt. The open pit in front of the mill in the upper photograph is where the scale for weighing the apples had been. (LA.)

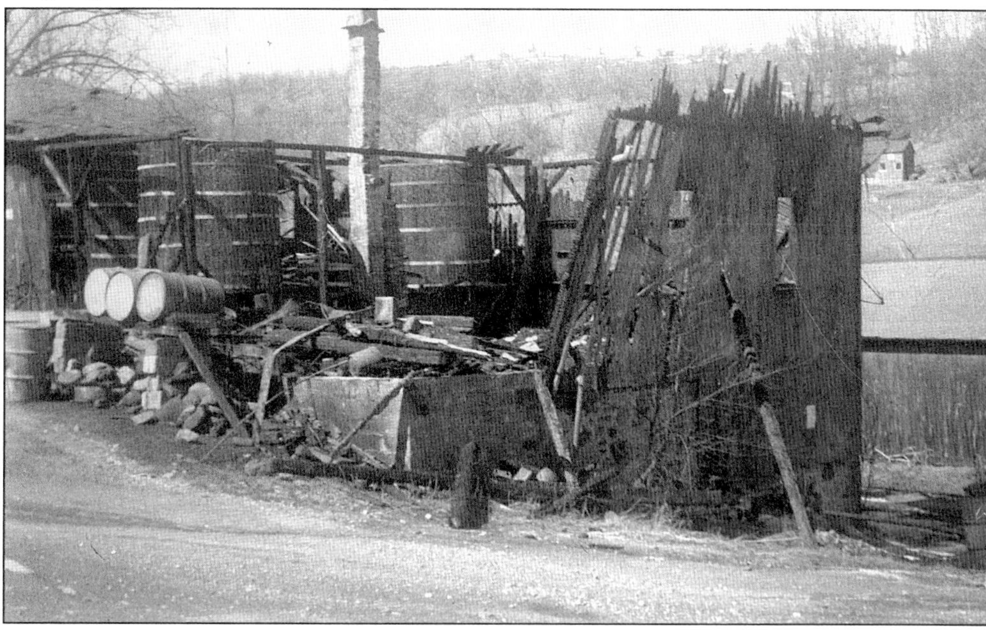

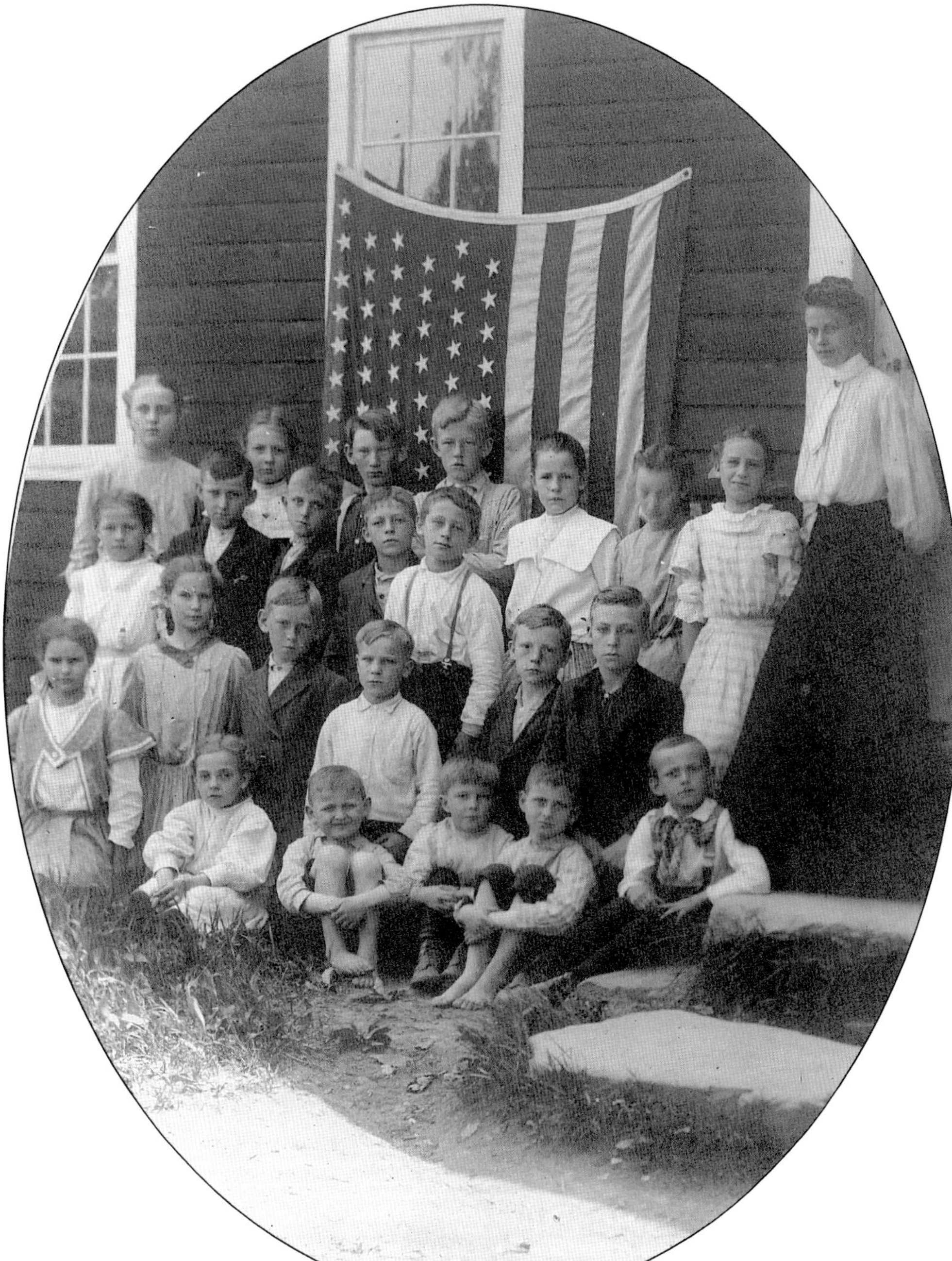

Fourth District School, 1909. Ethel (Canada) Barnes was the teacher at the District No, 4 School in 1909. Mildred and Ula Barnes are the two girls kneeling on the left side of the second row. To the right of them are Howard Alderman and Howard Mayers. Seated in front are Laura Horn, Oscar Tharau, Stanislaus Winalski, Rudolph Tharau, and Frank Fyek. Behind them are Josephine Seiffert, Henry and Paul Tharau, Henry and Herman Seiffert, Johnny and Joseph Horn. In the back row are Anna Tharau, Gladys Alderman, Clayton Hodge, Arthur Alderman, Anna Scheidel, Vera Hodge, and Bertha Mayers. (LA.)

Eight

The Woodland Under Water

A lively intersection near the Farmington River, at what is now Route 4 and 179, has been the site of some of Burlington's most industrious enterprises. From the earliest years, the trail north turned away from the Farmington River and went west through the valley up to the center of town. Later, the railroad along the river and roads met at this low elevation to bring people, goods, and services to and from Burlington and nearby Canton—until the flood of 1955 occurred. Today, on the banks of the beautiful Farmington River, this once thriving hub is quiet and peaceful. The river and the road remain, but the buildings previously at the level of the railroad bed and the tracks are no longer there. Thirty feet higher above sea level is the home of the Mullin family. Helen Hartigan Mullin, the daughter of William H. and Gertrude Hartigan, lives with her descendants in the family home, once the hub of a thriving business with many facets. This chapter shows the other buildings and the Woodland Hotel, later to be called New Woodland and Burlington Inn. When the flood of 1955 came, it was the Burlington Inn that was under water. These photographs may suggest the sounds and sights of an earlier time in terms of the work that transpired here and the fun and relaxation available at the Woodland Hotel.

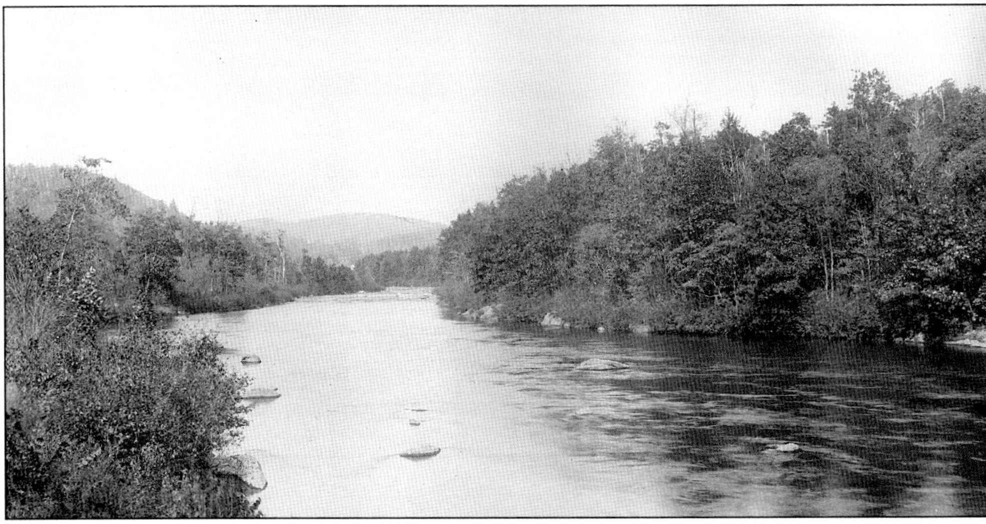

Farmington River Below Burlington Station. The Farmington River was designated a "Wild and Scenic River" in 1996, but has been admired for its beauty since man first beheld it. It is peaceful most of the time and only occasionally a raging torrent; the river is inspiring at all times and seasons. (LA.)

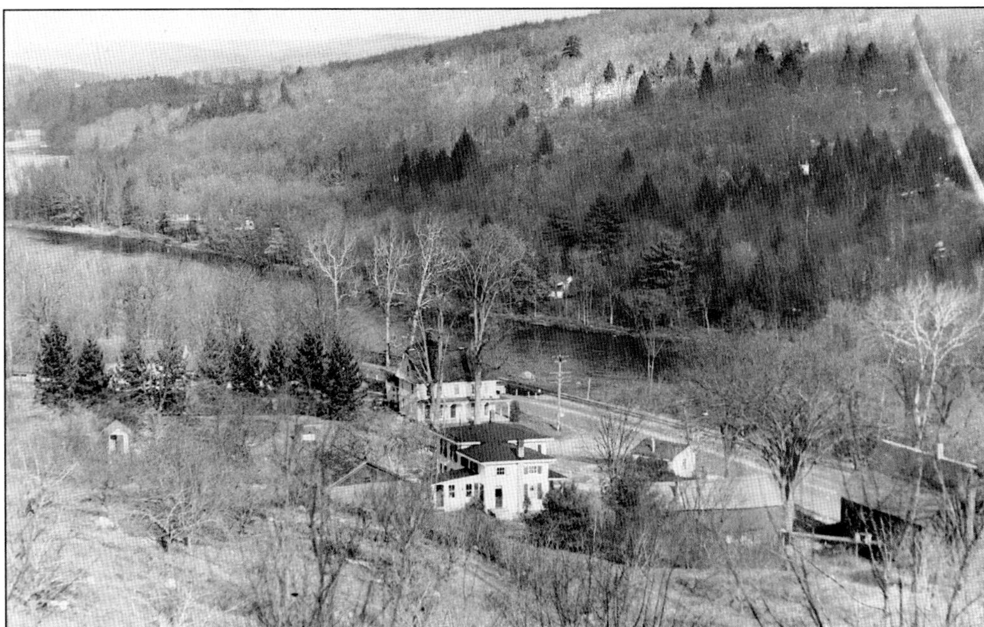

The Hartigan Place Above Farmington Depot, c. 1939. Before 1955, this intersection was a busy "home place" for members of the Hartigan family. The Farmington River flows past from Collinsville to Unionville; the trains go by several times a day on the tracks between the river and the road, and Route 4 turns west while Route 179 continues north. Here, the Hartigans made a good living. The large building on the right was the turning shop. A barn, a garage, and a fruit stand were near the road. The house is in the center foreground, elevated about 30 feet higher than the building seen above it, the Burlington Inn. Behind the inn, surrounded by evergreens, was a pond. Viewed from up a steep hill in the winter or early spring, it appears quiet. It was not always so, as the cover photograph shows. (HHM.)

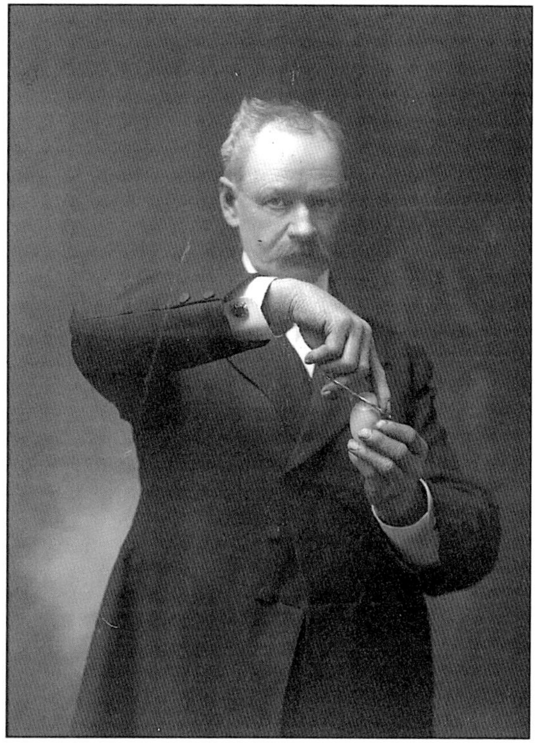

WILLIAM R. HARTIGAN THE INVENTOR. Born in Burlington in 1852, W.R. Hartigan was creative and enterprising. Educated at Unionville High School, he worked for John N. Bunnell in Unionville during the summers to earn funds to pay for his schooling. At age 17 in Burlington, he established himself in the trade of wood turning. A fire destroyed his business six years later. He began turning wood again and, as a skilled mechanic, added machine work, forging, and enameling on wood and metal to his talents. He was also an inventor. Here, he demonstrates his egg cutter. In 1879, he married Annie S. Barnes, and they had one son, William Horton Hartigan. Together, they ran the Woodland Hotel, which was famous for its partridge and other game dinners. (HHM.)

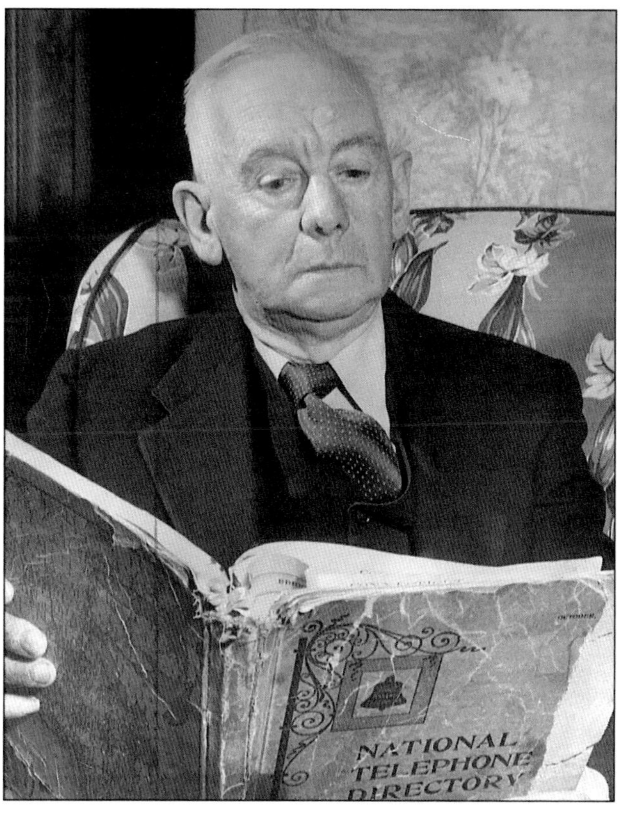

THE NATIONAL TELEPHONE DIRECTORY, 1950. William H. Hartigan retired as tax collector in Burlington after 42 years. He was also a successful fruit grower. As a tax collector, he prized the National Directory of Names and Telephone Numbers and declined several offers to sell it to the telephone company. He continued the wood-turning business, William R. Hartigan and Sons, which his son, Gerald H. Mullin, operates today around the corner. (HHM.)

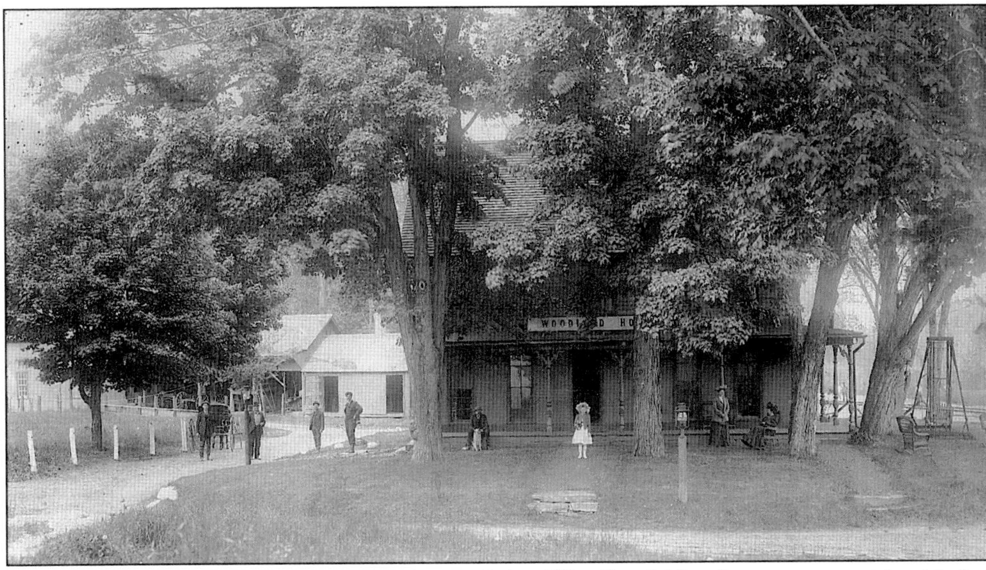

THE WOODLAND HOTEL, 1905. In front of the Woodland Hotel is a young girl with her bonnet and purse; four gentlemen are on the left in front of the coach and carriage house; another sits on the porch, holding his dog still for the photographer. Two ladies are on the right in front of the porch; on the far right, past the empty rockers and glider, are the railroad tracks and river. Electric wires are overhead. Oil lamps stand as beacons at the front and sidewalks. The original photograph is owned by Shirley Johnson Tibbetts. (BPL.)

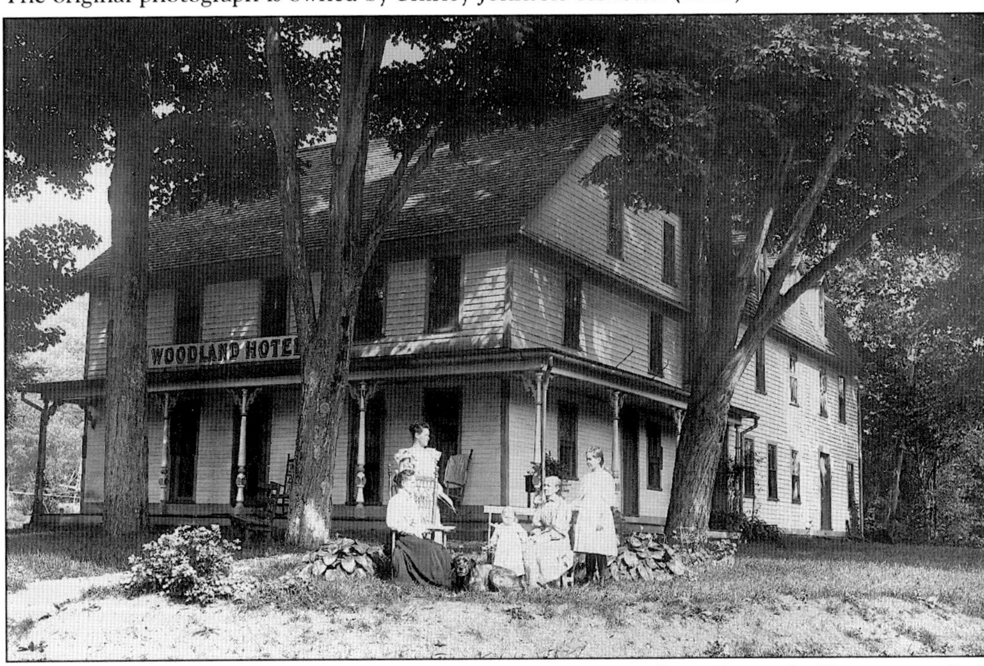

THE WOODLAND HOTEL, FROM THE BRIDGE, C.1924. Seated are Gertrude Hartigan, wife of William H. Hartigan, who was born in Germany in 1892, her daughter Helen, and Annie B. Hartigan, wife of William R. Hartigan. Written on the back of the photograph is the following: "Those standing could be Sophie (who worked for Annie H.) and her daughter." Sophie Uliasq is seated on the hood of the car in the cover photograph. (HHM.)

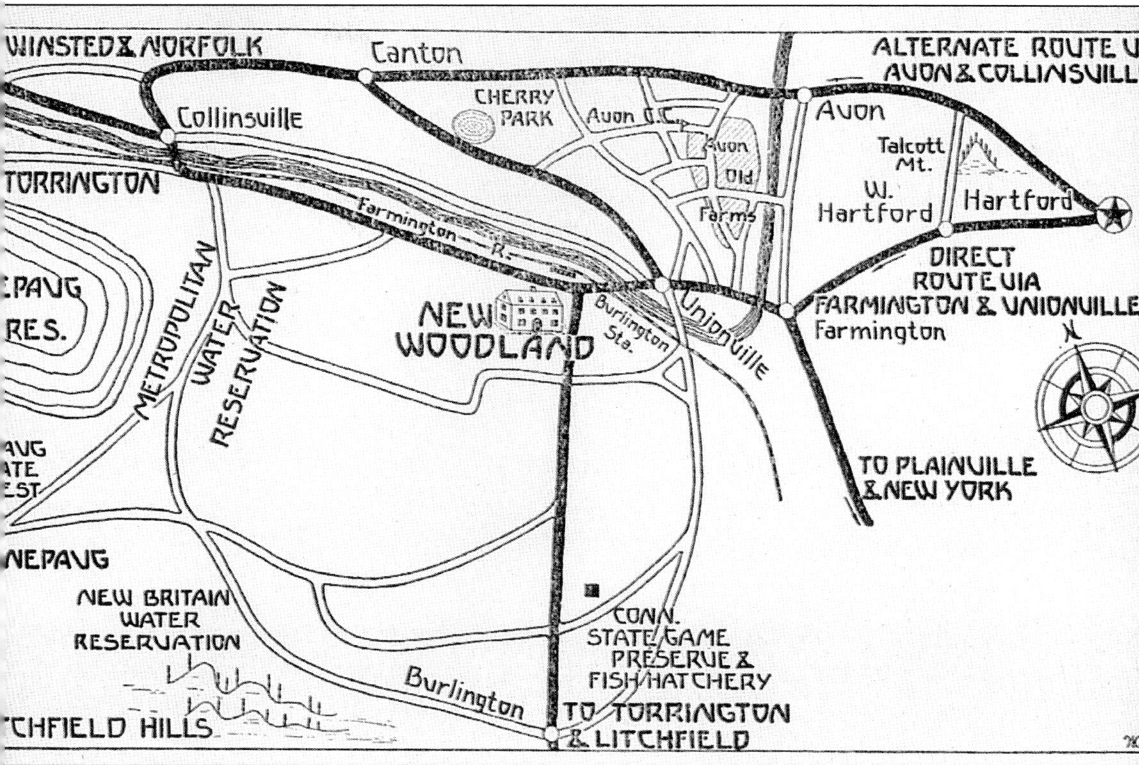

NEW WOODLAND MAP, C. 1920. This promotional piece for New Woodland gives the overview of the roads from the center to Canton and from Hartford to Collinsville. Not to scale, it also shows the roads and railroad tracks most heavily traveled in the early days of the automobile. (HHM.)

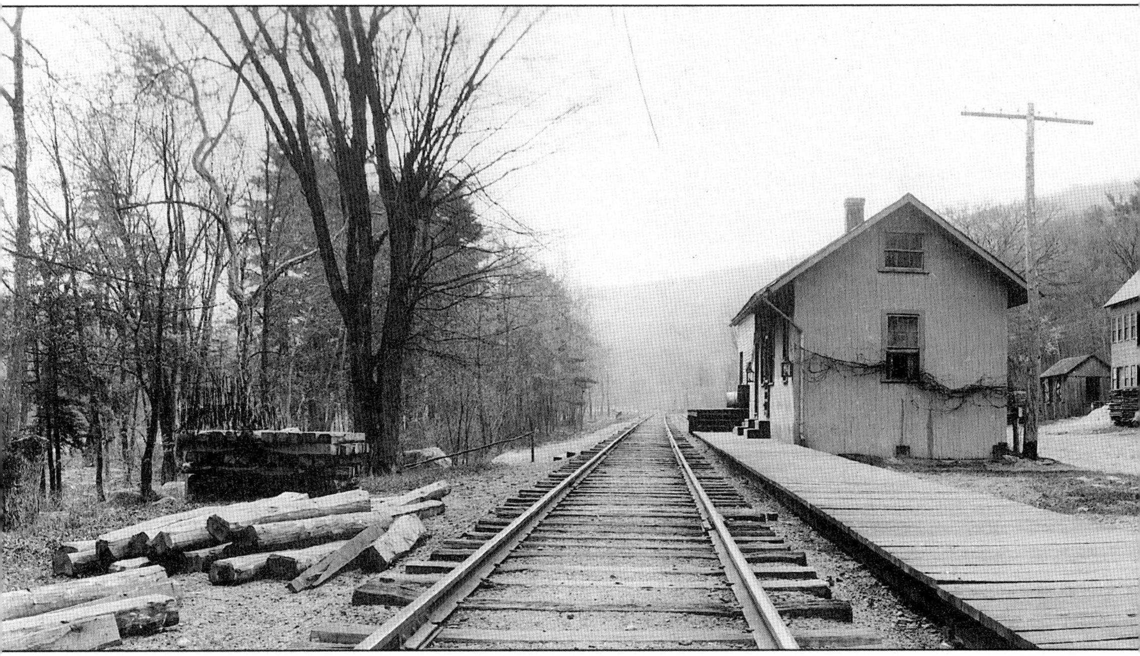

A Postcard of Railroad Tracks, Looking South. On May 12, 1911, as one looked towards Unionville along the tracks, railroad ties were on one side and the boardwalk platform for the depot on the other. Beyond the depot and across the road at the same level, was

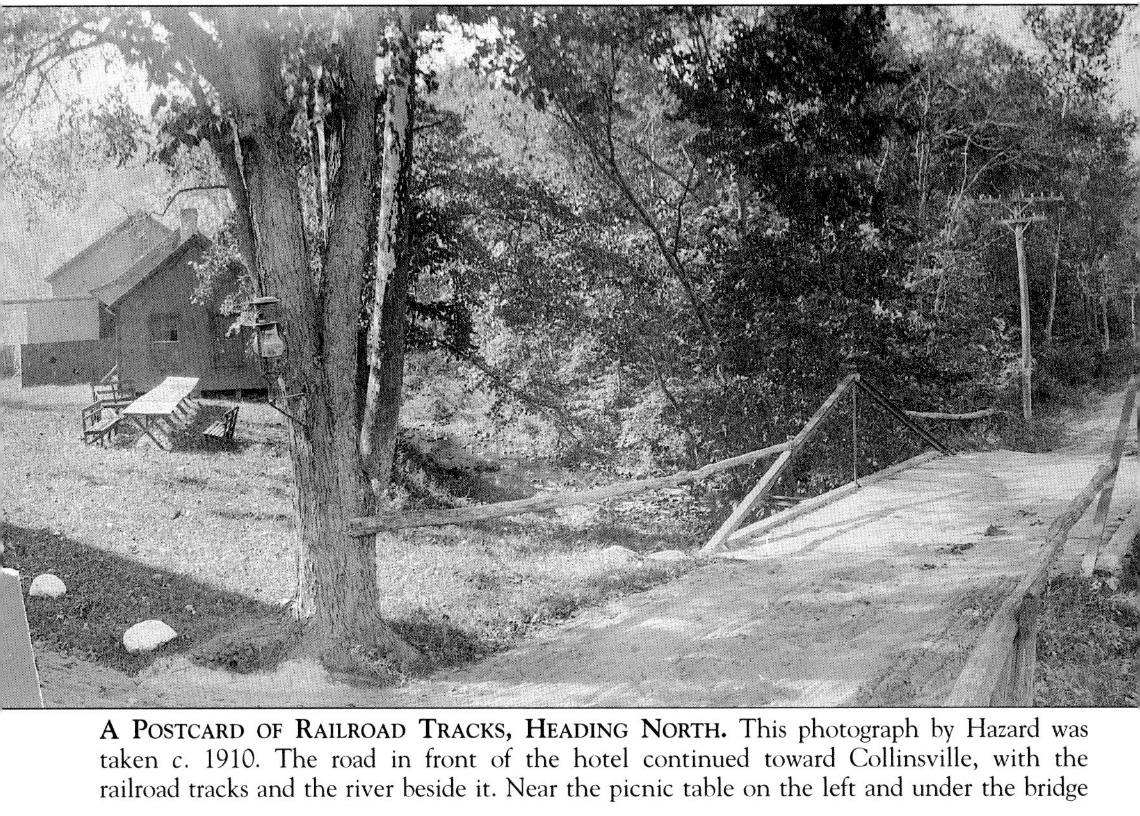

A Postcard of Railroad Tracks, Heading North. This photograph by Hazard was taken *c.* 1910. The road in front of the hotel continued toward Collinsville, with the railroad tracks and the river beside it. Near the picnic table on the left and under the bridge

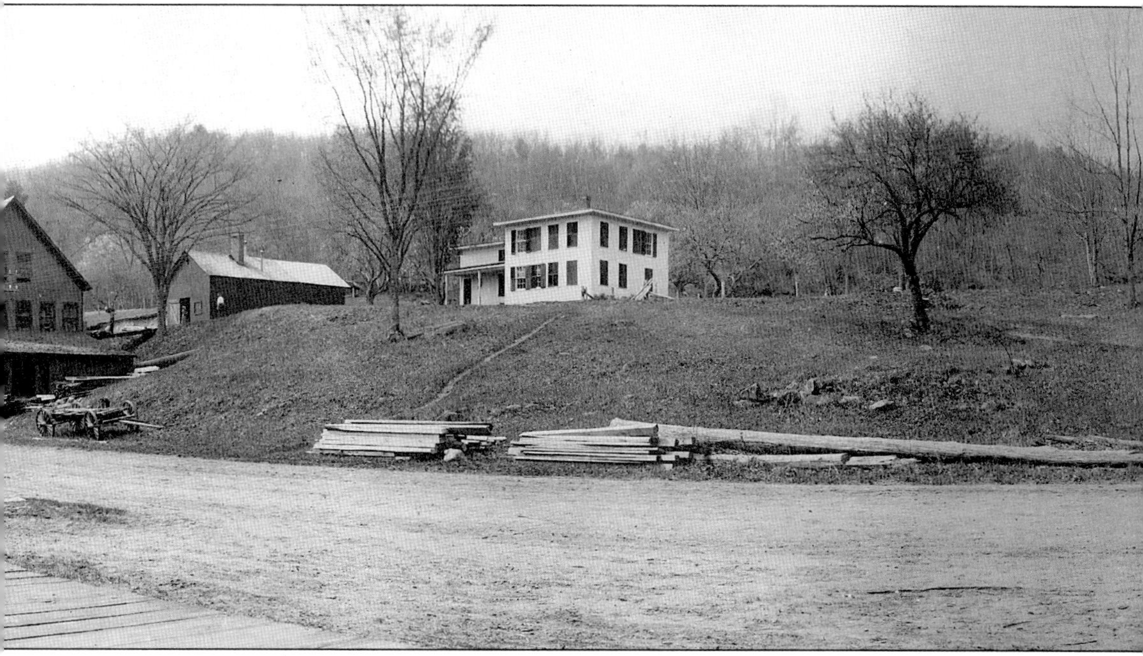

W.R. Hartigan's wood-turning shop. About 30 feet higher were his garage and family residence. Just out of sight to the right was the road into Burlington center. (LA.)

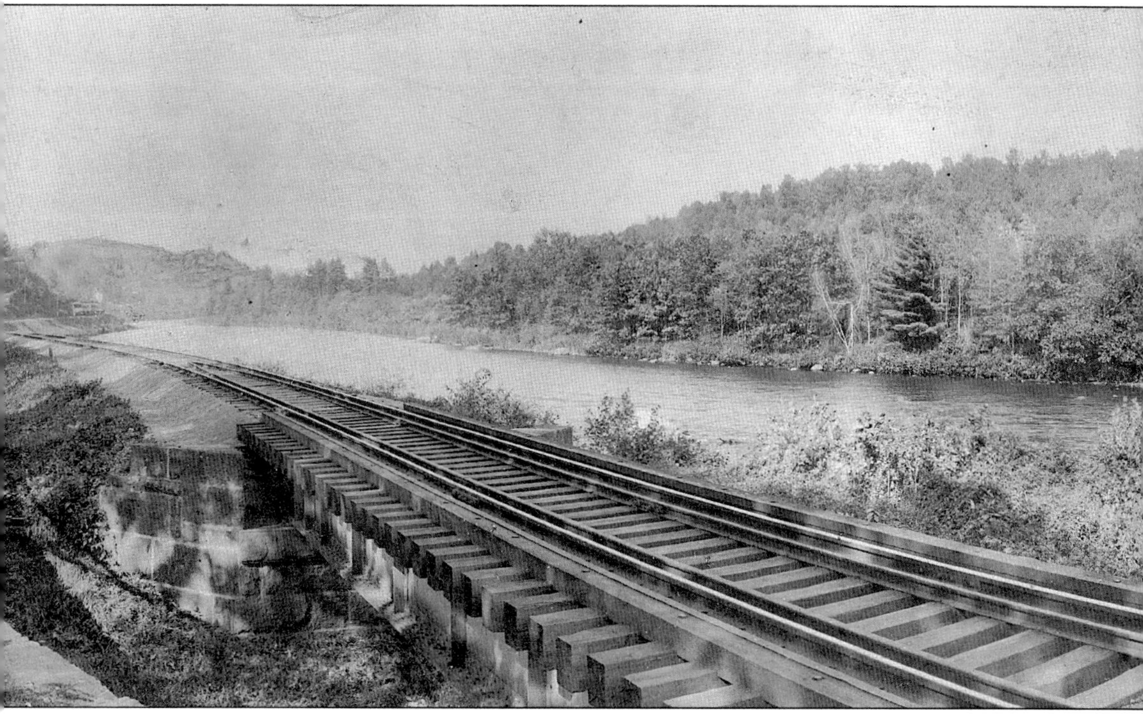

flowed the brook with water from the Alderman mills as it emptied out of the flume on its way to the river. (HHM.)

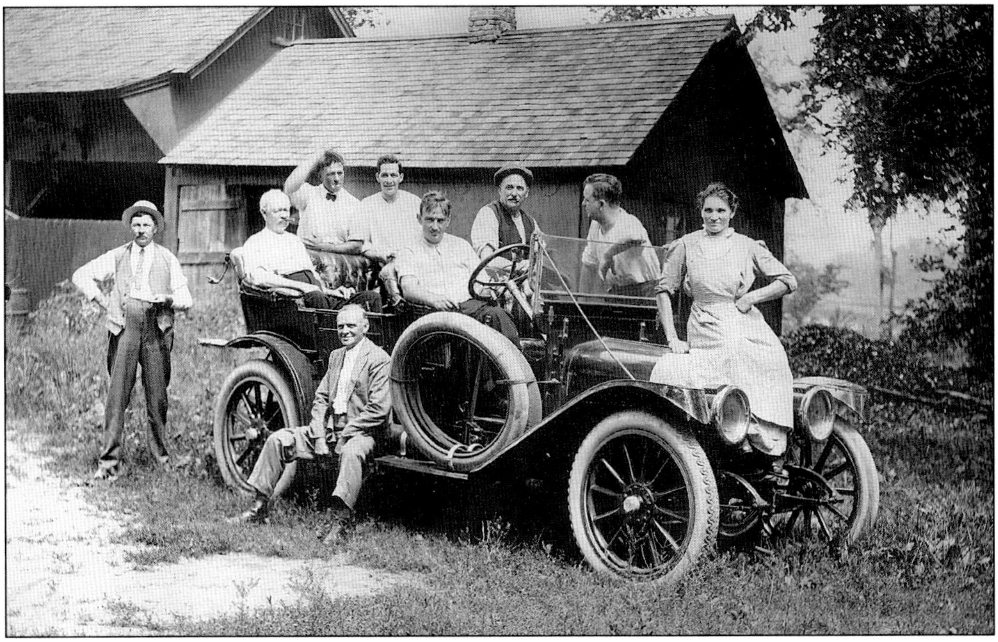

A PHOTOGRAPH OF W.R. HARTIGAN AND FRIENDS. Sitting on the hood of the car is Sophie Uliasq; Hartigan is the gentleman in the back seat with a cigar. The others are unidentified. The car is parked in front of the same sheds that are seen in the first Woodland Hotel picture. Part of this shed is said to have floated off its foundation and landed behind the inn in the flood of 1955.

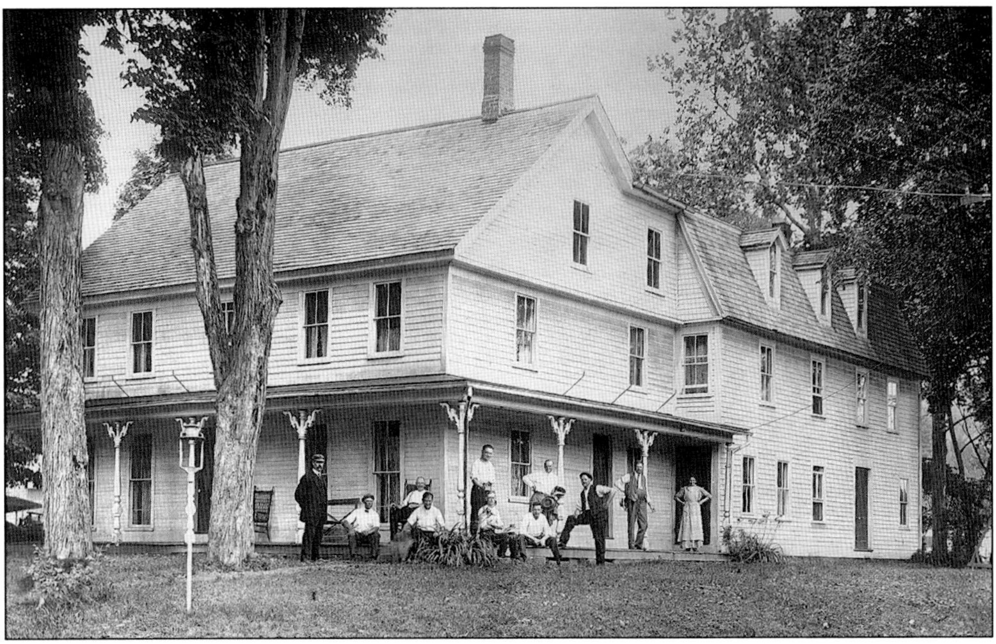

A HOTEL WITHOUT A NAME. The hotel signs have been removed but the supports remain on the porch roof. Standing in the doorway on the right is the only woman in this photograph, Sophie, with arms akimbo. Nearest to her is W.R. Hartigan, with a cigar. The other nine men are unidentified. (HHM.)

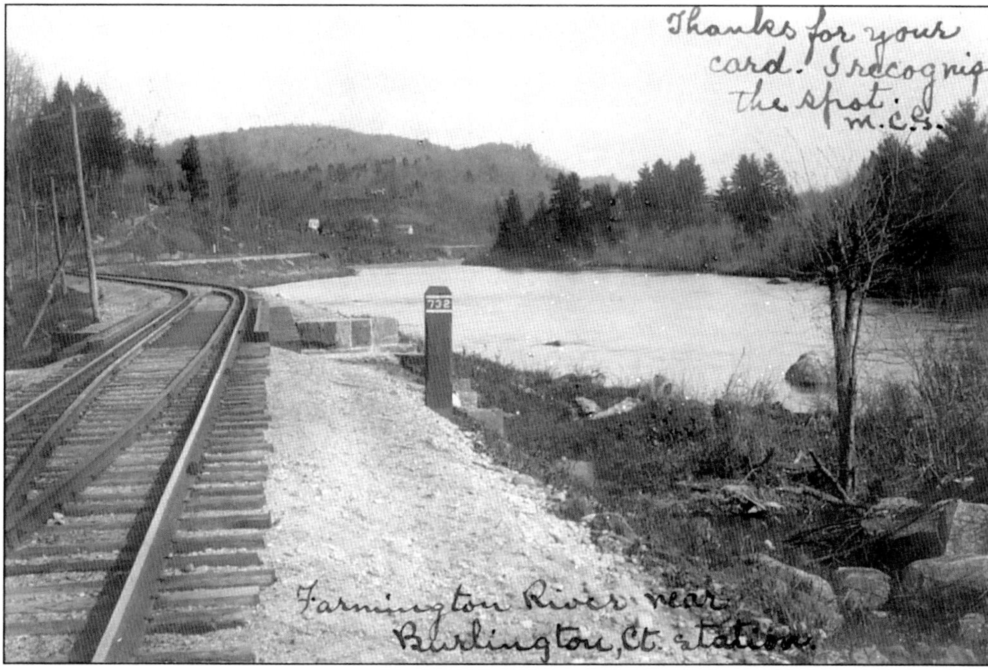

A POSTCARD OF MILE MARKER 732. On August 20, in Troy, Pennsylvania, Mrs. George Van Horn received this card with an August 18, 1906 postmark from Bristol, Connecticut. Good service for one penny! The address and stamp with postmarks fill the back, and the message is written on this side, "Thanks for your card. I recognize the spot. M.C.G." and "Farmington River near Burlington, Ct. station." (CA.)

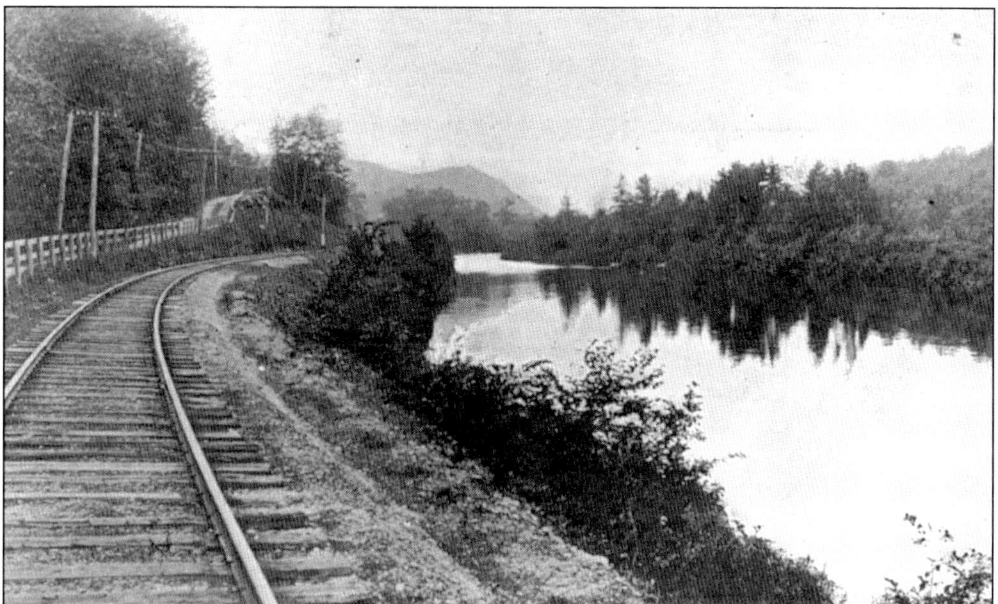

A POSTCARD "TWILIGHT ON THE RIVER," 1906. This card is No. 13 in the series of bicentennial postcards. While "Near Burlington Station," it was taken farther north than the previous photograph as the road begins to ascend the hill toward the sandbank. (BPL.)

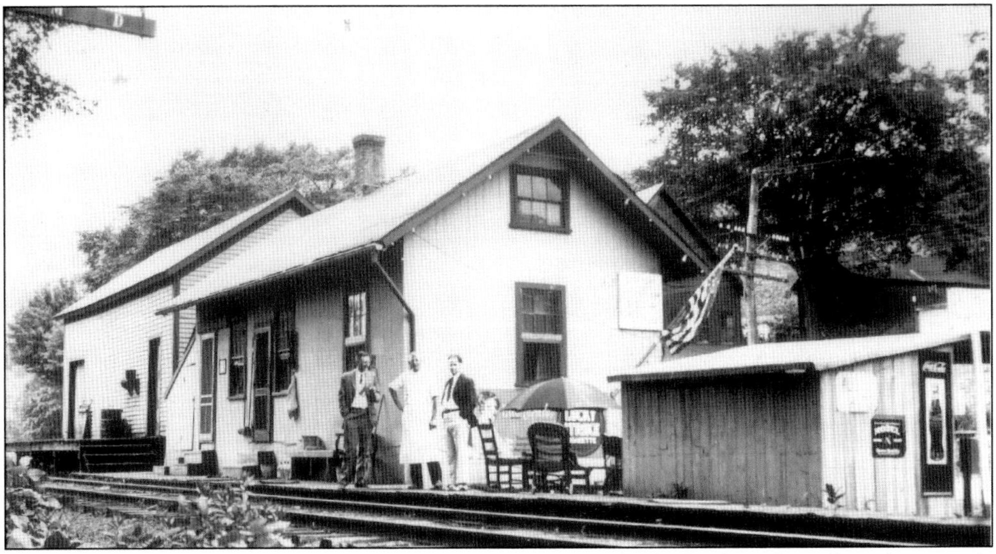

Burlington Station, c. 1900. Helen (Hartigan) Mullin helped us date this photograph because she recognizes her father, William Horton Hartigan, on the left in this trio in conversation on the boardwalk. She thinks he looks about 20 years old. We have been unable to identify either the man in the long white apron or the other gentleman. The station looks inviting with a table and chairs under an umbrella and barrels and benches along the platform. Beyond the flag and the shed with the Coca-Cola sign can be seen the roof of Hartigan's woodturning shop and garage. (HHM.)

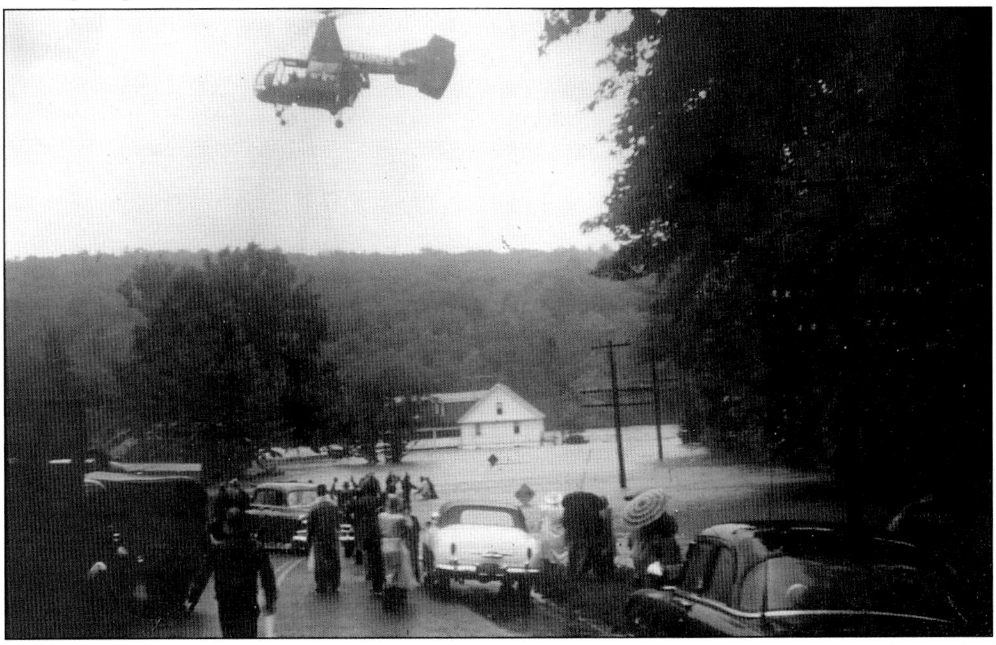

The Flood of 1955. In this photograph the helicopter was rescuing people from the roof of the Burlington Inn at Routes 4 and 116. The Farmington River was above the first story of the hotel. The depot platform, tracks, bridges, and roadway were about 10 feet underwater. Leonard Alderman took this picture on August 18, 1955, as the rescue missions continued up and down the river. (LA.)

THE ROAD HAS DISAPPEARED. The inn and the fruit stand sit high above the roadbed as the bulldozers began to fill in the road. The wood-turning shop roof is seen in the distance. (HHM.)

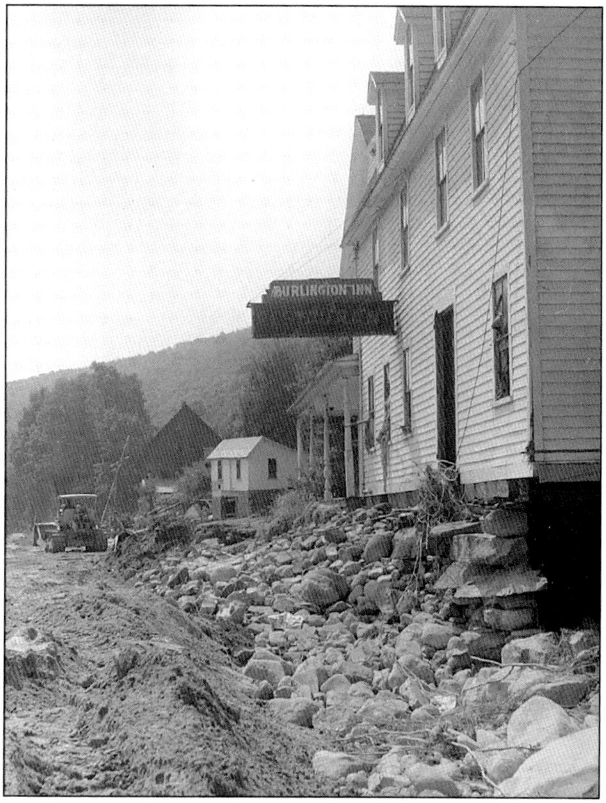

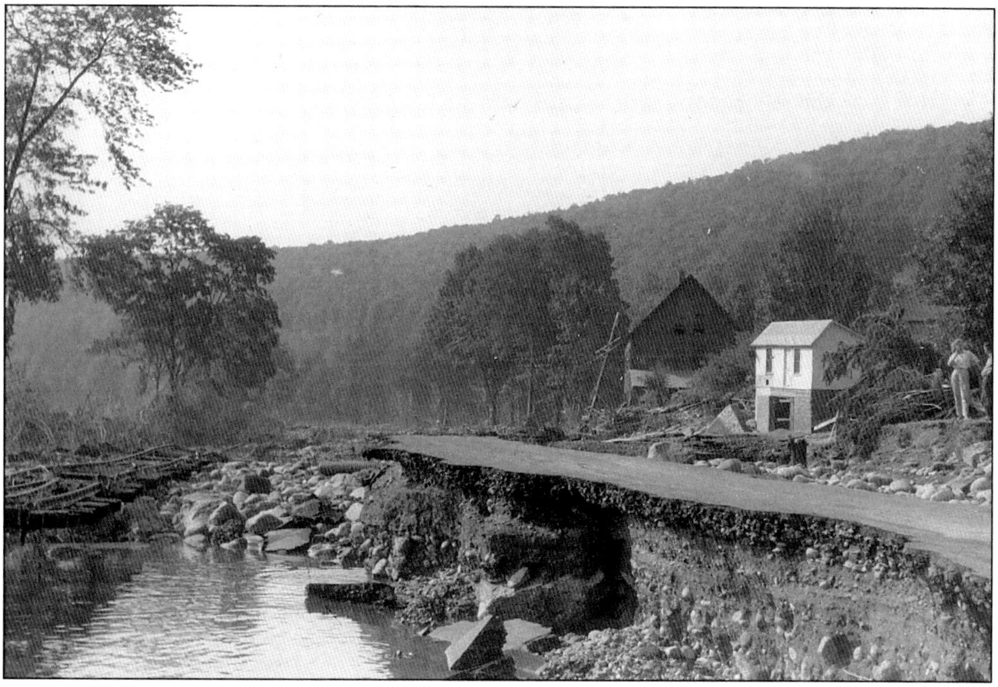

AUGUST 20, 1955. Looking toward Unionville from between the railroad tracks and Route 4, the fruit stand and the roof of the shop are visible. (BPL.)

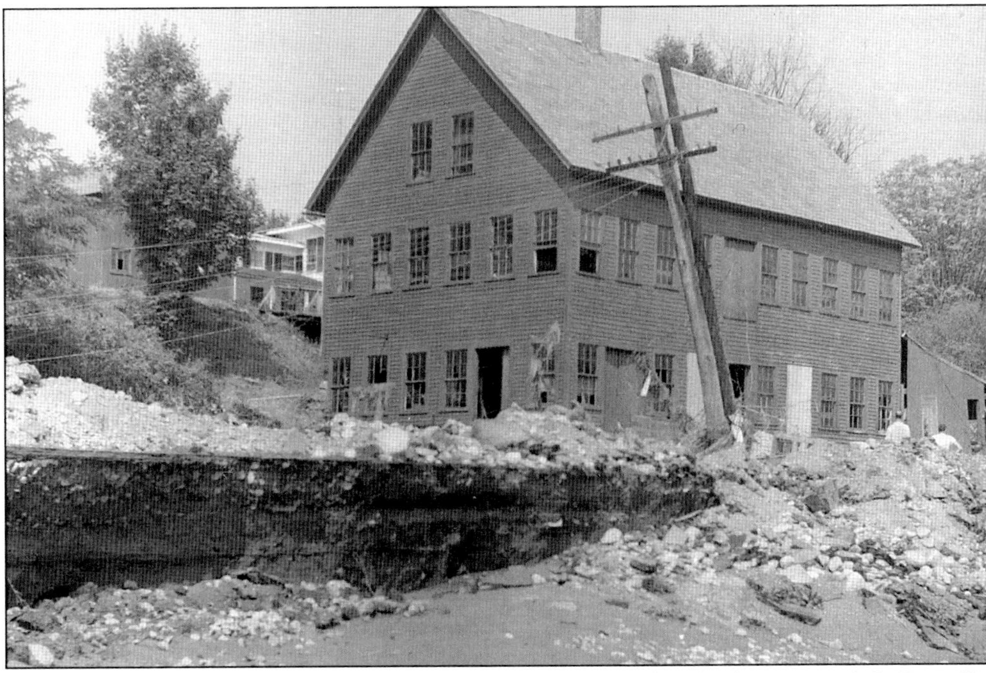

The Shop and the Inn. Both of these photographs were taken looking toward Collinsville. One shows the wood-turning shop sitting above the washed-out roadbed. The other was taken from between the road and the railroad tracks and shows the inn in the distance. (HHM.)

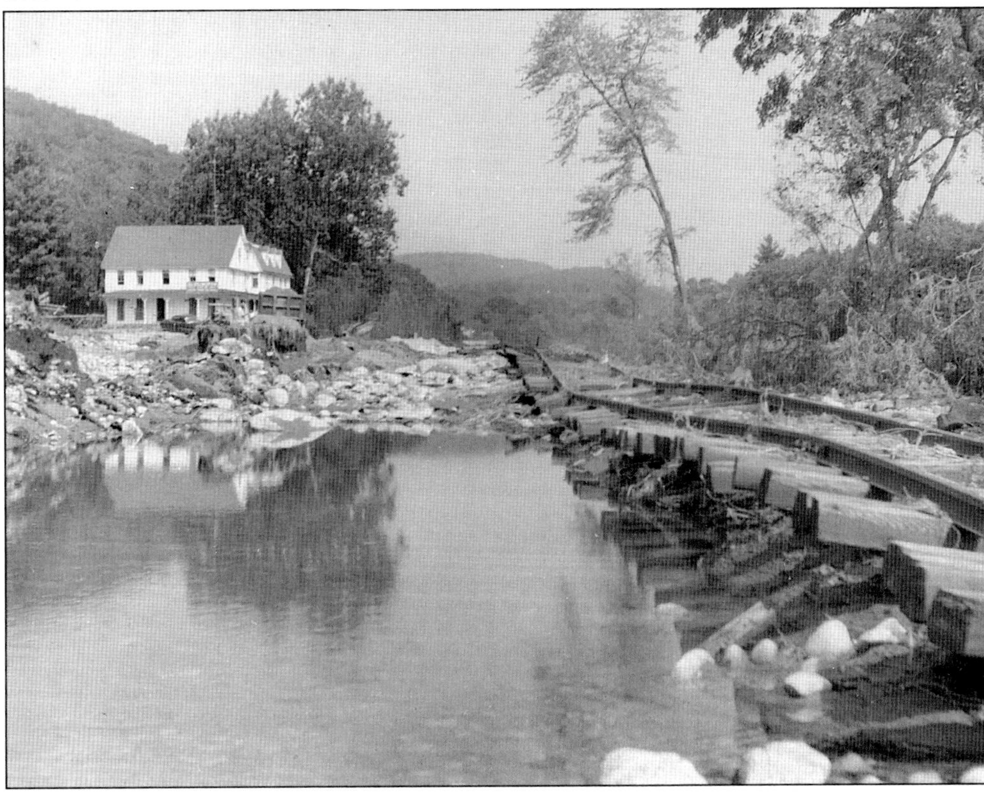

Nine

The Whole Dam Story

To enter Burlington from the northeast, one must cross a bridge in Collinsville. The last building in Canton is the rectory of the Catholic church, and the first building in Burlington is St. Patrick's Church. Until 1925, when the old church burned and the new stone church was built on the other side of the rectory in Burlington, this order was reversed. Continuing into Burlington, up the mountain a short ways is Nepaug Reservoir, behind the Nepaug Dam. Before the dam was built, the land was farmed and barns, houses, and mills thrived. This chapter records the building of the Nepaug Dam and shows one home and some families who lived there during the 1800s. The building of the dam across the Farmington River is also shown in this chapter. The Collins Company began building its power dam in 1911 and finished it in 1914. The dam was a short distance from Sand Bank (Riverside) School, where Hortense I. French was the teacher until 1918. Many of the children of the Polish and German construction workers were in her classes, and in her writings she recalls how "adept at drawing and artistic work" the children were. Photographs in this chapter show the building of the Collinsville Dam as the children must have seen it on their way to school from this side and, perhaps after school, from the other side of the Farmington River. Two other dams are shown in this chapter.

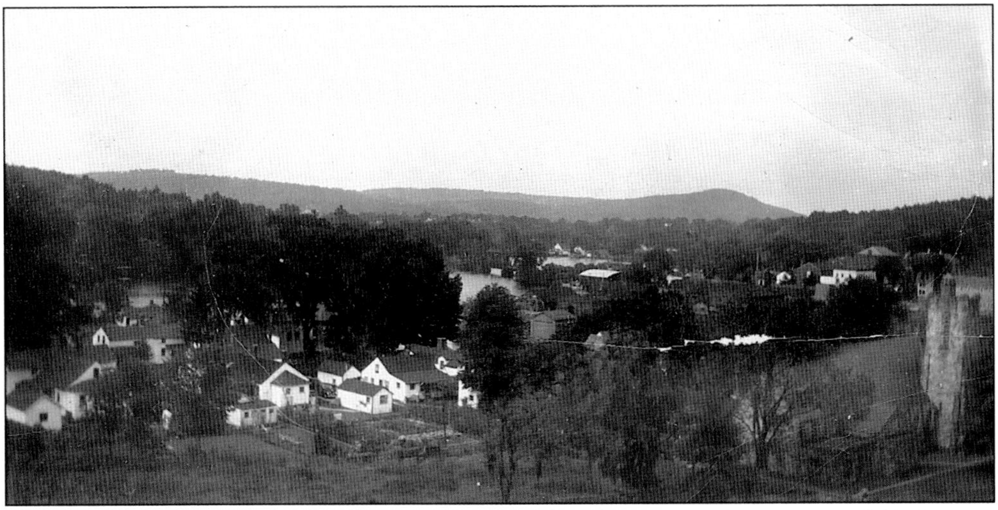

THE FLOOD AT ST. PATRICK'S CHURCH, 1955. The Farmington River covered Burlington Station and the low-lying regions for miles upriver. This view of the floodwaters is taken looking north over Collinsville from Burlington's Claire Hill Road. The "new" St. Patrick's Church, in Burlington, is seen from the back in the lower right. (WABS.)

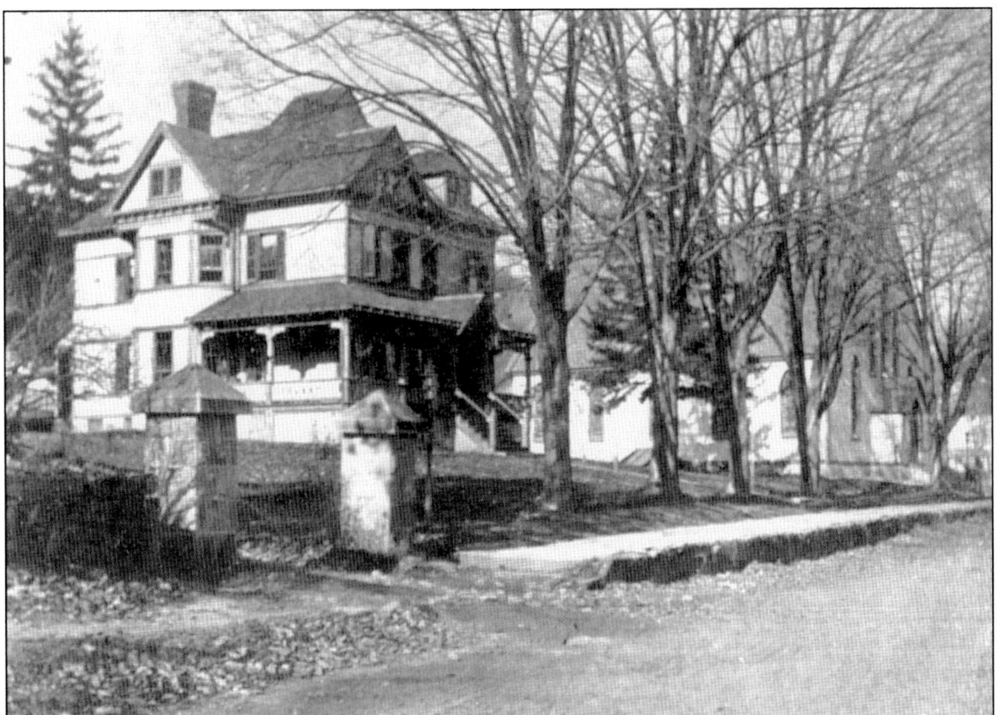

THE RECTORY AND OLD ST. PATRICK'S CHURCH, C. 1910. The rectory is the same in this picture as it is today. However, it has been moved to the location of the church seen on the right side of the postcard. This is one of the few photographs of the old St. Patrick's Church before it burned in 1925. (WABS.)

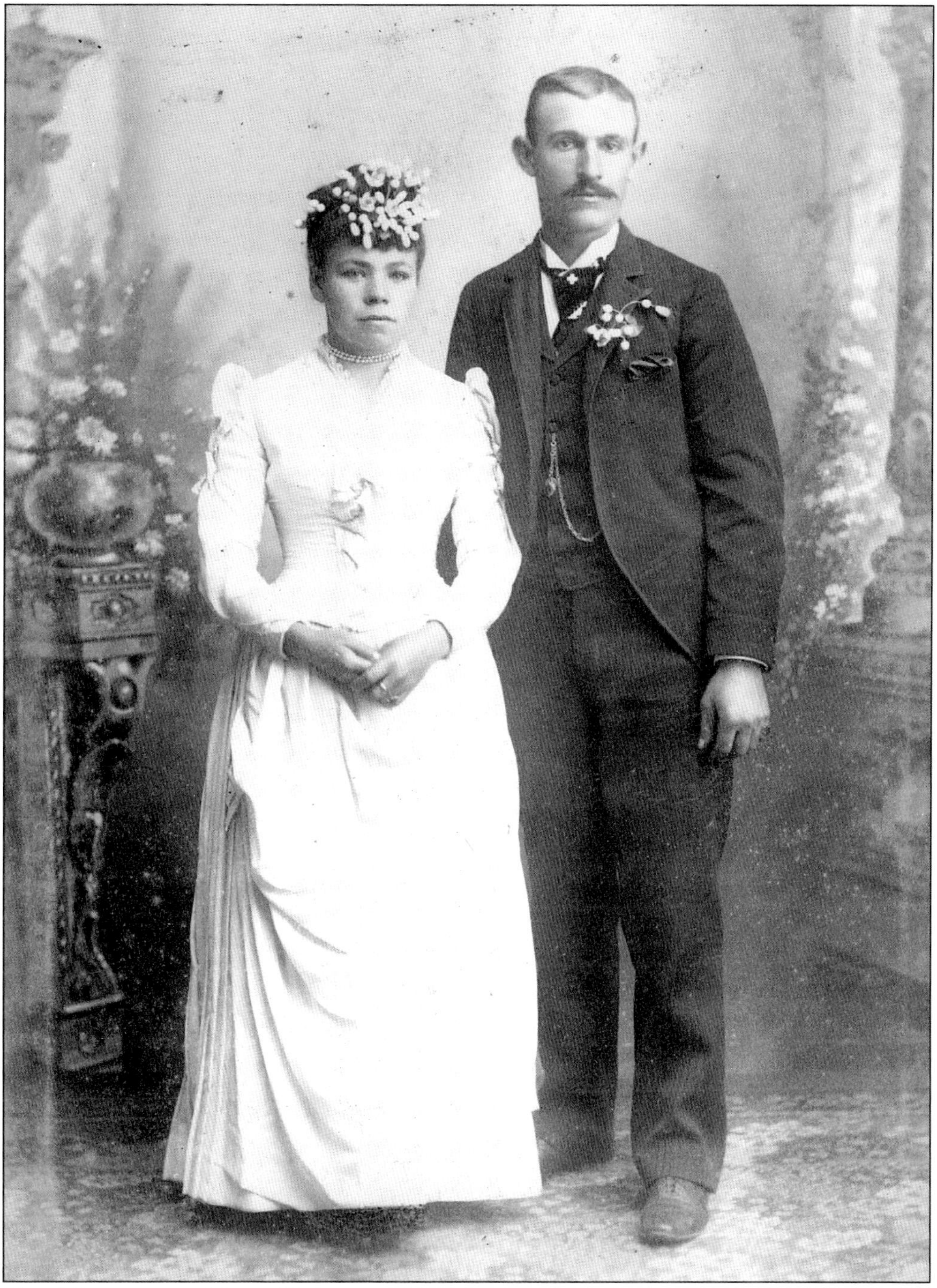

THE WEDDING OF MARY HORN AND BEN SCHEIDEL, LATE 1800S. St. Patrick's Church was the site of the Scheidel wedding. Mary Horn was born in Alsace in 1871 and came to Burlington once her mother, Agathe Arnold, was able to send for her. Ben Scheidel, born in Burlington in 1869, was the son of Joseph Scheidel, who emigrated from Germany. After their wedding, they made their home together near the southern end of what is now the Nepaug Reservoir. (ML.)

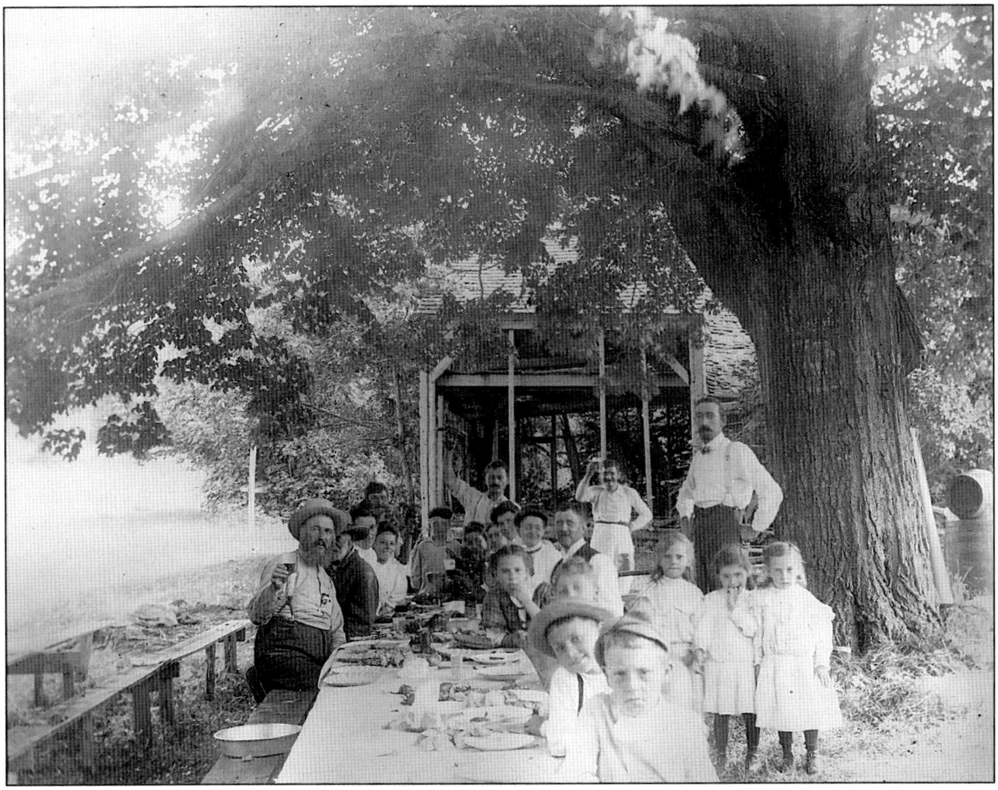

THE SCHEIDEL ANNUAL CLAM BAKE, 1910. The family, gathered for a clam bake and reunion, included George and Mary's Scheidel's family from Wilkinsville (on the Farmington River's edge). The group sat at the picnic table under the shade of a large maple tree in the backyard of Joseph Scheidel's home. Tilly, Louise, and Agatha are the three girls in the right front. Their Uncle George is the man with the beard on the left. (HWS.)

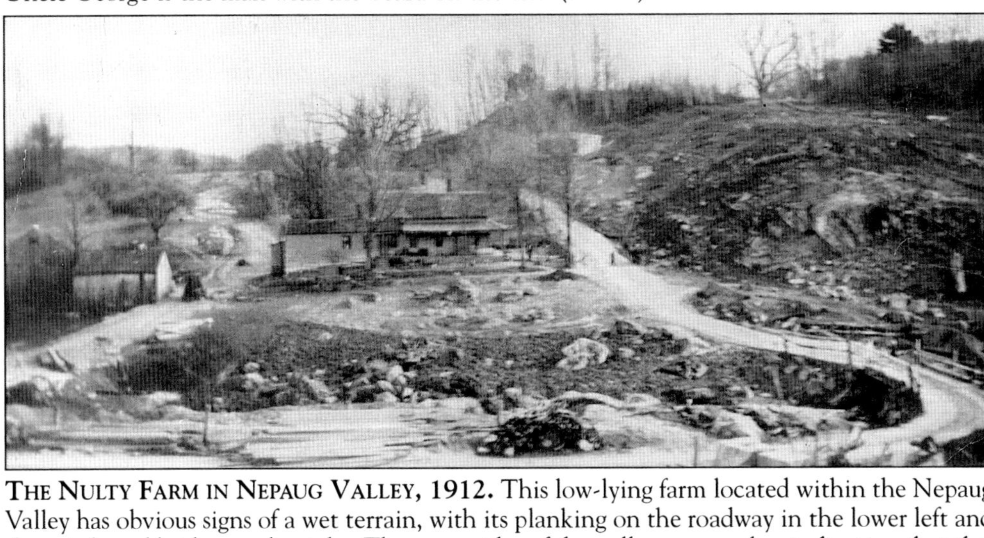

THE NULTY FARM IN NEPAUG VALLEY, 1912. This low-lying farm located within the Nepaug Valley has obvious signs of a wet terrain, with its planking on the roadway in the lower left and the reinforced bridge on the right. The steep sides of the valley are another indication that this natural basin was a logical choice for a reservoir to serve nearby urban areas. Nepaug Valley was flooded when the Phelps Dam was completed. (LA.)

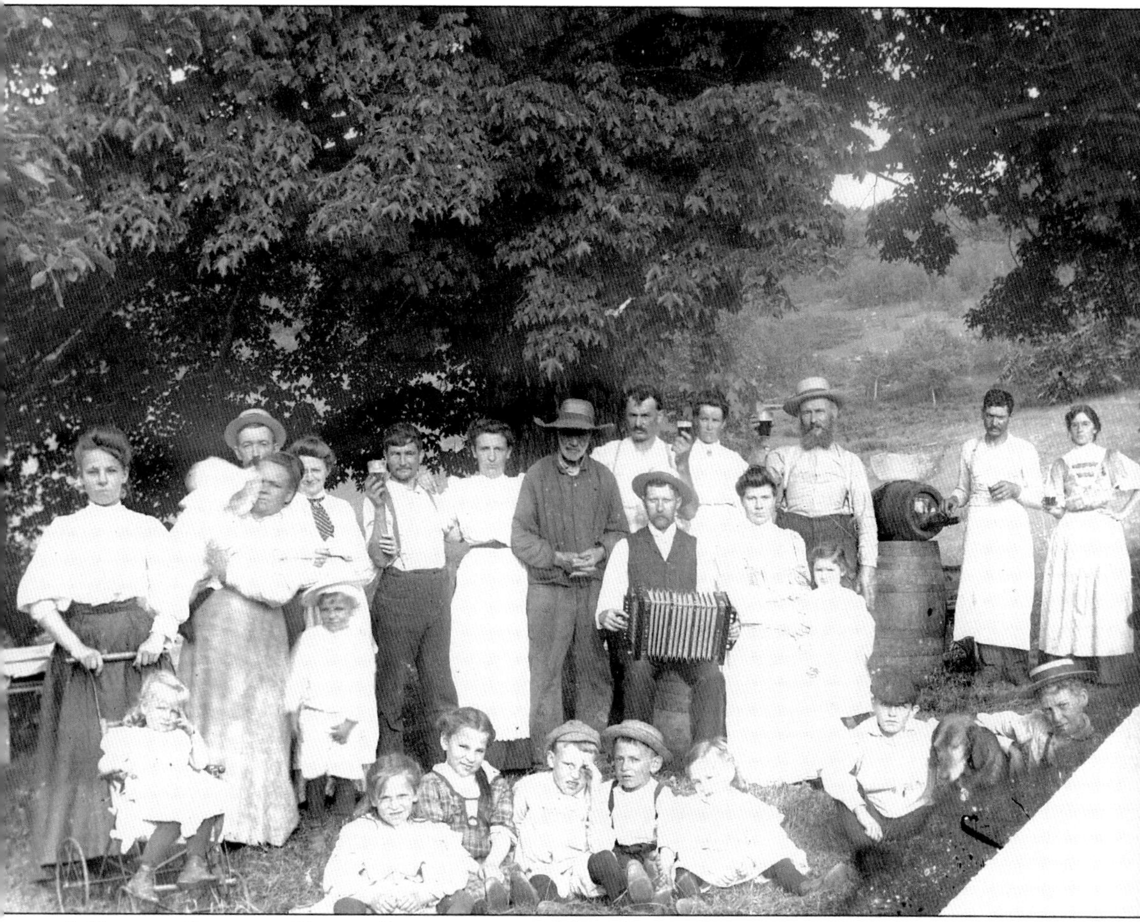

A FORMAL SCHEIDEL FAMILY PHOTOGRAPH. Taken the same day, this picture brings together members of several generations and a "popper," a hired hand and woodchopper, seen in the dark shirt and straw hat. The children, at the front of the picture, and their dog have enjoyed a day of food, music, and story together. Mary Horn Scheidel is the mother holding the baby; George is behind her, wearing the straw hat. Their daughter Jennie holds on to the carriage with her little sister, Johanna, in it. Joseph is near the keg and barrel, holding up the glass. George Warnecke played his accordion, and the woman next to him is his wife, Frances Scheidel Warnecke. (EE.)

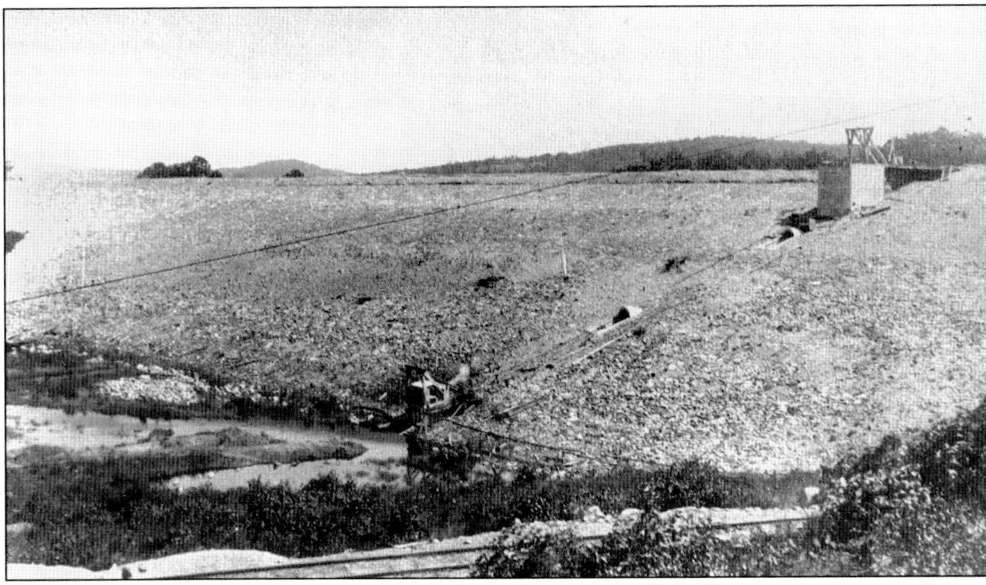

BUILDING PHELPS DAM. These two views show the interior of the dam as it nears completion. A temporary railroad line was installed to bring in the supplies needed for the dam and to move the earth from the center to the dam where it was piled upon the cement. The stone and cement core was covered with wooden shingles made at Schwarzmann Mill before piling on the dirt. The ends of the three outlet pipes, each 42-inches in diameter, are visible beneath the square control tower. These pipes at three different levels are capable of delivering water to West Hartford. (LA.)

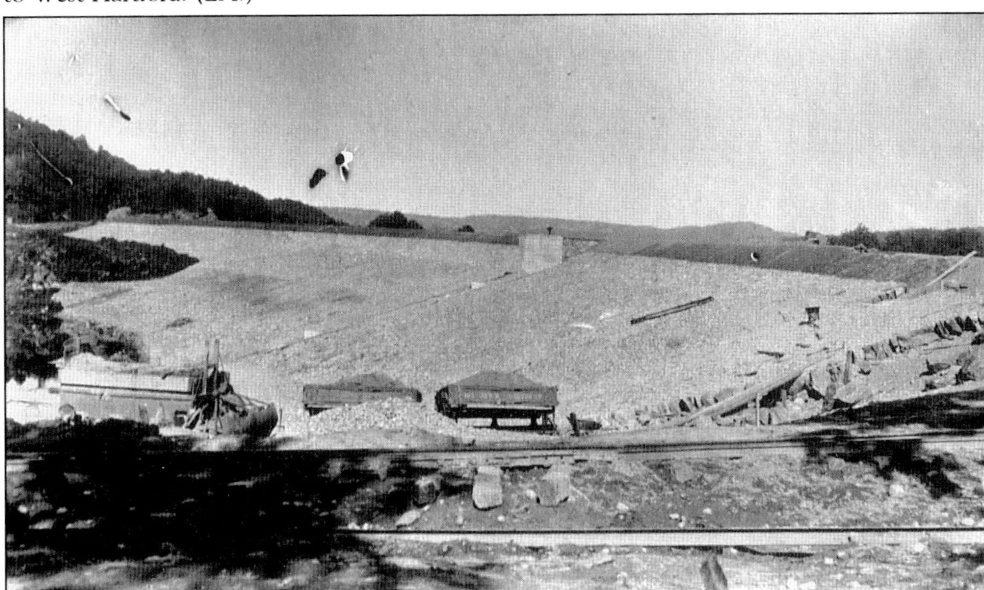

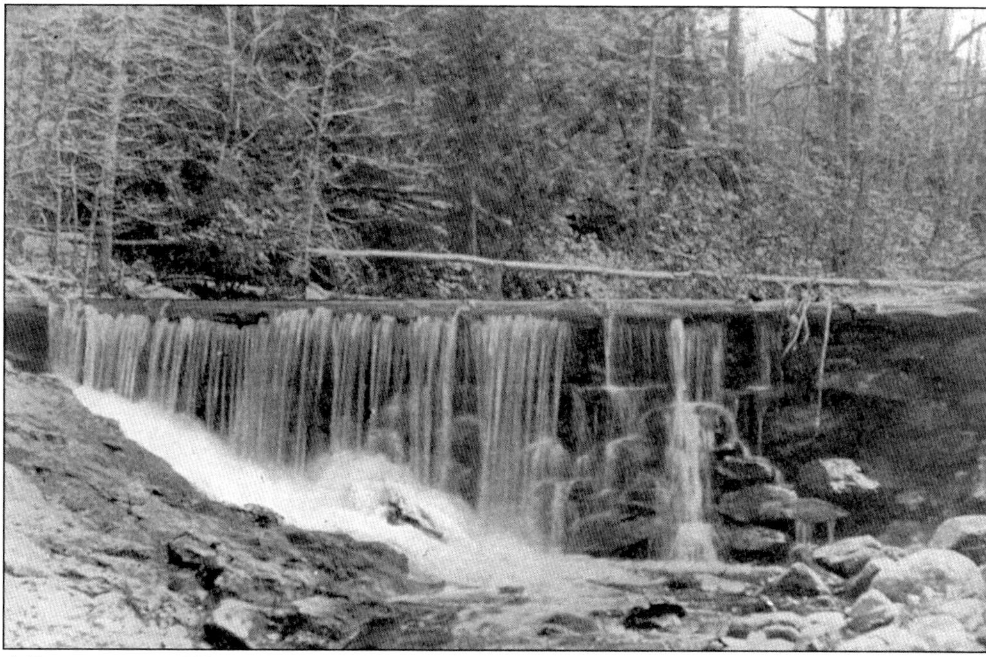

A POSTCARD OF WILKINSVILLE DAM, 1906. Wilkinsville was a community of houses near the river in Burlington, not far from Collinsville. This centennial postcard No. 14 shows the dam, which held back the water in times of heavy rainfall. (BPL.)

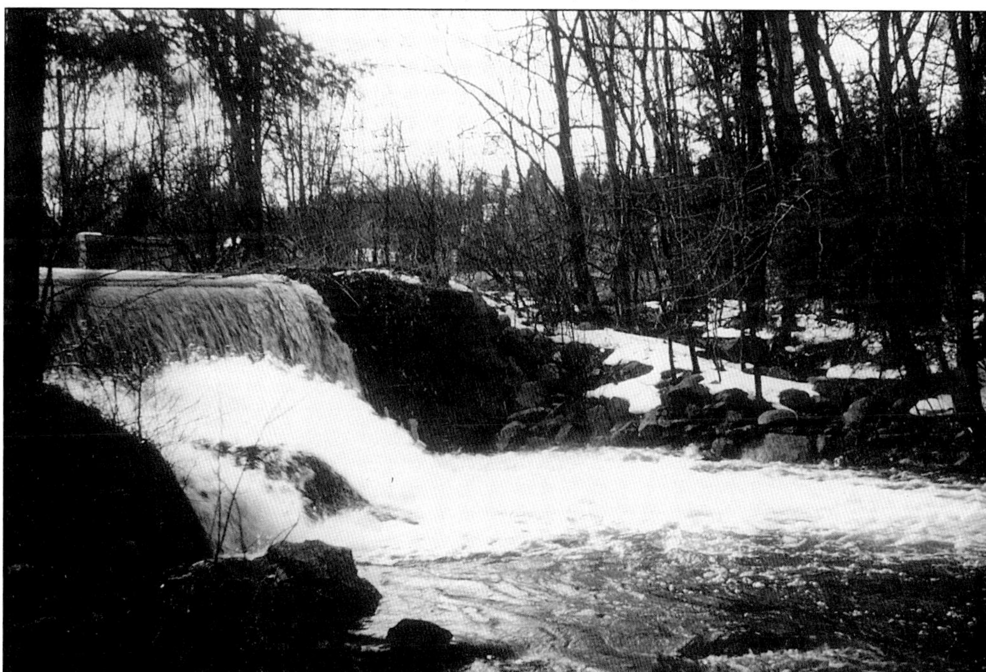

HARTIGAN'S DAM, MARCH 3, 1953. The power to run the wood-turning shop was generated by this dam over Burlington Brook. The race for this water ran beside the road and the indentation is still visible on the south side of Route 4 just after one turns west and begins to climb toward the center. (LA.)

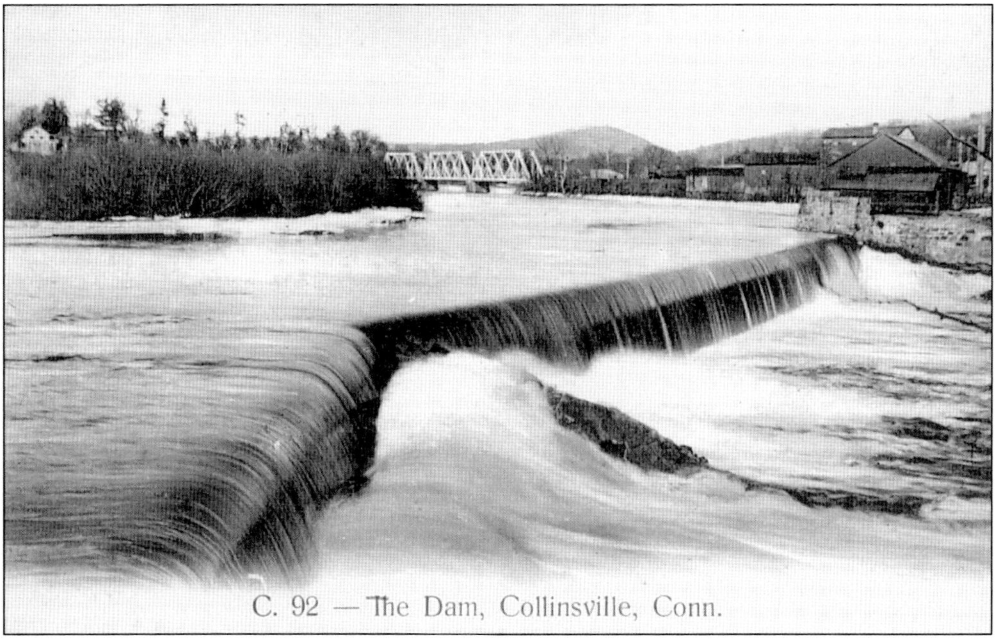

THE COLLINSVILLE DAM. This dam is in Collinsville and is the first of two across the Farmington River. The next dam, which is smaller and a few miles south, was built in 1912 to provide power for the Collins factory. It is the building of the lower dam that is shown in the following images. (BPL.)

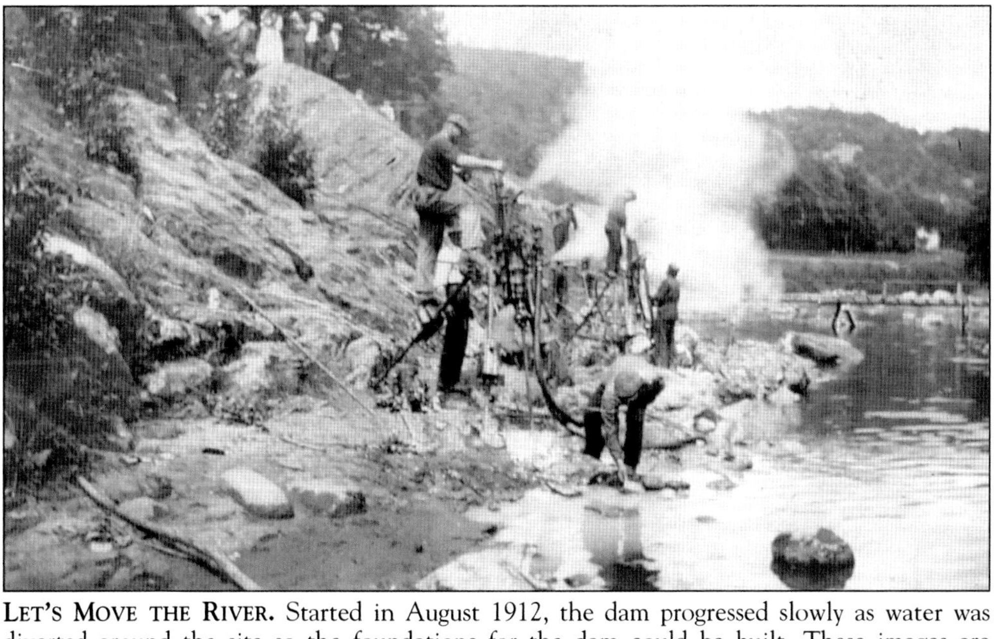

LET'S MOVE THE RIVER. Started in August 1912, the dam progressed slowly as water was diverted around the site so the foundations for the dam could be built. These images are postcards that show the workers and machinery; the dates are written on the reverse. (BPL.)

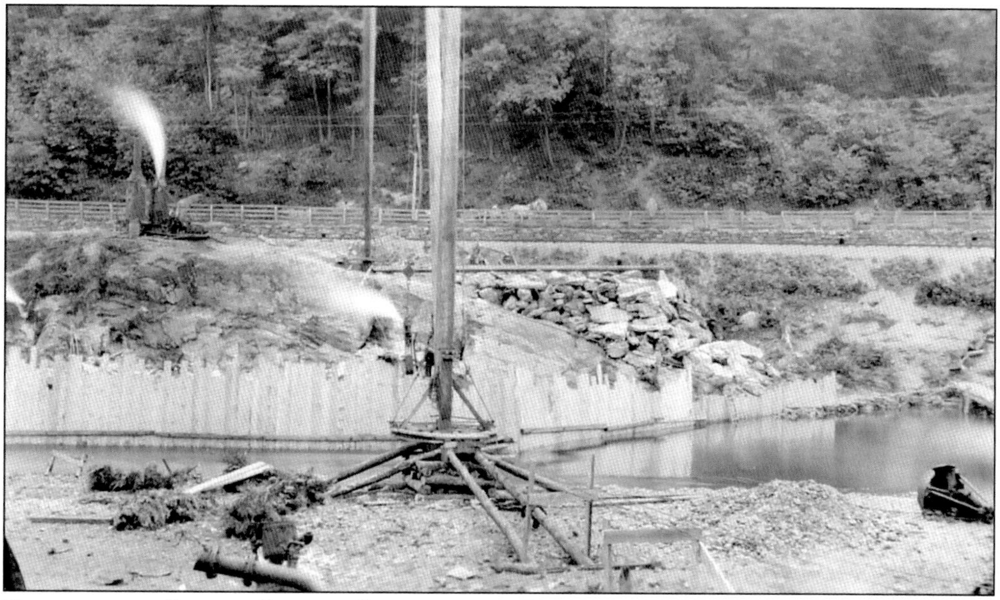

BUILDING THE LOWER COLLINS COMPANY DAM. In late August, equipment is in place and board walls have been built to hold in the crushed rock before the cement is poured for the dam. The steam engines generate power on the site. When no steam is visible, they are not in operation. Most of the images taken from the Collinsville side of the river show the fence along Route 4. Those with trees and no fence are from the Burlington side. (BPL.)

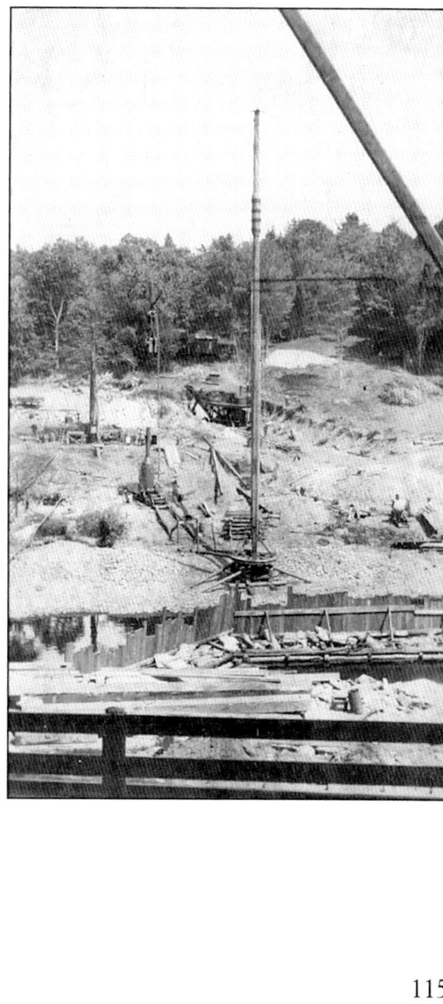

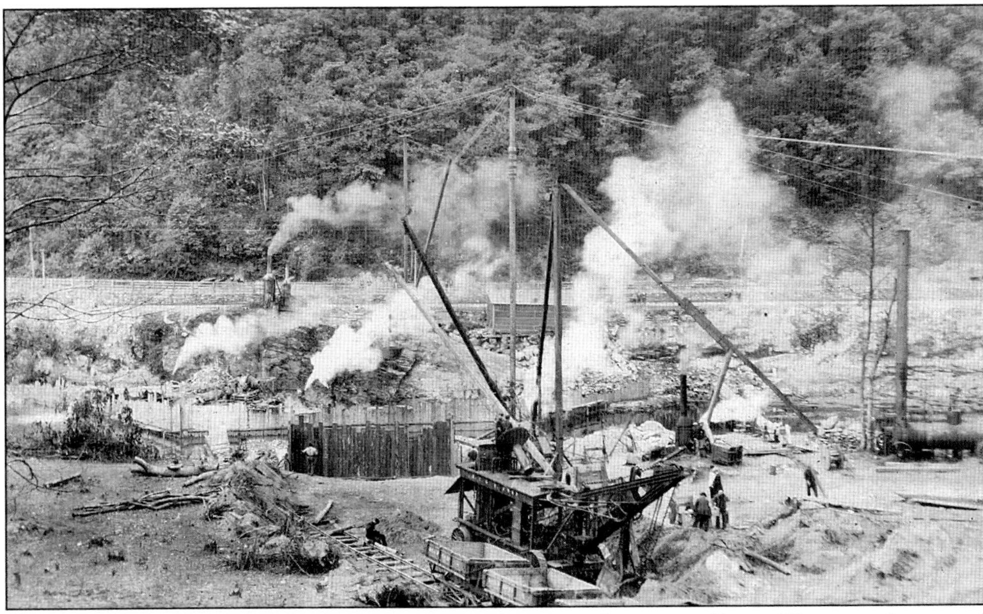

Postcards of the Construction of the Collins Company Dam. The top photograph was taken on September 15, 1912, from the Collinsville side of the river. It shows the work in progress, with steam engines at full power. The lower view, dated October 20, 1912, shows workers on scaffolding on the poured concrete on the left and others at work preparing the rocks before the next layer of concrete is poured on the right. Jackets hang on the steel reinforcement rods. (BPL.)

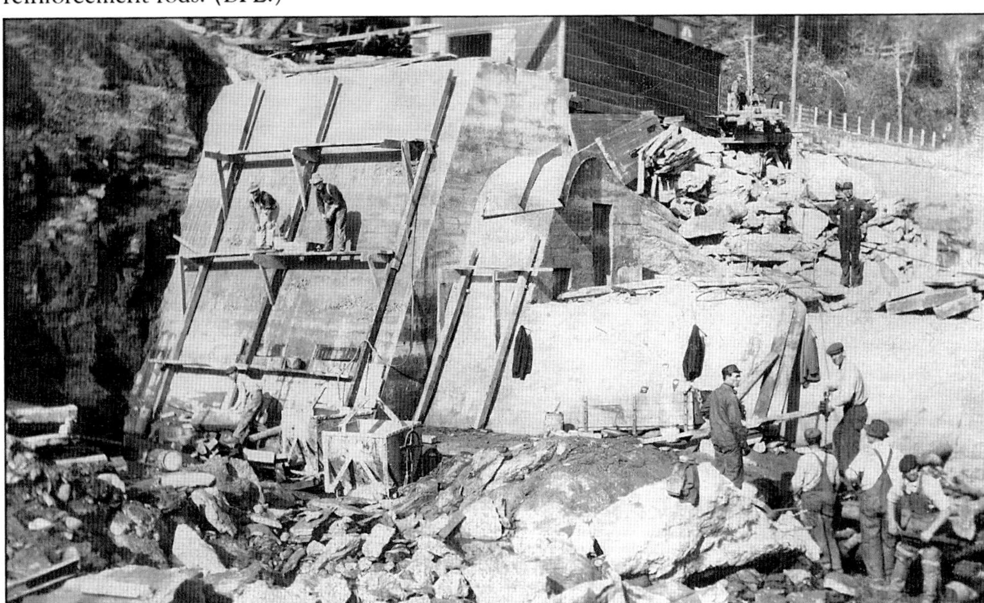

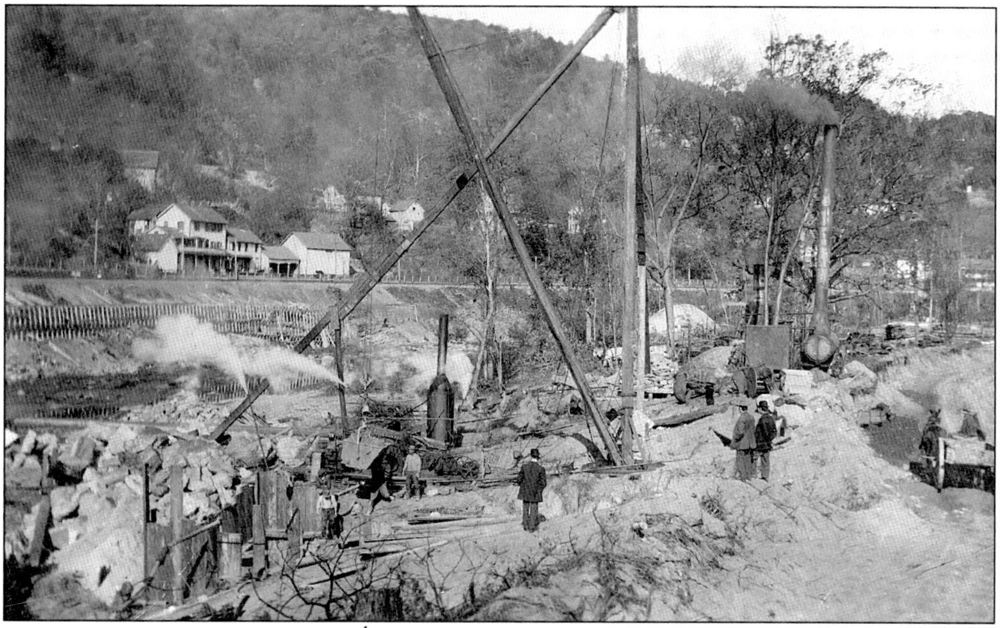

Dam Building and the Café Roof. In the upper photograph, the roofline for Café Sand Bank and its barns is visible above the fence, which kept the traffic away from the river's edge. (BPL.)

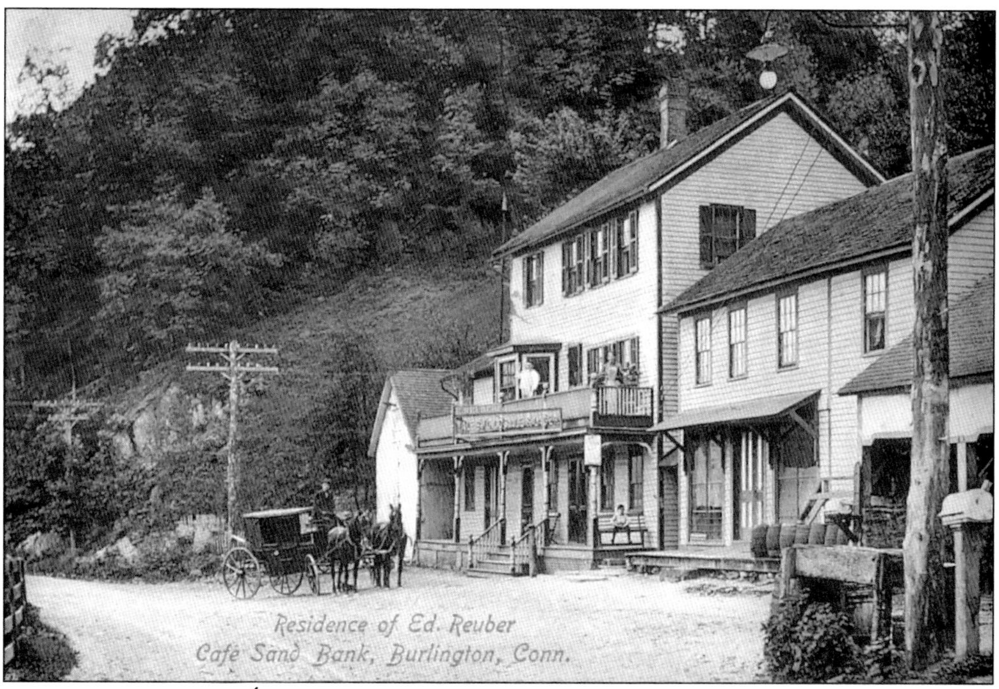

A Postcard of Café Sand Bank, c. 1910. After a day of building the dam, workers welcomed refreshments at the café. On the far left, the fence, built for the construction of the dam, is visible. The family of Ed Reuber lived and worked here; some of the family members are on the porches. This card was hand-colored, with green trees and red roofs. (CM.)

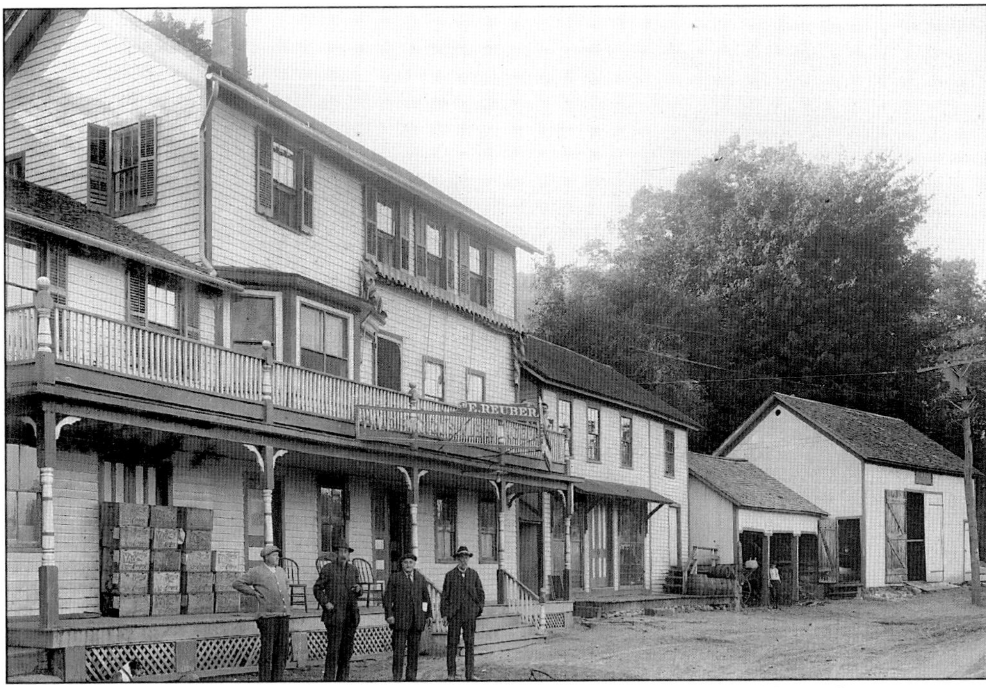

THE REUBERS, OCTOBER 12, 1915. This photograph is not a postcard but a larger image in sepia, dated on the back. Two of the four men are identified; they are George Scheidel, second from left, and Zygmund Winalski, on the right. Scheidel also appeared in the two family clambake photographs. (LA.)

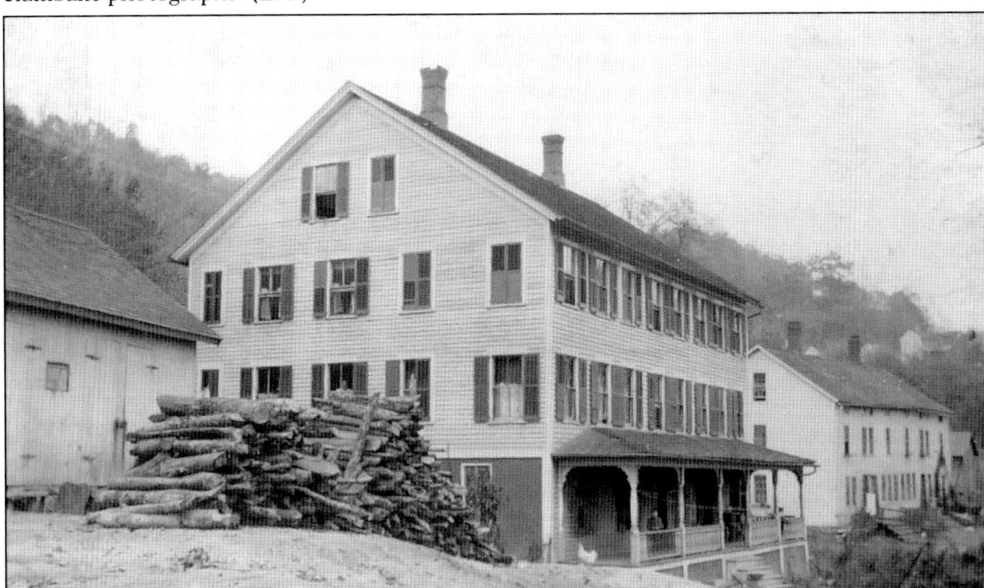

RIVERSIDE AVENUE AND CLAIRE HILL ROAD. These two large buildings were used both as businesses and as residences. Some of the shuttered windows in the near building have curtains; at least one face peers out at the photographer. A white chicken near the porch and a clothesline suggest that this is someone's home. None of these buildings are on the site today. The first photograph in this chapter was taken from near this spot. (BPL.)

Ten

Main Street

The only "Main Street" in Burlington is in the southern section of town, in an area once called Poverty Hollow. Starting at Milford Street near Lamson Corner, Main Street ran southeast to Jerome Avenue. Whigville takes its name from a banner, made for a convention in Hartford, which stated that the supporters, who belonged to the Whig party—a forerunner of today's Republican party—were residents of Whigville. The largest copper mine of the state was discovered here in the late 18th century by Theopolis Botsford. In both Burlington and Bristol, it was worked intermittently during the 19th century and was closed in 1895. Whigville is an eighth of a mile southeast of the site of the New Britain Reservoir. It was once lushly forested with chestnut and maple trees. Where a busy corner store, clock shop, and the Smith brother's wood-turning shop were is today a rural area with a few houses, barns, and outbuildings. The Whigville Grange and Schoolhouse, now both residences, were once popular gathering places. An anonymous student remembered, "In September 1913, with freshly scrubbed body, a starched dress and ribbon bows in my braided hair, I made my one mile trek to the Whigville School House for my first day of school. I felt like a very important person, a little apprehensive, but also eager. My brothers, on a few occasions, had taken me to visit the school when something special was planned. It was a big day for me. I don't remember how many kids started the first grade that year, perhaps five or six, which was a big first-grade class." Then, she tells us about her teacher, Maude Hinman, the mother in the family portrait in chapter six, "She lived on a farm on what is now Milford Street." Her husband started the sawmill that is still in operation. He was also in the dairy business. The Hinman sawmill still operates but there are no longer any cows in that dairy barn nor in the remaining barns in Whigville.

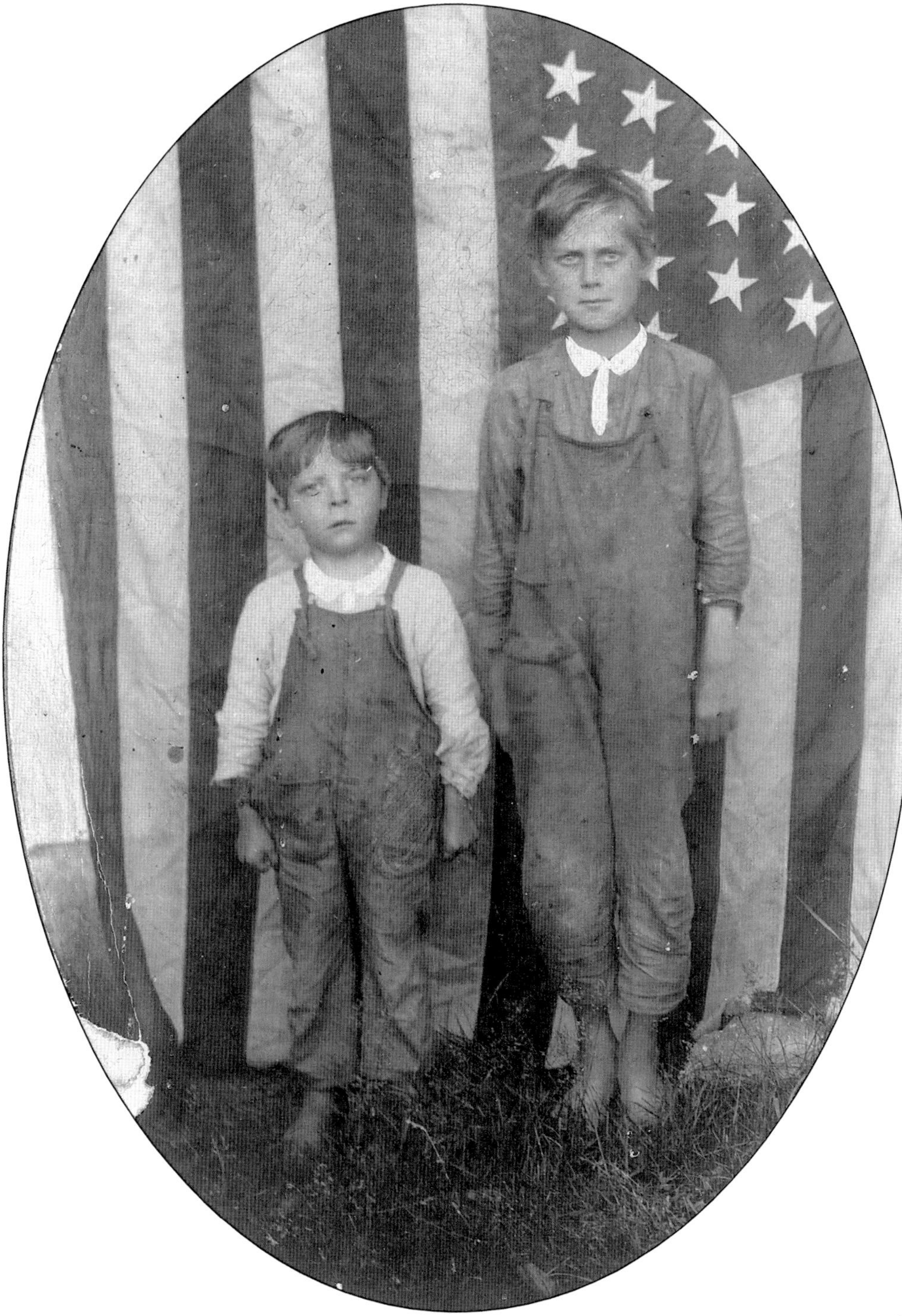

TWO BACKES BOYS, 1909. Joseph and John Backes stood in front of the flag-draped Whigville School for a portrait. The two sons of Joseph W. and Augustina Backes and their little sister, Augustina, lived with their parents on a farm on Bradley Road. Backes was a town assessor for 12 years and a farmer. (ABP.)

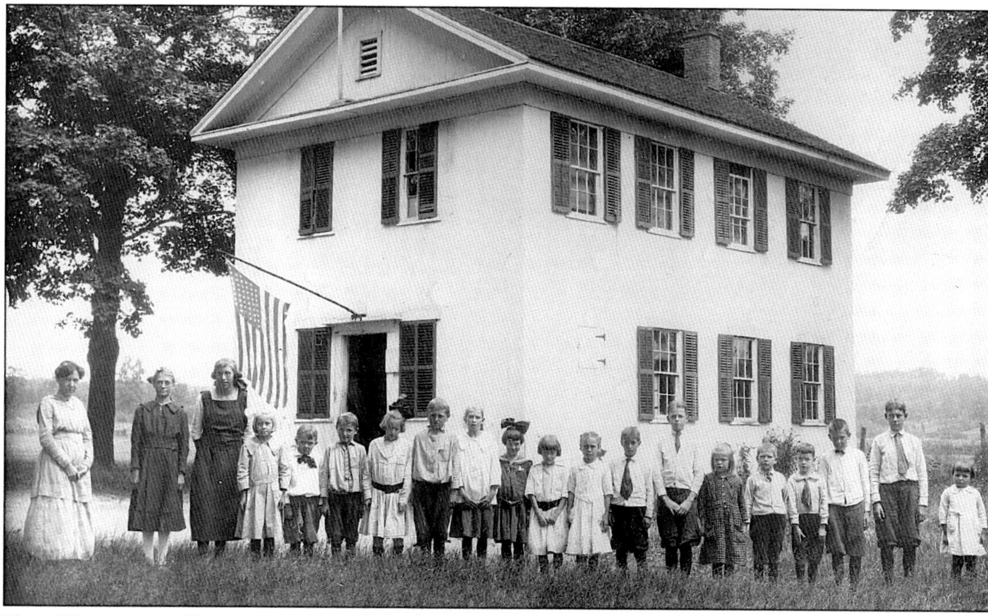

THE WHIGVILLE SCHOOL, 1920. Standing next to teacher Ella Winston is Augustina "Gussie" Backes. The other students, from left to right, are Augusta Bredefeld, Edna Semeroe, Nelford Scarrett, George Pavlik, Hazel Lourey, Frank Pavlik, Lillian Simroe, Dorothy Bradley, Ester Lourey, Alma Woike, Oscar Bredefeld, George Newhaurer, Lillian Leide, Richard Leids, Carl Scheding, Wilbur Lourey, Harold Lourey, and Julia Pavlik. (ABP.)

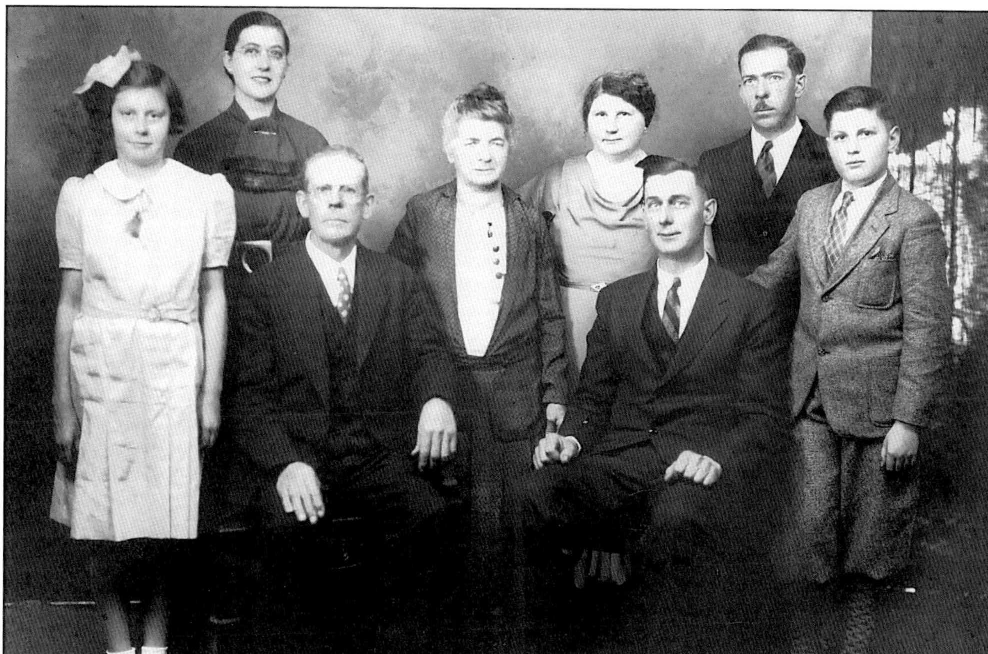

THE BACKES FAMILY PORTRAIT, C. 1935. Family members, from left to right, are Elizabeth, John's daughter; Gussie; Joseph William Backes Sr.; Augustina; Mary (Wagner), John's wife; John A.; Joseph W. Jr.; and Joseph W. III. (ABP.)

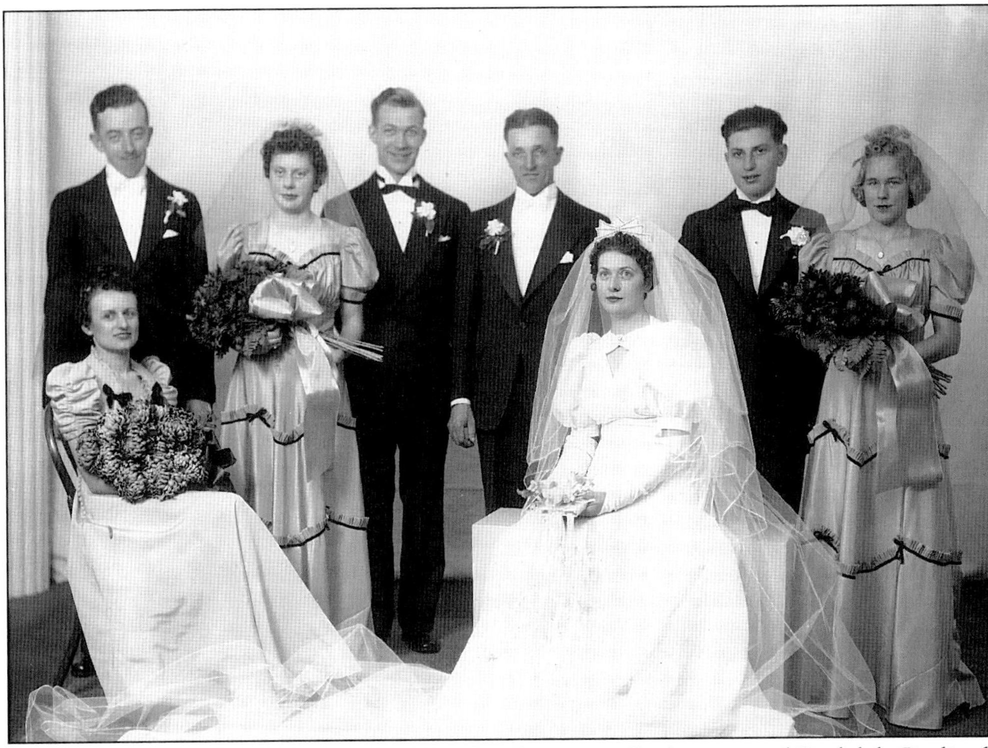

The Backes-Poglitsch Wedding. In 1939, Augustina Backes married Rudolph Poglitsch and chose her niece and nephew as attendants. The wedding party included, from left to right, Elizabeth Rucki of Bristol, Paul French of New Britain, Elizabeth Backes, Andrew Wackovetsky of Brooklyn, the groom and the bride, Joseph William Backes III, and Veronica Rusczyk of New Britain. (ABP.)

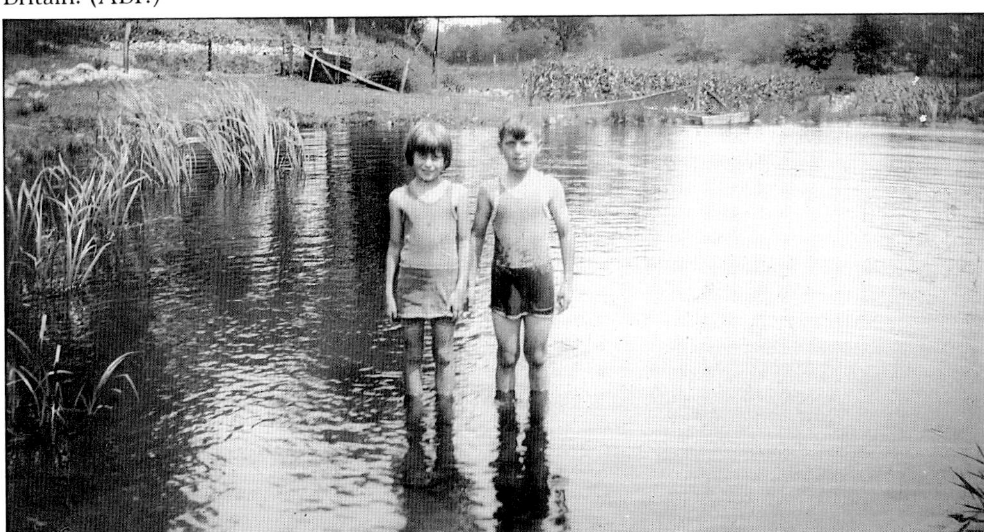

The Pond on Main Street. Elizabeth and Joseph William Backes, the children of John Backes, stand in Clover Pond, on South Main Street in Whigville. Filled in long ago, the pond was across the street from the clover mill. Backes Power Equipment is in the old mill now. (ABP.)

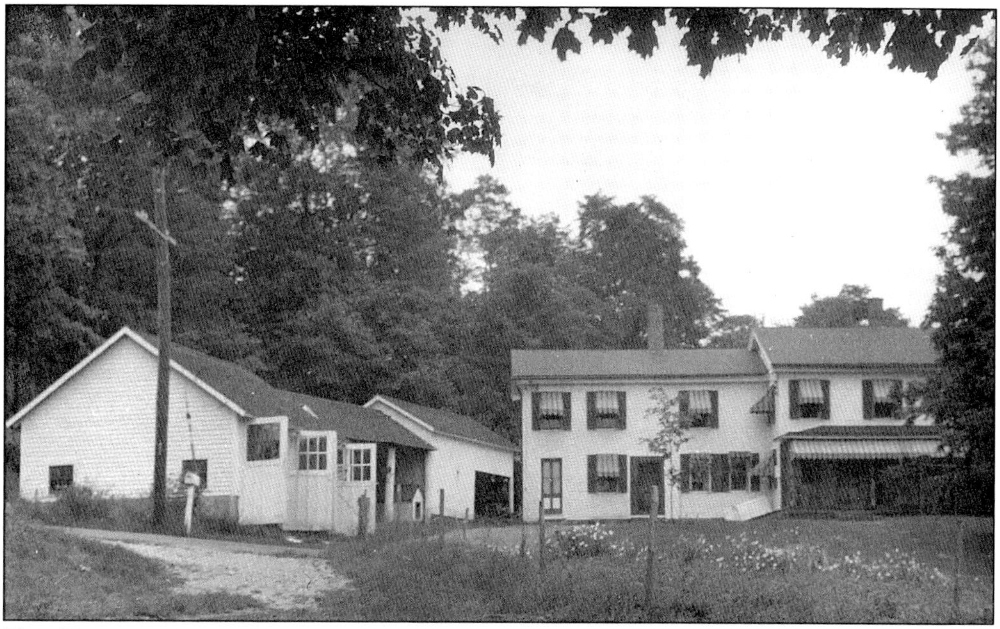

THE FARMHOUSE ON BRADLEY ROAD, c. 1930. Gussie Poglitsch still lives here with her daughter's family. She retrieved these family and Grange photographs from her attic so the Burlington book would show "at least one Whigville family." (ABP.)

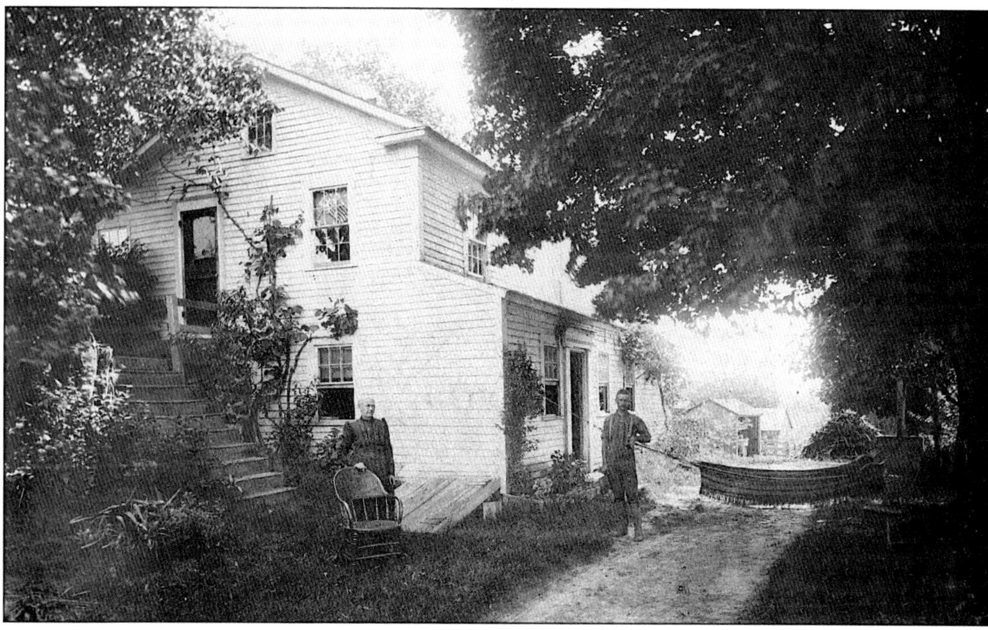

THE HILLSIDE HOME OF THE MATTHEWS FAMILY. Frances M. "Fanny" (Lamberton) Matthews and her son Edwin are outside their home. Edwin Matthews was a farmer and was active in both Burlington and Bristol civic and social affairs. He was superintendent of Union Sunday School in Whigville. Twice married, he lived first in this house and then in one he built on the other side of the driveway. He had two sons, Adrian and Charles, by his first wife, Henrietta Moses of Unionville. In 1922, he married Ella Mae Winston, a teacher at North Chippens Hill School. (MFD.)

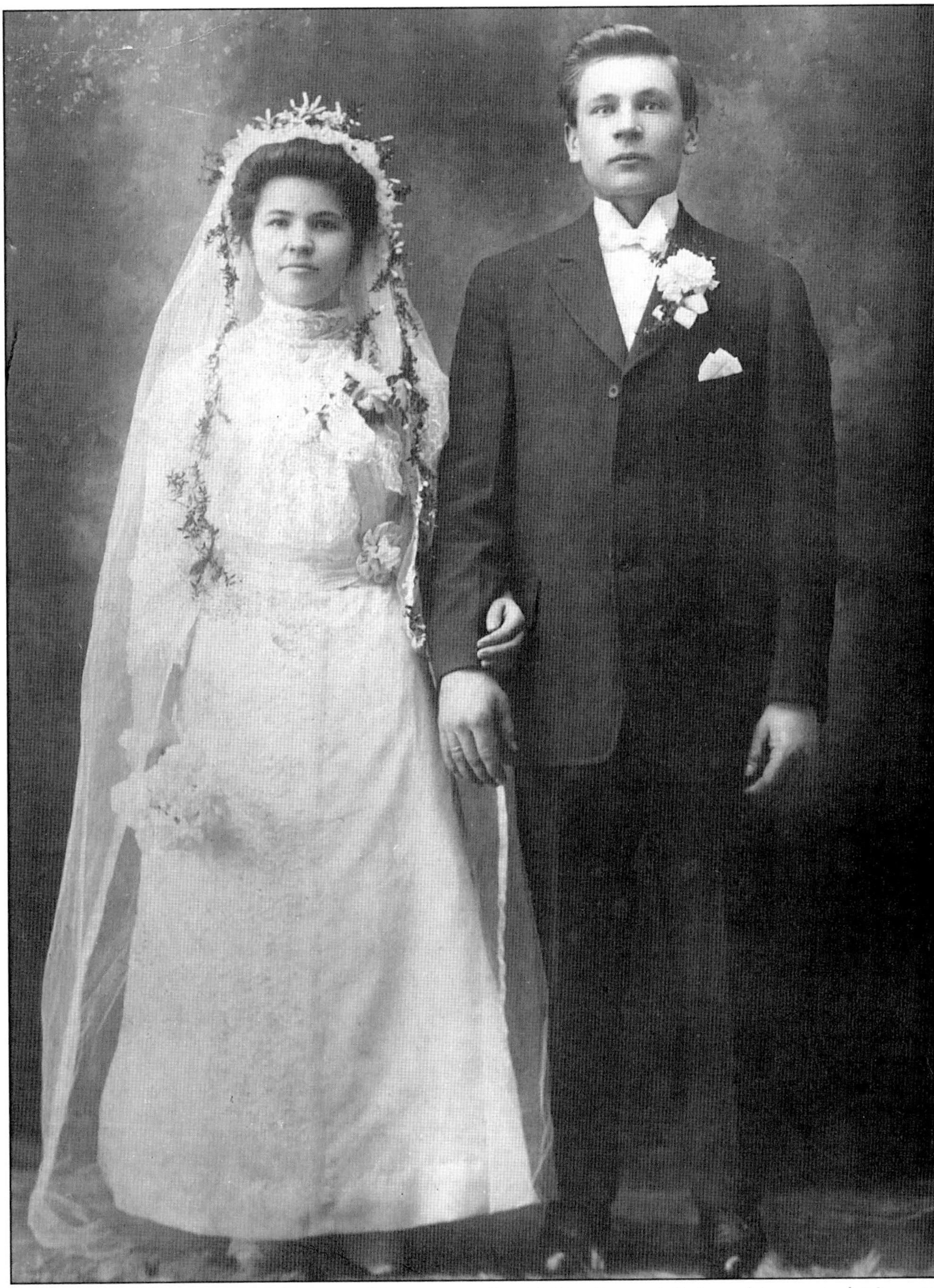

The Marek-Sakowski Wedding Portrait. In 1913, Antoni Sakowski married Victoria Marek. Together they operated the Walnut Grove Dairy Farm from 1934 until 1958. Their five children helped on the farm on Jerome Avenue and attended the Whigville School. (MSK.)

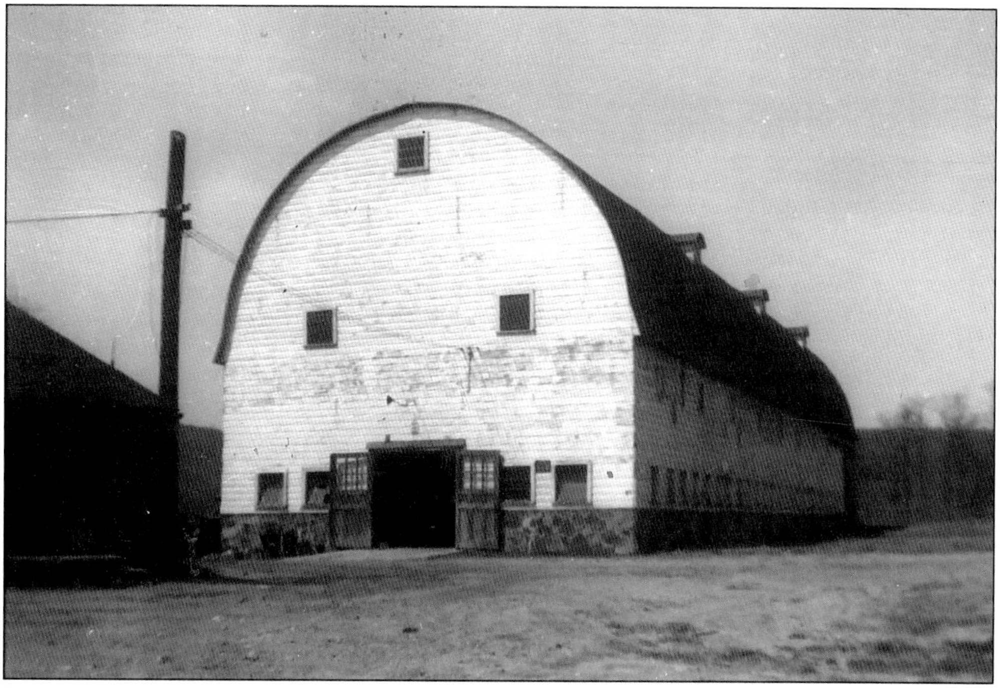

THE WALNUT GROVE DAIRY BARN AND TRUCK, C. 1942. The new barn, with a rounded roof, was built by the Sakowskis and their friends. It still stands on Jerome Avenue. Joe Kobylarz, on the left, and Walter Krawiec, on the right, hold up a bottle of milk. A.F. Sakowski's milk truck has a Bristol phone number since the dairy is closer to Bristol than to the center. The Bristol post office delivered mail in this part of town as well. (MSK.)

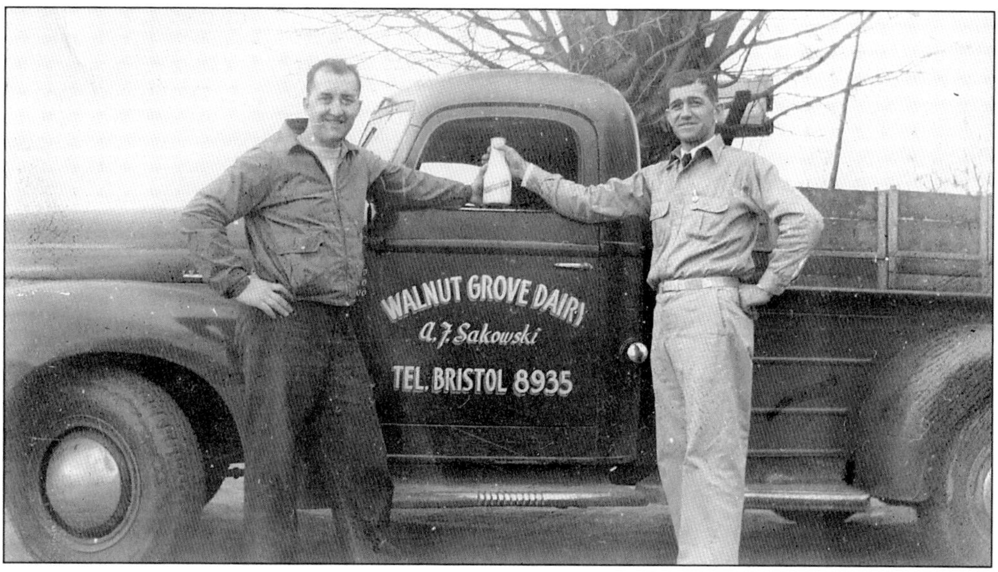

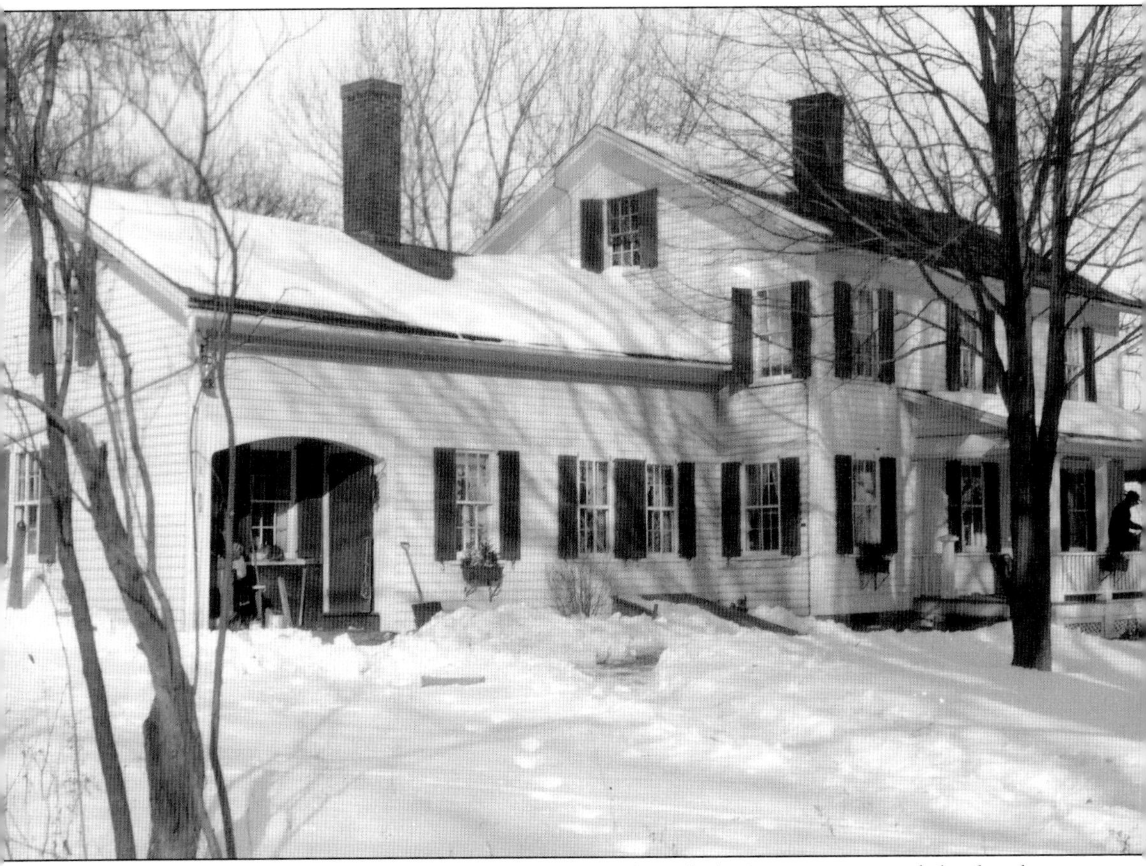

BLACK WALNUT ACRES, AFTER 1939. George and Rachel Merriman restored the farmhouse, just off of Milford Street, for their young family after World War II. They are standing on the porch in this snow-covered scene. (LMF.)

A Leafy Black Walnut Lane. Like most of the other side roads in Burlington before they were improved and paved, this lane was beautiful in the summer and autumn and a nightmare in the winter and spring. (LMF.)

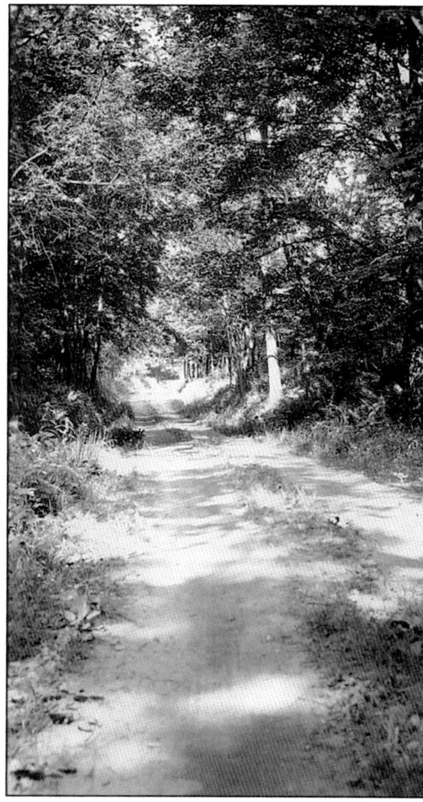

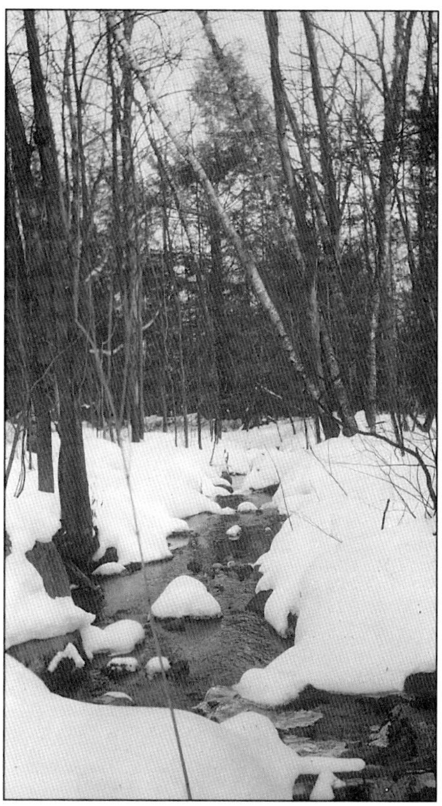

The Brook on Black Walnut Lane. This brook, like the others in town, is a quiet reminder that nature is generous and precious and that to preserve the gifts we have been given is an honor and a responsibility. The photographs of Black Walnut Lane are in the care of Lucretia Fortier, granddaughter of George and Rachel Merriman. (LMF.)

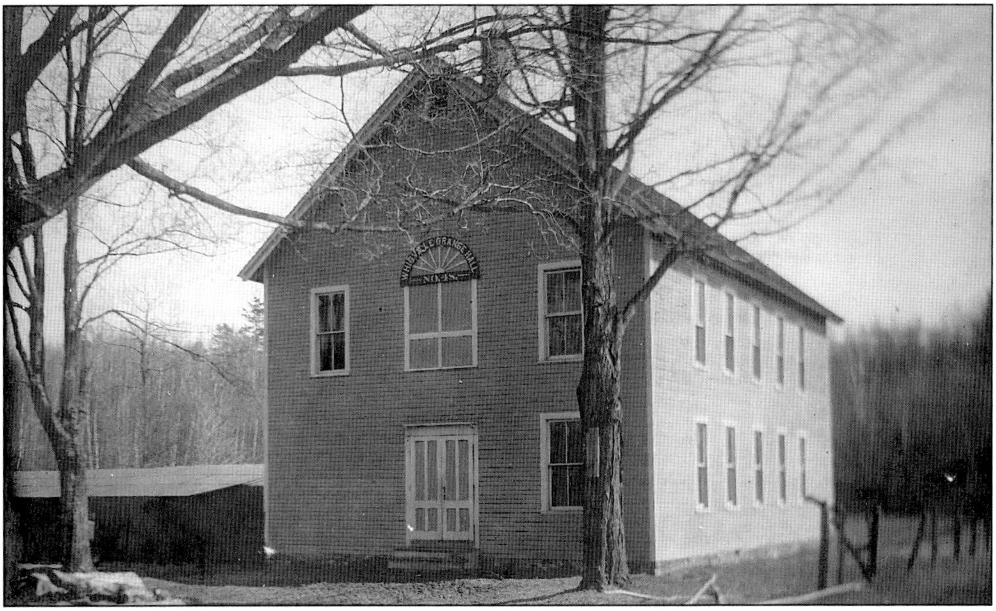

WHIGVILLE GRANGE NO. 48, C. 1900. Whigville Grange was organized on June 2, 1886 to "debate and research the best farming methods and provide domestic subjects for the wives of the members." Music, literature, drama, and history were encouraged for the 40 charter members from West District, Farmington, Burlington, and the north part of Bristol. The meetings were held on the second floor of the school until 1893. The Grange Hall was built on land given by L.L. Lowrey with about $1,000 in member contributions. (LA.)

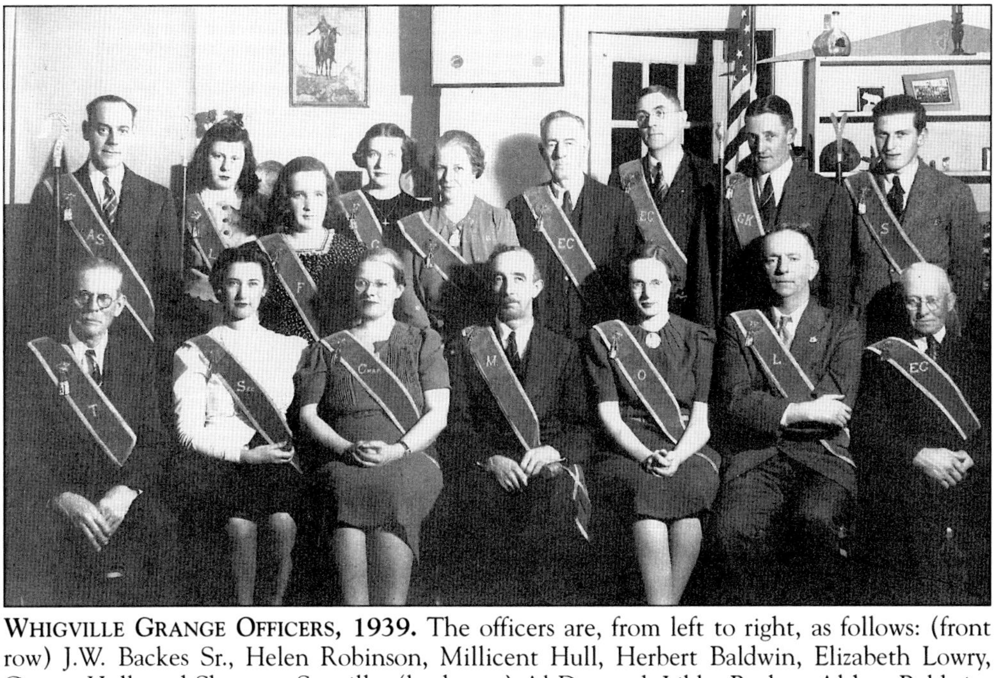

WHIGVILLE GRANGE OFFICERS, 1939. The officers are, from left to right, as follows: (front row) J.W. Backes Sr., Helen Robinson, Millicent Hull, Herbert Baldwin, Elizabeth Lowry, George Hull, and Sherman Scoville; (back row) Al Douyard, Libby Backes, Althea Baldwin, Gussie Poglitsch, Rachael Merriman, George Merriman, Walter Porch, Rudy Poglitsch, and Joe Backes III. (ABP.)